Without the architects and their inventions which propelled the dialogues in the first instance, there would be no book. To Ben van Berkel, Rem Koolhaas, Peter Kulka with Ulrich Königs, Daniel Libeskind, Alvaro Siza, whose work is featured here, I am indebted. They encouraged an open dialogue between engineering and architecture and their stimulating collaboration was the fertile ground upon which *informal* took hold. As with all creativity there are no boundaries and their architectural imaginations influenced my own explorations.

edited by
Christian Brensing

Prestel
Munich · Berlin · London · New York

informal

Cecil Balmond

with Jannuzzi Smith

to Ove Arup

PREFACE: CHANGING ARCHITECTURE

Whenever there is a revolution, or fast change, in architecture professional barriers break down as specialists exchange roles. Architects become sculptors, engineers become designers, artists turn into architects, and all these job descriptions become fuzzy. This happened in the Early Renaissance, during the building of the dome for Florence Cathedral, when Ghiberti and Brunelleschi switched professions from goldsmith to sculptor and artist to architect. It happened countless times in the 19th and 20th centuries when the avant-garde was reconstituted again and again. It happened with Eiffel and Tatlin, with Duchamp and Le Corbusier, and indeed it is one good measure of an avant-garde. If professionals do not give up their job descriptions, their trade union, there is no avant-garde, no breaking of barriers, no radical creativity. The work of Cecil Balmond again proves this rule. Engineer, designer, architect, thinker with numbers, speculative mathematician, writer: what is he if not all these things. Why? Because he is part of the creative edge that is moving architecture. Architectural movements, as the metaphor suggests, move the boundaries of the discipline and they characteristically do this by challenging assumptions, the conceptual framework behind the profession.

Of course Balmond does this coming from the profession of engineering, and the unusual office that Ove Arup set up in London 55 years ago. This is an extended organisational framework of collaboration, of teams of engineers with a certain flexible autonomy and democracy. Rather than the old customary hierarchy, it is one of the first examples of that type which has become prevalent today, the network organisation. In terms of pay scales, responsibility and decision-making, it shares more with Microsoft than the old Ford Motor Company, and the success of this model confirms the original idea. New ideas, creativity and excellence in design emerge when barriers are momentarily broken in order to be reformed in new configurations.

If one asks what Balmond does in the inception of a building, then he is part designer, part catalyst, part the unseen hand behind the structure. Usually the engineer's role is highly visible, especially in big buildings. Think of Nervi's stadia, or the work of Santiago Calatrava today.

What are they if not powerful diagrams of structural forces, and organic metaphors turned into emphatic form. The engineer often gets his identity, and pay, for making architecture into giant structural expressionism. The High Tech movement did this either with the exoskeleton, as in the Hong Kong Shanghai Bank, or with the construction joints, as in the famous 'gerberettes' of the Pompidou Centre – or with both, as in Lloyd's. Structural fetishism can be a beautiful thing, and all art fetishes those parts of a work on which it focuses attention.

But this does not mean, as is often thought, that the designer-engineer always has to express the structure of a building as if it were a crab or turtle. A good engineer has to have a paradoxical skill, the ability to extend structural invention while, at the same time, suppressing its expression for the sake of other architectural ideas. Indeed, it was this more subtle ability that led to Cecil Balmond's first important collaboration, that with James Stirling on the Neue Staatsgalerie in Stuttgart in 1977. Whereas a more repetitive, structuralist approach had been suggested by the previous engineers working on the job, Balmond came up with a solution that underscored the spatial idea and it was this innovation that Stirling used to make Stuttgart such a masterpiece of urban drama.

Balmond, as the sketches show below, often is present at the creation of an architectural idea. His thinking thus has partly shaped the buildings of Rem Koolhaas and Daniel Libeskind, Alvaro Siza and Ben van Berkel, not to mention a host of good mainstream architects such as Arata Isozaki and Philip Johnson. In 1997, when I had to list the fifteen most important buildings and projects that were changing architecture, I found to my amazement that Balmond scored higher than any architect on the list – that is, if one is to credit the engineer with partial creation.

And this raises the contentious issues of attribution, power and control. It is the rare architect who, like Le Corbusier, depicts the collaboration of architect and engineer as two interlocking hands, as a partnership between equals. Moreover, Cecil Balmond, like the architects on my list, has a sophisticated idea of the new paradigm. This is due, no doubt, to the fact that it is coming from the sciences of complexity, and engineers have to be conversant with the sciences.

The new paradigm is, inevitably, characterised in different ways; as Complexity or Nonlinear architecture, as Emergent or Cosmogenic architecture. None of these terms would make you leave home, always the test of a good label. Computer designers have called it Animate, Blob, Digital and Fractal architecture, or more simply Cyberspace. Scientists themselves debate whether the new paradigm should go under the label of Complexity or Chaos Theory, or Nonlinear Dynamics. Balmond adds his special use of 'informal' to the lists, to the jousting of terms, to the Darwinian competition of labels. Perhaps, because the new paradigm is so closely allied to pluralism, this heterogeneity of usage is appropriate and a single winner will never emerge.

Nevertheless, there is a broad coherent movement, a discernible, referent for these terms. The way 'informal' illuminates the territory is in stressing patterns that emerge from new assumptions. The customary way of conceiving a structure and space is formal, that is through the Phileban solids (such as spheres and cubes) and the grids that are based on them. From the beginnings of Chinese and Egyptian architecture right up to the present, this formal system has dominated cities and design. While not rejecting this approach, the new paradigm puts it in its natural place as part of a much greater whole. Formal patterns do underlie some of nature – spherical planets and hexagonal snowflakes, for example – but most of the cosmos shows nonlinear organisation. Brain waves, heartbeats, or the growth of galaxies show patterns that are fractal and dynamic. Through feedback slight variations, or sudden jumps, are introduced into organisational forms. The old paradigm was epitomised by the maxim 'less is more', the injunction of Flaubert and Mies van der Rohe, whereas the new is characterised by 'more is different'.

This is the phrase of the Nobel laureate and scientist Philip Anderson. It refers to the ubiquitous property in nature of emergence, of phase change. Add more energy, or information, or mass, or whatever, and a system will reach a critical point and jump into a new regime. The basic insight, not much more than twenty years old, is that under these conditions new patterns of organisation can emerge spontaneously.

Cecil Balmond brings this new understanding to the collaboration of engineer and architect. With Daniel Libeskind at the V&A in London he has worked out both a new chaotic spiral organisation and a new system of tiling, the 'fractiles'. With Rem Koolhaas he has developed acentric cantilevers, and new roof structures. He, like they, turns columns into beams and floors into walls and roof. The continuous structural surface, the hybrid floor-ramp-wall, has become an identifying mark of the new paradigm, as conventional as the glass and steel curtain wall was for Modernism. Balmond has developed this with Dutch architects, but it is just one more result of his nonlinear approach. He characterises this as thinking in terms of surface not line, zones not points, scatter not equal support, and moving locus not fixed centre. These are the hallmarks of his 'informal', a recognisable style tending towards the biomorphic and free form. In this sense he is a leading part of that broad movement in architecture whose most visible exponent is Frank Gehry.

On every design on which he has collaborated he has pushed the structure in different ways, or allowed new assumptions to interact, so that surprising patterns emerge. Patterns are what underlie mathematics and our various conceptions of beauty. The problem of old patterns, and particularly formal ones, is not that they are ugly but unchallenging. We already know many of their combinations and, if we are not fatigued by this knowledge neither are we stimulated by it. Aesthetic and intellectual appreciation demands a minimum provocation, something that spurs us to see and think anew. If the architect allows it, Balmond never leaves a structural and spatial idea unchallenged, where he found it.

By convention, and even law, the engineer is not meant to receive equal credit for the architecture, and Balmond is careful not to claim this. Often chief designers on a building have their role passed over in silence and it is clearly time we devised more accurate methods of assigning authorship than those that prevail today. But, as a critic and historian, I have to say that in the long term Balmond's contribution will come out and he will be mentioned as an important force behind so much contemporary architecture of significance, and take his place with the Brunels, Eiffels and Candela.

Charles Jencks

PREFACE

Cecil Balmond has, almost single-handedly shifted the ground in engineering – a domain where the earth moves very rarely – and therefore enabled architecture to be imagined differently.

As perhaps only a non-European could, he has destabilized and even toppled a tradition of Cartesian stability – systems that had become ponderous and blatant... Instead of solidity and certainty, his structures express doubt, arbitrariness, mystery and even mysticism. He is creating a repertoire that can engage the uncertainty and fluidity of the current moment.

He is involved in the most intimate moments of the architectural processes and has spawned a generation of hybrids of engineering and architecture, where previously separate identities have merged.

Through his work, engineering can now enter a more experimental and emotional territory; if architecture ever wants to evolve beyond the ornamental status it currently enjoys, it is through the thinking of Cecil Balmond and others that offer both a new seriousness and new pleasures.

Rem Koolhaas

INTRODUCTION

When we conjure up impressions, ideas, and images of the engineer we tend to think of an ingenious individual and Promethean spirit who overcomes huge obstacles to realise the most daring constructions. The tallest, the biggest, the largest, are the records set by the great engineers. The Isambard Kingdom Brunels, the Gustave Eiffels become the heroes in our transgressions of Nature. In the public mind the engineer turns into the supreme technological legislator – a hard person of science – who makes the impossible work.

This romantic notion of the engineer conspires to keep art and science separate. Engineering as a catalyst to inspire a creativity is not the generally held view. But in the Greek word 'techne' the unity of engineer-architect describes a sharing of design values, the diagram and calculation, the concept and proportion being viewed as cycles of noetic invention.

At first I assumed a certain subservience in engineering, as an enabling science to the act of putting up buildings. There was satisfaction in negotiating its precisions, and only I had X-ray eyes to see into the equations and numbers. Then I began to question what these regular framings of closed squares and rectangles were; were they containers of an empty inanimate space?

I looked again. I did not believe in this restriction.

I found answers in early Greek mathematics, in its proportionate rules leading to sub-assembly and grand-assembly and in its procession of orders, producing interior balance. Their notion of *symmetria*, a concept of liveliness in concurrent measured rhythms, was not that far removed from the contemporary idea of complexity as an unfolding, simultaneous and self-similar pattern. Fascinated by arithmetic and geometry, as if for the first time, I also looked into the modern instabilities of mathematics where uncertainty principles and fractional geometries were opening new worlds. Chaos theory produced impossibly beautiful structures; could such animation be brought to building science, a loose or travelling geometry giving shape and form?

Geometry is never mentioned in the normal course of designing a building; it is taken for granted as a system of isolated bounded shapes. Appearance and externalities seem to be all that matters – there is no sense of interiorisation or working from a theoretical base of form towards a configuration; *symmetria* has turned into non-speculation. Space is left empty and barren, trapped in rigid containers. Seen as necessary evils out of a Cartesian logic, columns are placed in diminished regular grids. Structure is assumed to be a reduction and a regulation. The mindset is also the negative behind many a desperate underpinning of free-form; subtle transpositions of shape that fashion strength out of apparent feebleness are not well understood.

There is a lot more to structure than strict post and beam. Slabs may fold and act as lines of vertical strength, beams may bifurcate and change shape, columns can serve as beams, the ingredients are all there to evolve form in fascinating ways. The challenge is to make structure the new discipline in a re-examination of space.

Now the computer opens a door and gives unparalleled freedom to explore – the result is a bewildering and mind bending free-for-all where anything goes. But cool new shapes and blobs are nothing more than mere façade if they are propped up by standard post and beam constructions. To create an integrity in the establishing of a free shape a new method is needed for configuration with flexible start points. Instead of line – surface; instead of equi-support – scatter; instead of fixed centre – a moving locus; and instead of points – zones.

Such scenarios cover the range of projects in this book, from a villa to a great station hall, from normal frame to flow diagrams or algorithms, from orthogonality to spaces that fold over themselves. And there are common characteristics: in each case the intervention that influences the design is a local forcing move, or a juxtaposition that stresses rhythm, or two or more events mixing to yield hybrid natures. As the effects are multiplied by extension or overlapping, surprising and ambiguous answers arise. Because there is no hierarchy, only interdependence, I call this template of ideas *informal*.

But in a building form that is static, where are the dynamics, what is the non-linearity?

This is a difficult question. To my mind the answers lie deep in configuration. As we are made of patterns, both random and regular, both physical and emotional, probing the archetypes of pattern is important – in its recognition and resonance we may find an element of beauty. In the past beauty was conditioned by aspects of purity, fixed symmetries and pared minimal structure being accepted as norms. As long as our brain kept to tramlines of reasoning the model persisted. Now that the world is being accepted as not simple, the complex and oblique and the intertwining of logic strands gain favour. Reason itself is finally being understood as nascent structure, non-linear and dependent on feedback procedures. Beauty may lie in the actual processes of engagement and be more abstract than the aesthetic of objecthood. Ultimately it may really be a constructive process.

We are in a time when anything goes and there is no basis for a manifesto – post modern has come to, ultimately, no meaning. With little understanding of the motivation of form, modernism runs into minimalist dead ends and by continuing to look to the outside the seduction with objecthood and architecture as art is perpetuated. Geometry is not invoked; no one peers within and asks questions about the archetypes of form. These are forgotten. Instead, instant realisations are sought from computers with form-finding that is software dependant.

But there are stories to tell. Searching for a form, an exploration of instinct against pre-conception, starts several interrogations. The chapters in this book catalogue such a search. A cycle of invention and post rationalisation runs from one start to another – and in between are the judgements and criticisms one makes. What remains constant is the motivation to keep entering that creative dialogue between architecture and engineering, and the writing of new stories.

Cecil Balmond, London, January 2002

17

Some people keep a diary.

Others, like me, find the daily minutiae too meaningless to record with its small traffickings up and down. But if one looks back over time and runs a memory record of a project through one's mind, a diary of sorts takes shape. In serial fashion, key events milestone the project – changes, dead-ends, parallel lines of enquiry, the conclusion and the ambitions of that first inception – moments of importance that turn into only a few days of recollection. Looking back on the Bordeaux project, I remember only Eight Days. And with each day the long hours of criticism, the short seconds of inspiration, the tug of all those movements that push and pull each way as what we call 'The Project' ticks on.

Rem Koolhaas phones me. As usual the voice is urgent, full of convictions and ambitions, the language poised beautifully on extreme polarities. He has an unusual request, to make a villa in Bordeaux 'fly'.

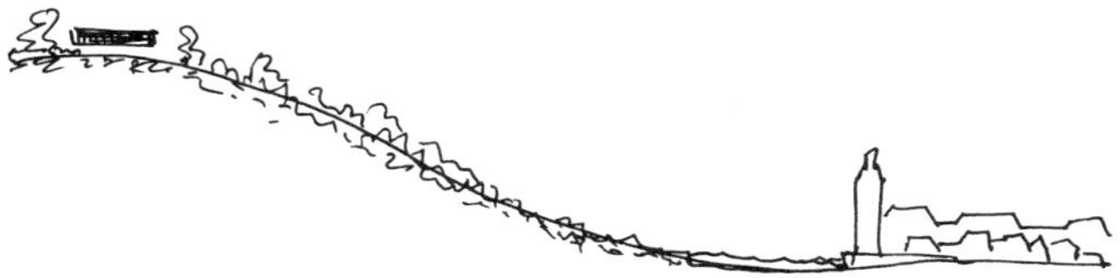

The project is on a fantastic site with panoramic views over the rich, wine-laden city stretching along the river.

Rem says the client is seriously disabled from a recent car accident but is fighting back, determined to have a new life. And the house has to be a special one that can accommodate his needs with those of his wife and two children. They have a large town house, but now under different circumstances the family wants a new villa, up on the cliff edge, overlooking the city.

And I had that reaction when one first hears of a project – the immediate excitement, a new challenge and with it the start up fear – will it succeed?

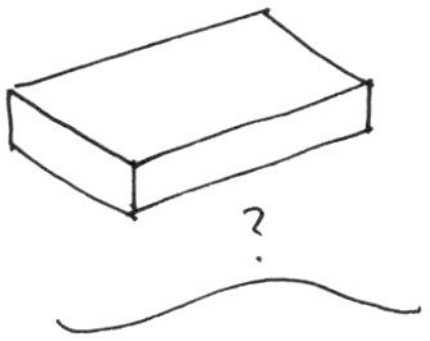

In the event, the answer was quite unexpected.

Generic Issues

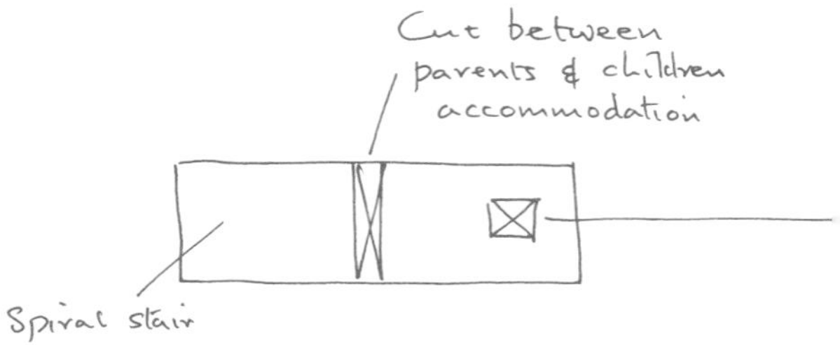

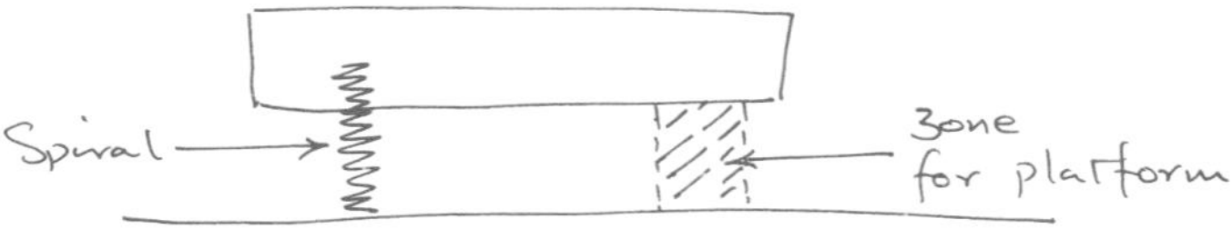

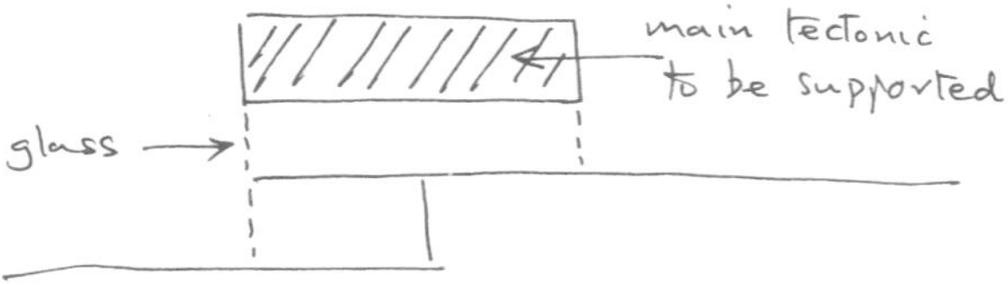

We meet in Bordeaux. The setting is something else – a hotel designed by Jean Nouvel overlooking the fields of Floriac, just a few miles outside the city.

We work at first in a ground floor reception room. No one seems to be about. OMA's team of Jerry and François are here and sketches of the site and ground plans lie all over the place. They outline the brief to me.

– hole for lift platform through ground and first

A family house, for husband and wife, plus two children. The design must give access to the disabled person, to release the full potential of the house. The principle tectonic is to be a box, up in the air, where the bedrooms will be located. Below this are the living spaces, surrounded by glass. The glass may open out onto the landscape and vanish; below the living space is a partial basement, cut into the earth on one side but open to an entry courtyard on the other. There is to be a special lift, a moving part of the house really to reach all levels.

INTERROGATION:

To ask a mass to levitate is not a new question; there is always an architectural demand for a lightness of being, *tabula rasa* visions with nothing to account for gravity. Structure in these situations simply gets in the way, becoming an enemy of promise.

But gravity is a tyrant. Its pull cannot be avoided, and the usual response for supporting a load in the air is to configure legs to hold the weight up from below. There is a directness of purpose to this configuration but there is also a complacency to look for nothing else.

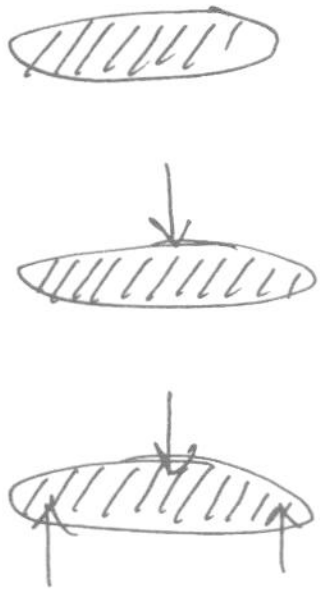

And the paradigm of 'table' brings with it implicit acceptance of a static symmetry.

A classic reference to this assumption in modern architecture is the Villa Savoye, Le Corbusier's pristine vision of a white box of light floating over the fields of Savoye.

Pilotti, concrete rods of a machine-like elegance, staple the form into the earth and anchor it, unmoving. Perhaps that is what the architect wanted, an altar forever fixed in space. Its mnemonic is temple. Such icons of form exert a stranglehold on future perception.

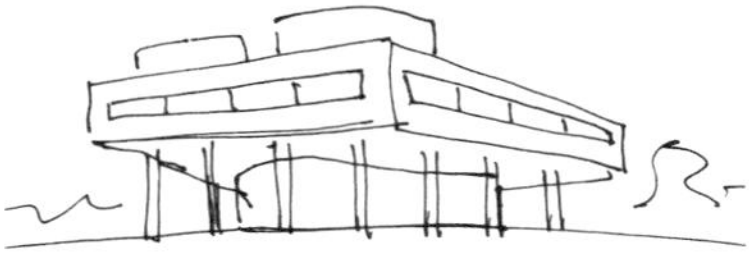

Countless imitations kill off speculation.

Now the question was being asked again, how to make a tectonic mass elevate, even fly. But did it need to? We went up to the site to have a look.

We cut through the heavy growth, finally emerging at the top. The views were terrific. The sun was going down, flooding the river with colour. Lights came on in the distance; it was that time of the day when cities turn into fairylands. If this were my house, I too would want a magic carpet up here, to look out on a twinkling land – the word 'hover' came to mind.

DAY TWO

If a weight suspended above the earth should somehow levitate, the risk-answer must lie in the breaking of symmetry.

I sketched out various solutions, trying to set the mass 'free'.

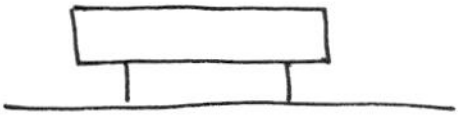

Columns were stuck well underneath to give a feeling of free edge:

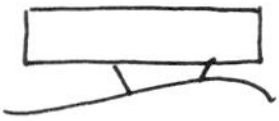

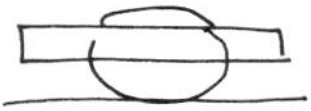

In some cases the ground came up to disguise the support:

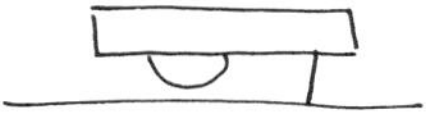

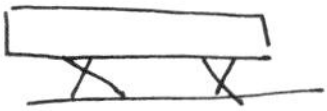

In other instances raking columns initiated oblique lines to take away the feeling of direct support.

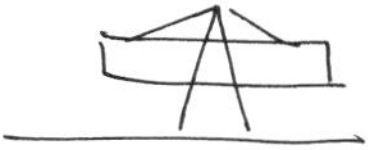

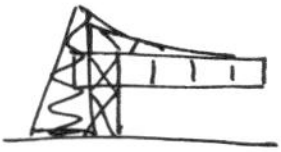

I tried top hung support as well but that felt alien and inappropriate for the site.

None of the ideas really satisfied. I still felt confined. The picture of the site kept imposing its own dynamic, challenging a better solution. No matter how the columns were placed beneath the load the generic concept of table came back, and with it the imprint of an 'anchor' killing off the ambition.

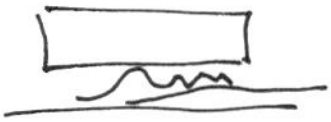

Something else was needed.

The idea of *launch* came to mind, to energise the building as momentum. Two lateral moves broke with symmetry.

Move one:

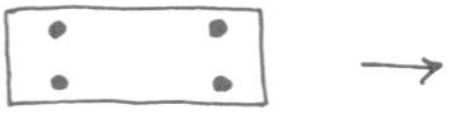

what if the supports in plan are displaced beyond the boundary, well outside the box?

Move two:

what if the supports 'flip' in elevation, one top hung, one bottom fixed?

Suddenly we had the dynamic we wanted. The side-way shifts in plan and jumps in elevation brought a skewed tension to the solution. They stretched the concept of balance to the edge of the predictable, towards a moment of instability, setting up a precise danger point.

At one end the box sits on a shelf beam. At the other end its weight hangs off a roof girder, precarious and scary. The cable that restores balance is placed outside the plan, mimicking the movement of the displaced column at the shelf support end. Each cross-section is the reverse of the other.

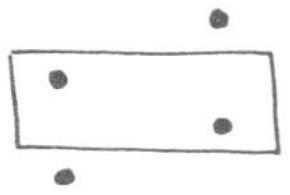

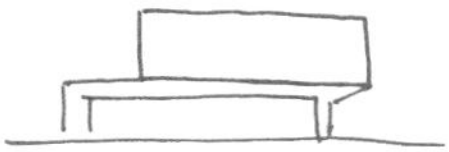

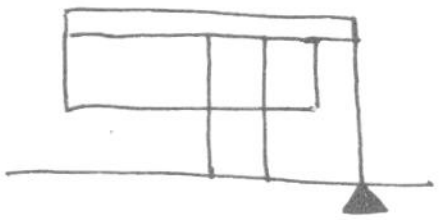

A contradiction is offered in how the load is perceived. The solution pulls one way and then the other. The weight of the box is both supported from the ground and hung up in the air, in plan and elevation the exaggerations deny any conventional reading of balance.

The idea of a table is destroyed. Instead, the dynamic is *launch.*

In my mind's eye I already saw the villa flying.

Imagine a ball at the bottom of a concave curve. It nestles securely, unmoving. That is the pragmatic response to the support of load – a secure base, a stable configuration.

The reverse of this is a moment of insecurity at the top of a curve, inherently a position of instability. A slight push at the summit, one way or the other and the ball moves off and away.

The two diagrams serve as a metaphor for design; tried and tested, or new?

At the bottom of the valley, there is the point of tradition and solid reference. No matter how far we experiment and get away from that location and move up the slope, we fall back to the bottom and settle at the origin. Analysis always brings us back to the zero point. The solution cannot get away from its original reference. The Villa Savoye belongs to the valley diagram in its configuration of structure.

But at the summit of a hill the point is one of departure, the outcome unpredictable. There is no way back to the origin. We roll into the unknown to chart a new course. In the cliff top scenario there is not the safety of past reference, only the certainty of unfamiliar territory ahead.

The Bordeaux Villa belongs to this second category of diagram – its future interpretation yet to come.

This day was one of balance, working out the top support which picks up the wall beams.

At one end, the villa has a core running through it, a shaft that encloses a spiral stair. It is deliberately offset to add drama.

Such an eccentric support would cause a mass to tip over.

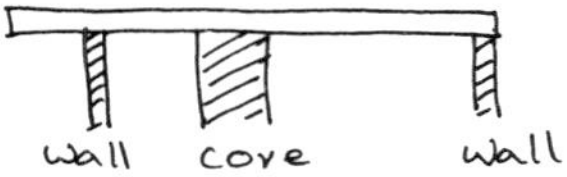

The diagrammatic is:

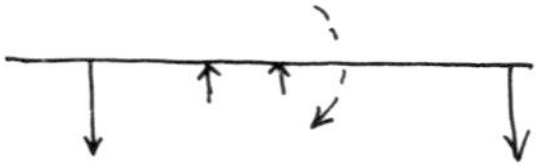

A tie down is needed at the extreme end to restore stability.

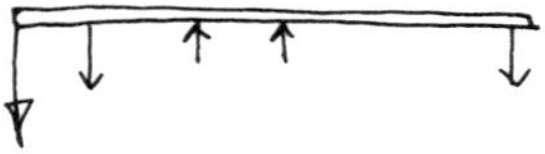

In the Bordeaux Villa this is given by a cable, providing tension through a counter weight buried in the ground. The trick is to keep the cable under tension all the time. A hot day, for example, will increase the length of the tie due to thermal expansion, slacken it, and tend to tip the box over to one side. So the cable is over tensioned to compensate and be taut under this condition keeping the mass to the horizontal. Asymmetrical loading of snow, or wind, or people can also induce slackness in the cable; and for each of these conditions calculations were made to ensure tension, at all times.

What happens if the cable is cut?

The box will tilt to one side; but the deflection is calculated and the material proportioned in such a way as to keep the structure stable in this extreme condition. Due to the elastic nature of materials (even concrete) once the cable force is reinstated the structure will ease back to the horizontal!

Calculation Sheet

48919	FIGURE 1

LOAD SYSTEM ON CABLE

Title: BORDEAUX VILLA

Member/Location

Drg. Ref.

Made by CB/RP Date NOV 95 Chd.

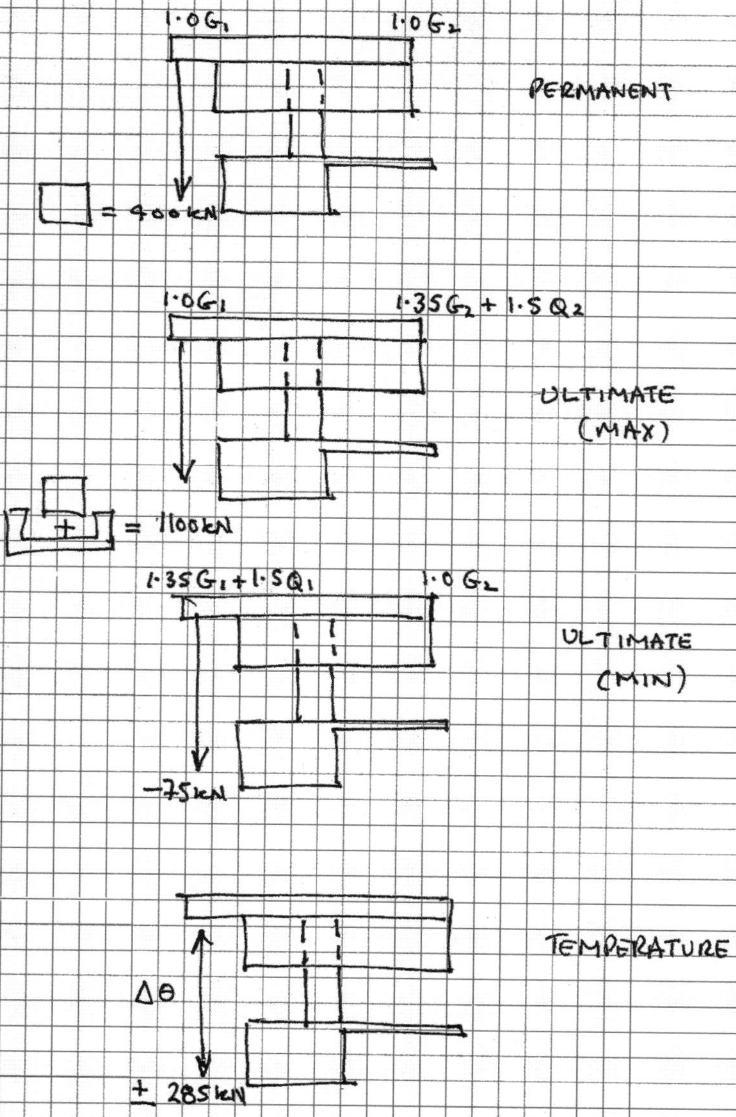

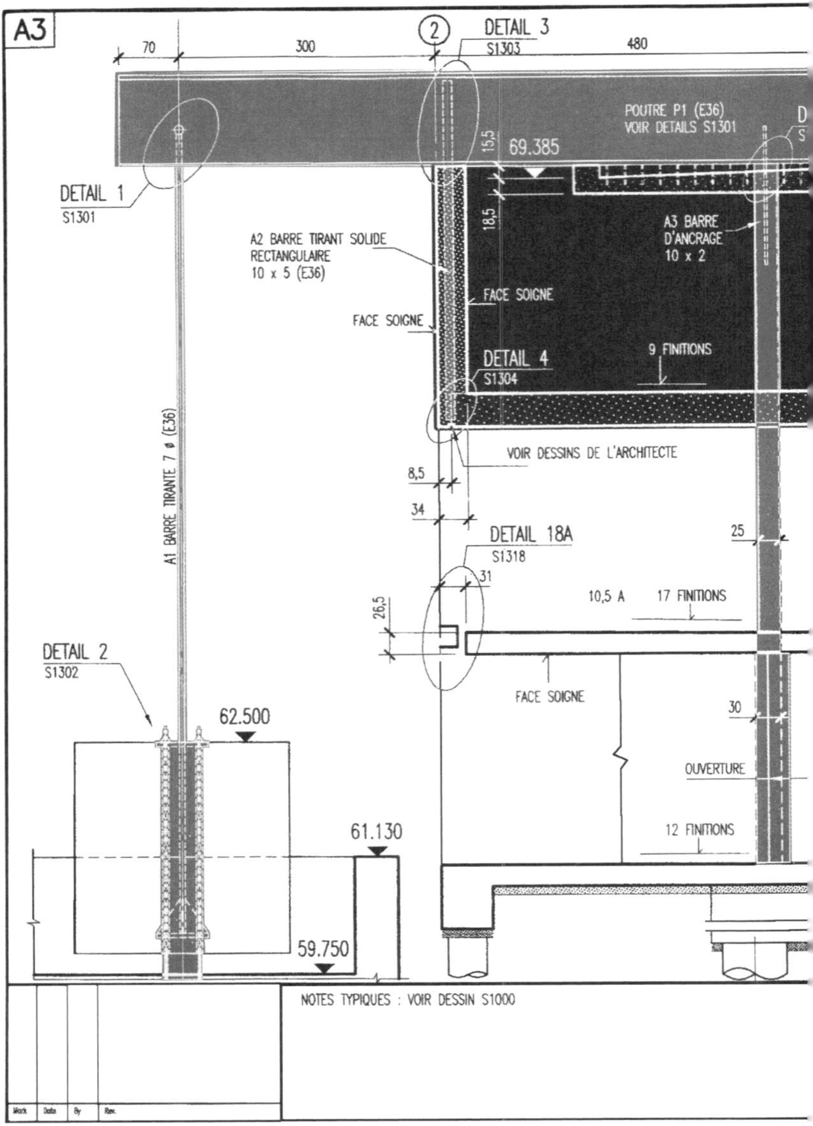
A3
70
300
480
2
DETAIL 3
S1303
POUTRE P1 (E36)
VOIR DETAILS S1301
15,5
69.385
18,5
DETAIL 1
S1301
A2 BARRE TIRANT SOLIDE
RECTANGULAIRE
10 x 5 (E36)
A3 BARRE
D'ANCRAGE
10 x 2
FACE SOIGNE
FACE SOIGNE
DETAIL 4
S1304
9 FINITIONS
A1 BARRE TIRANTE 7 ø (E36)
VOIR DESSINS DE L'ARCHITECTE
8,5
34
DETAIL 18A
S1318
25
31
10,5 A
17 FINITIONS
26,5
DETAIL 2
S1302
FACE SOIGNE
30
62.500
OUVERTURE
61.130
12 FINITIONS
59.750
NOTES TYPIQUES : VOIR DESSIN S1000
Mark
Date
By
Rev.

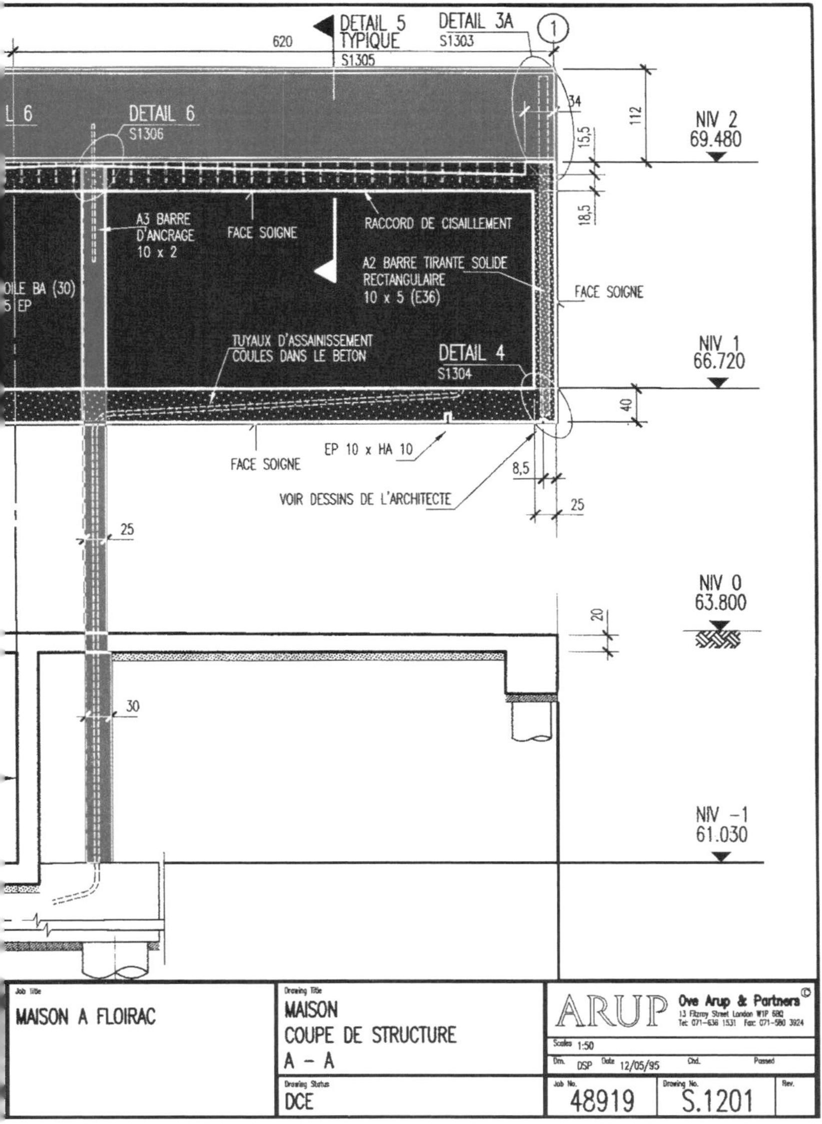

Job Title	Drawing Title	
MAISON A FLOIRAC	MAISON COUPE DE STRUCTURE A – A	ARUP Ove Arup & Partners © 13 Fitzroy Street London W1P 6BQ Tel: 071-636 1531 Fax: 071-580 3924
		Scales 1:50
		Dm. DSP Date 12/05/95 Chd. Passed
	Drawing Status DCE	Job No. 48919 | Drawing No. S.1201 | Rev.

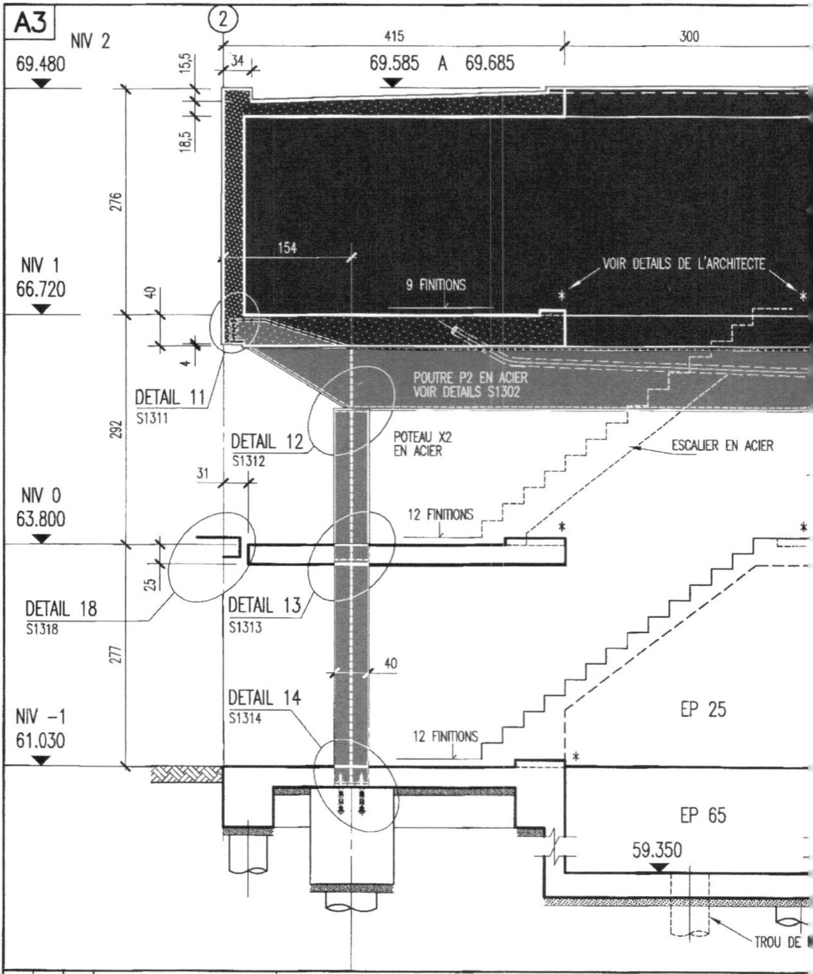

Mark	Date	By	Rev.

NOTES TYPIQUES – VOIR DESSIN S.1000

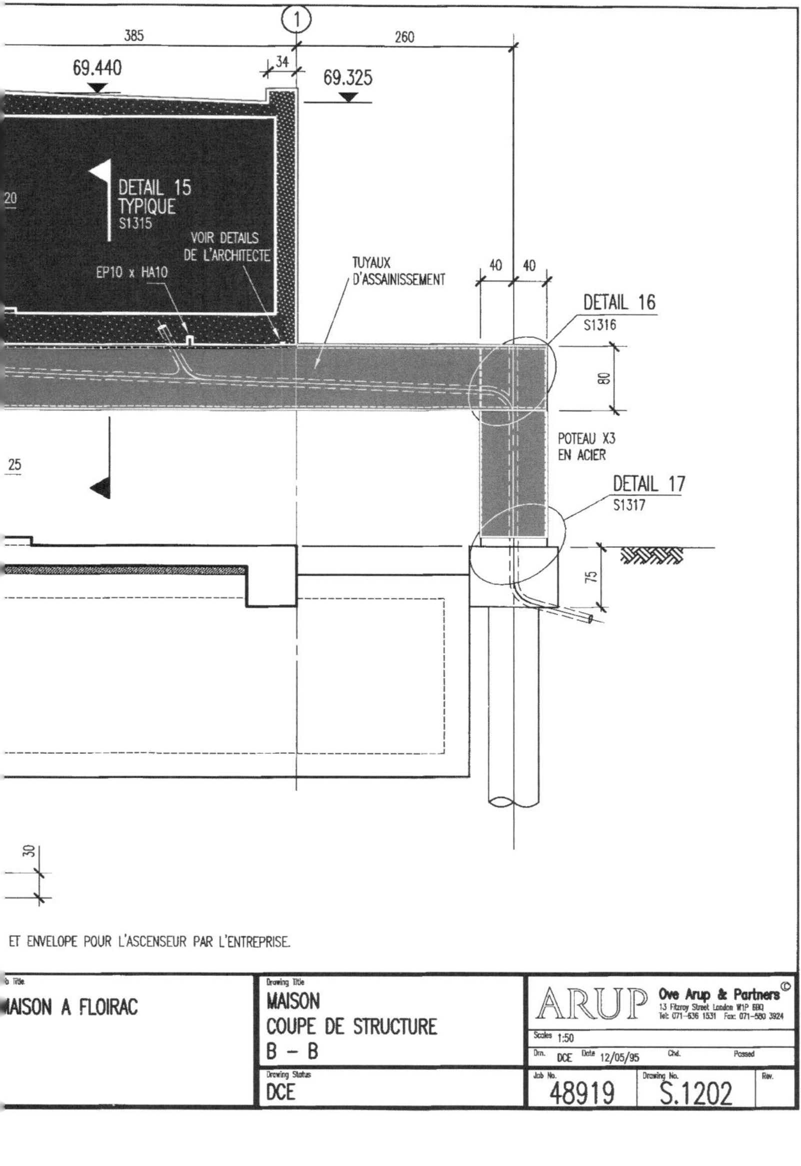
385
260
69.440
69.325
34
DETAIL 15
TYPIQUE
S1315
VOIR DETAILS
DE L'ARCHITECTE
EP10 x HA10
TUYAUX
D'ASSAINISSEMENT
40
40
DETAIL 16
S1316
80
POTEAU X3
EN ACIER
DETAIL 17
S1317
75
20
25
30
ET ENVELOPE POUR L'ASCENSEUR PAR L'ENTREPRISE.
MAISON A FLOIRAC
Drawing Title
MAISON
COUPE DE STRUCTURE
B – B
Drawing Status
DCE
ARUP
Ove Arup & Partners
13 Fitzroy Street London W1P 6BQ
Tel: 071-636 1531 Fax: 071-580 3924
Scales 1:50
Drn. DCE Date 12/05/95
Chd.
Passed
Job No.
48919
Drawing No.
S.1202
Rev.

I proposed a seamless winding of material for the elevated box, a concrete culvert.

Specification: 40 cm floor; 20 cm roof; 25 cm walls.

The roof and floor spanned 11 metres onto longitudinal wall beams. These beams in turn had two supports, and cantilevered beyond them at each end. Though thin in section the depth of these walls gave adequate stiffness and the gable ends of the box could be kept open if needed. On the wall beams, lines of principal stress were marked so that holes could be cut out without complications to the structural action.

Keep it simple – that was the aim.

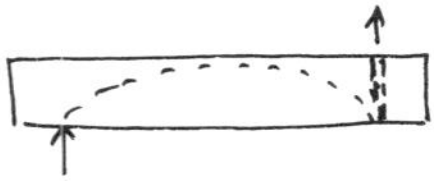

A grid was plotted on the wall elevation to allow a random solution. Rem speculated that small porthole-like windows scattered throughout the elevation would look terrific. We floated small circles, like soap bubble experiments, through the elevation as we tried various punctuations – low level portholes for the client in a wheelchair, and high level vista points for the others. Views were calculated and prescribed. A beautiful drawing, like a wind rose, took shape in OMA's office.

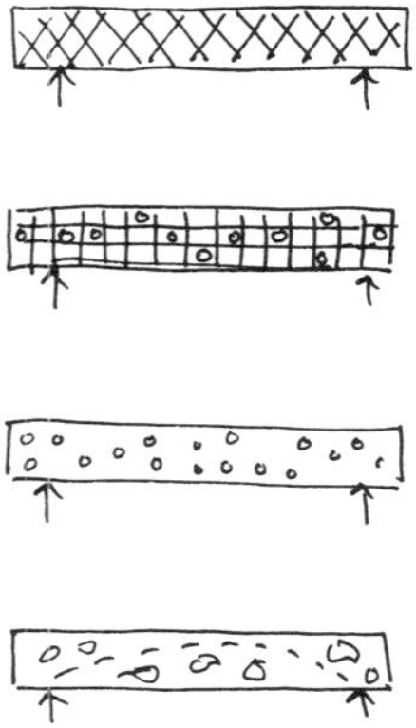

The design, we thought, was progressing well. The shape, size and configuration were solved, the materiality agreed: we were into the 'Avant Projet Détaillé' stage of design, prior to tender.

Then came the problems.

The floor slab looked too heavy, the roof too light. The free edges along the cuts in the slab were deflecting significantly and the walls were felt to be too thin.

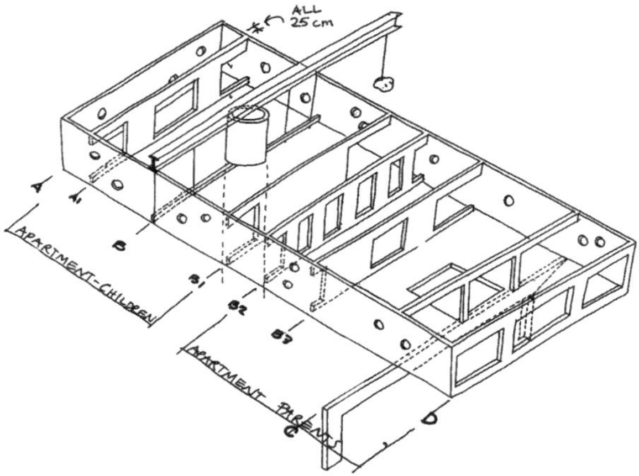

Strategies were looked at to lighten the floors; conventional beam and slab framing methods/void formers in polystyrene/rib systems/etc. Use of the stairs from ground to first floor as a prop was even considered so that all key dimensions could be maintained; but the stair was too weak and located badly, to take any significant load.

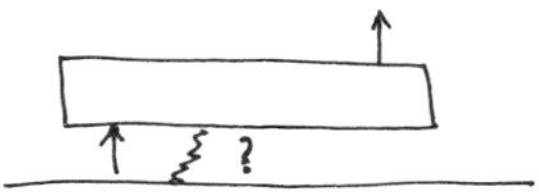

Various initiatives by our respective teams grew, challenging the concept.

Suddenly it all seemed too difficult. That uneasy moment arrived when the initial idea began to turn into a grave doubt. The culvert form was abandoned. Internal Vierendeel type beams were introduced to stiffen the roof and floor, allowing more slender dimensions for slab elements, but the Vierendeel solution meant intrusions below the soffit, reducing headroom and a consequent heightening of the vertical dimension of the box. Did we want to do this?

If a few more millimetres were added to the height of the wall we saw the suspended form, from being 'heavy and just right', turning into 'massive and ugly'.

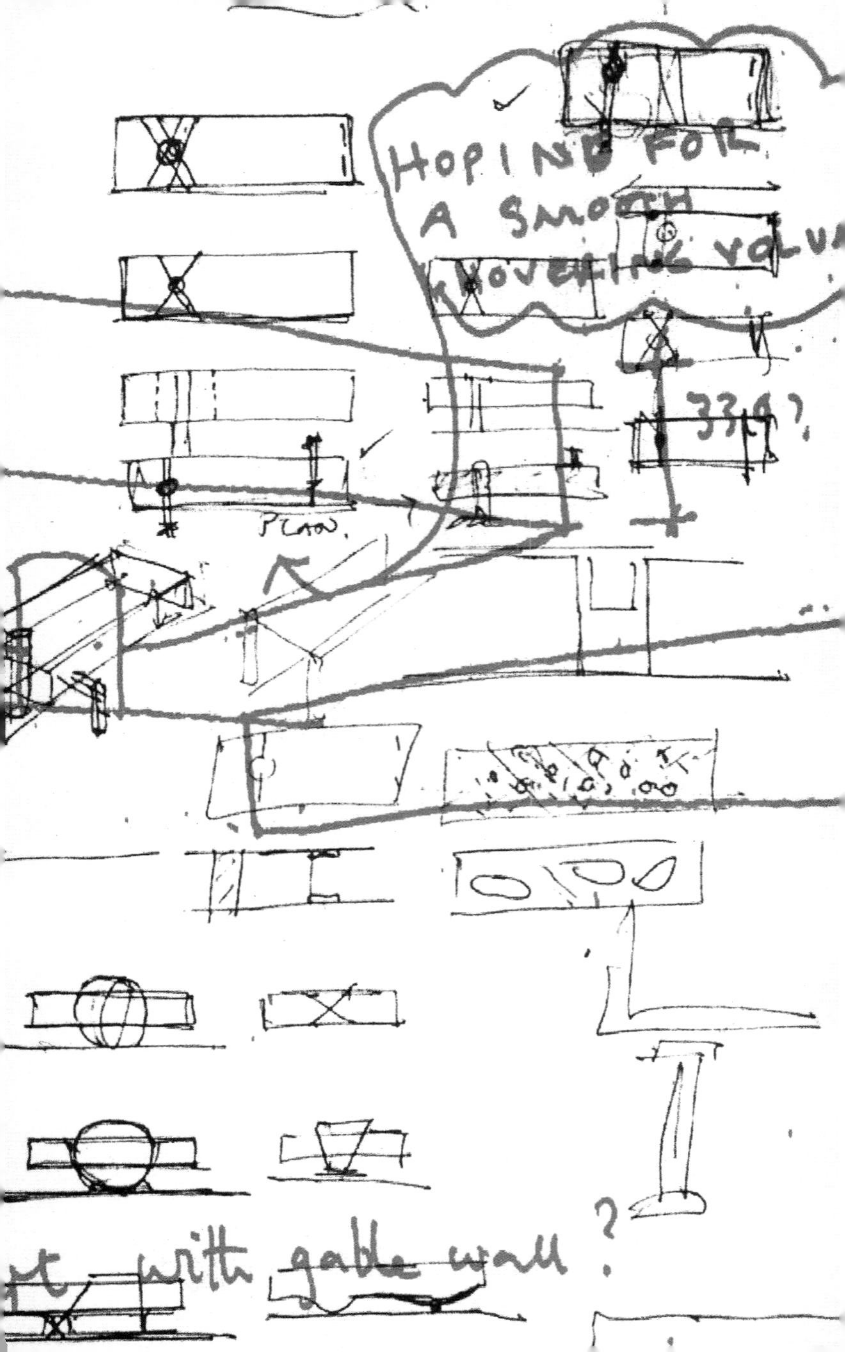
HOPING FOR
A SMOOTH
HOVERING
Plan.
33,9?
with gable wall ?

There were other technical problems as well.

The physical cut in both roof and floor slabs, gave a major discontinuity to the transmission of lateral loads. Normally the slabs would be considered as braced diaphragms, but now the walls had to act as horizontal ties, passing stability load between the core and slender verticals of the portal type shelf beam.

One side of the basement opened onto the landscape, the other side remaining buried against the cut earth...

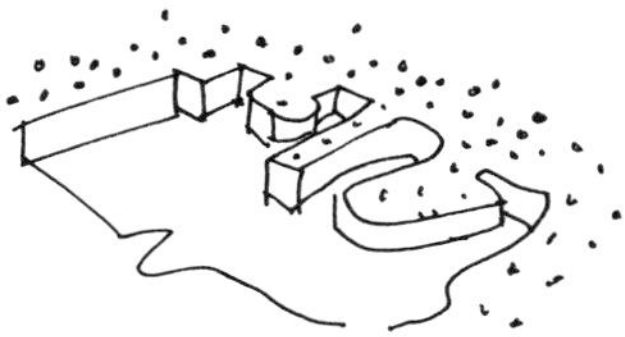

...this gave a horizontal force from the retained earth face that had to be resisted. Again, a problem of lateral stability.

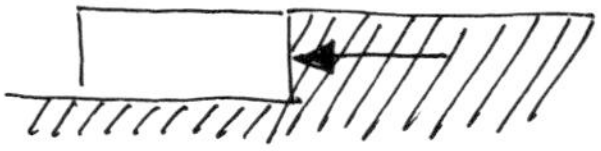

Other questions were asked such as how to make the glass walls at ground level 'vanish', and what chases and slots should be cut into the concrete slab to accommodate sliding rails? The very interventions that gave freedom to the people in the house, eroded the concrete section and weakened it, threatening more support or thicker dimensions. A meeting was called for.

It is the insanity of design 'rightness' that makes one stick to stubborn judgements and we returned to the initial concept despite the uncertainties. No one can account for such dictates but they dig in, convinced of their own *a priori* logic.

We decided to start afresh, drawing the simple culvert shape again; I restated the dimensions as if the questions against it had never been. Perhaps it was just the renewed focus that helped, for things quickly fell into place. The slabs worked, the beams worked. Conduits, slots for door slides, drainage falls, free edge deflections, were somehow all solved. We were back on track. What had the fuss been about? Impossible to say: how does a collective nervousness work to destroy a confident starting point? Reassertion of the concept seemed to steady the hand of the possible and work a minor miracle. The day looked good again.

DAY SIX

The main tectonic of the box solved, attention turned to the design and proportioning of the two main lines of support. If a mass has momentum, it should not be 'pinned' or held back. The supporting beam lines should not restrain, they must just touch.

TOP HUNG:

Rods buried in the concrete walls took the load up into the top steel beam. This girder was made to accommodate a double web so that the rod fixing passed between the web plates in secret. Similarly, the tension cable departed through a slot cut in the bottom flange. The roof connected via shear studs buried in a concrete plinth to give a seamless feeling between beam and slab.

The aim was to declare 'look no hands'; the apparent lack of 'nailing' or gussetting adding to a perceived moment of danger.

BOTTOM SUPPORT:

Here the proposal was for a portal type frame. Initially concrete was considered, but the dimensions of the beam grew, reducing headroom at ground level drastically. Transferring the wall load at the tip of the cantilever also produced a high shear stress. Steel with its greater strengths seemed more appropriate. A hollow section could also be developed for this beam, allowing a path for drainage pipes from the floor above. And steel provided sharp edges in contrast to the seamless wrap of concrete – a hard precision could be brought to the solution

A special feature was made of starting the taper from the centre of its supporting column, to emphasise an exact point of balance. The idea was to stress this coincidence against the more distributed aspects of the overall configuration.

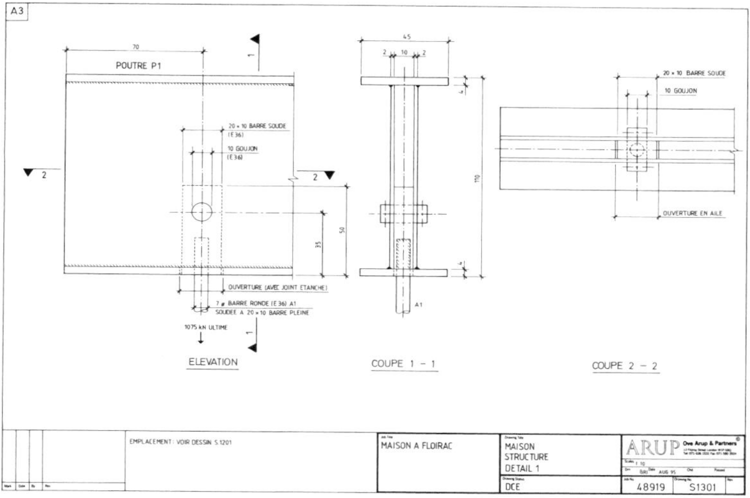
A3
70
POUTRE P1
20 × 10 BARRE SOUDE (E36)
10 GOUJON (E36)
OUVERTURE (AVEC JOINT ETANCHE)
7 ø BARRE RONDE (E36) A1
SOUDEE A 20 × 10 BARRE PLEINE
1075 kN ULTIME
ELEVATION
45
COUPE 1 – 1
20 × 10 BARRE SOUDE
10 GOUJON
OUVERTURE EN AILE
COUPE 2 – 2
EMPLACEMENT: VOIR DESSIN S.1201
MAISON A FLOIRAC
MAISON
STRUCTURE
DETAIL 1
DCE
ARUP
Ove Arup & Partners
1:10
AUG 95
48919
S1301

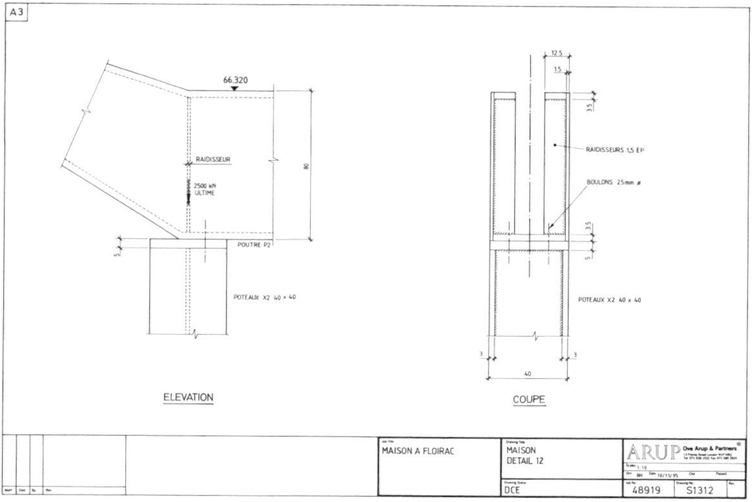
A3
66.320
RAIDISSEUR
2500 kN
ULTIME
POUTRE P2
POTEAUX X2 40 × 40
ELEVATION
12.5
RAIDISSEURS 1,5 EP
BOULONS 25mm ø
POTEAUX X2 40 x 40
40
COUPE
MAISON A FLOIRAC
MAISON
DETAIL 12
DCE
ARUP
Ove Arup & Partners
1:10
10/11/95
48919
S1312

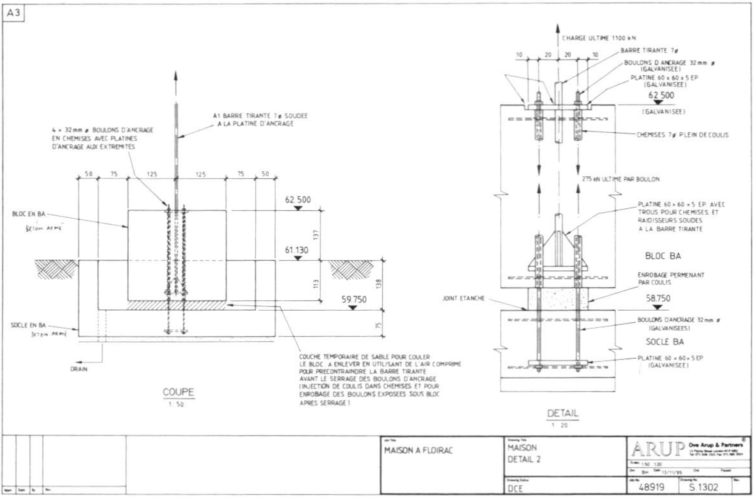
A3
A1 BARRE TIRANTE 7ø SOUDEE
A LA PLATINE D'ANCRAGE
4 × 32mm ø BOULONS D'ANCRAGE
EN CHEMISES AVEC PLATINES
D'ANCRAGE AUX EXTREMITES
50
75
125
125
75
50
62.500
BLOC EN BA
BETON ARMÉ
137
61.130
113
138
59.750
75
SOCLE EN BA
BETON ARMÉ
DRAIN
COUCHE TEMPORAIRE DE SABLE POUR COULER
LE BLOC. A ENLEVER EN UTILISANT DE L'AIR COMPRIME
POUR PRECONTRAINDRE LA BARRE TIRANTE
AVANT LE SERRAGE DES BOULONS D'ANCRAGE
(INJECTION DE COULIS DANS CHEMISES ET POUR
ENROBAGE DES BOULONS EXPOSEES SOUS BLOC
APRES SERRAGE)
COUPE
1:50
CHARGE ULTIME 1100 kN
10
20
20
10
BARRE TIRANTE 7ø
BOULONS D'ANCRAGE 32 mm ø
(GALVANISEE)
PLATINE 60 x 60 x 5 EP
(GALVANISEE)
62.500
(GALVANISEE)
CHEMISES 7ø PLEIN DE COULIS
275 kN ULTIME PAR BOULON
PLATINE 60 × 60 × 5 EP. AVEC
TROUS POUR CHEMISES, ET
RAIDISSEURS SOUDES
A LA BARRE TIRANTE
BLOC BA
ENROBAGE PERMENANT
PAR COULIS
JOINT ETANCHE
58.750
BOULONS D'ANCRAGE 32 mm ø
(GALVANISEES)
SOCLE BA
PLATINE 60 × 60 × 5 EP
(GALVANISEE)
DETAIL
1:20
MAISON A FLOIRAC
MAISON
DETAIL 2
ARUP
Ove Arup & Partners
Scales 1:50 1:20
BH
13/11/95
DCE
48919
S.1302

No one wants a day like this, but every project seems to have one – savings had to be made! The project was over budget and despite our attachment to the solution, some key features had to be redesigned.

Two cost reductions were agreed to.

1: Reduce the weight of the steel roof beam by making it much deeper, from 1.0 m to say 1.4 m.

We had spent a lot of time minimising the size of this top girder, keeping volume and bulk down, and every millimetre had been guarded jealously. If we accepted the contractor's proposal for a change, there would be a 40% increase to the vertical height of a key element. This was hard to swallow.

But the dramatic increase in height exaggerated the idea of 'beam', moving it towards another definition in Koolhaas' mind, of 'fascia'. The OMA team thought it would actually work better, and not for the first time in our work, out of a forced brutality a new inspiration was improvised.

2: Get rid of the counterweight.

Conceptually we wanted a very visible reading of 'anchor', a rock hanging freely from a cable. Through design development and concerns for safety the rock had turned into a concrete dead weight, located in a pit and held down further by a buried foundation. This was now too expensive. It was cheaper to bury the anchor they said, and have the cable tie disappear into the ground, fastened onto a lump of dead concrete.

This was a pity. The visible counterbalance underlined the drama of tipping over. But savings had to be made, and we reluctantly agreed to the change. Only a plate on the surface would denote passage through to the subterranean holding. It was expedient but not poetic, not our daredevil vision of a hung weight in space denoting a danger moment.

Construction was over. The shutters had been taken off, slabs depropped; walls were sustaining their design load and transmitting stress around the various window apertures. The thin box culvert spanned and cantilevered. Would the mental picture we had of the box 'flying' as it were, be there? Would the analogue of the actual building take shape and leap out at us?

The day I went to see the work, by luck, Rem was there. François and Jerry were there as well. The same people assembled in Bordeaux as on Day One. Was this the conclusion?

We compared notes. The skew supports gave configurations such that one end of the box literally seemed to launch itself off into space. Being released from the traditional securing of a centre of gravity, the mass seemed to power itself. We saw that symmetric supports would have been terrible, giving a static feel.

Wrenching the supports apart, moving them outside the plan, gave a degree of release.

Flipping the supports in elevation, one top and one bottom, added the second release.

The two movements taken together allowed the mass its own momentum – from tremendous to terrific. Almost scary at one angle, like a missile pointing over the edge, at another angle it looked a monster trapped against its will. Either way, the configuration worked. It was dramatic, brutal and exciting.

For Rem and I this was raw hypothesis made real, no adornment, no finish, just *structure*.

57

Trapped by a Cartesian cage I wanted to
break out.

The *informal* beckoned . . .

that opportunity came with Rem Koolhaas and
the Kunsthal in Rotterdam.

The Formal marches to strict rhythms.

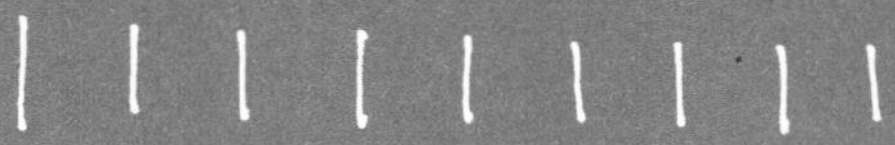

Why the necessity to space out structure equally, like soldiers marching on a parade ground?

Is the design of structural framing limited to the bar pattern of a cage; is space so dull that punctuating it means only the regular monotonous beat of verticals and horizontals? Why not relax and move towards a slip or jump in the arrangement of things?

Let the *informal* in. Have a syncopation – a rat-ta-ta-tat – instead of the dull metronomic one-two repeat of post and beam that rises up and runs along our buildings in stark structural skeletons.

Why not skip a beat? Incline the vertical, slope the horizontal. Or allow two adjacent lines of columns to slip past each other. Let space entertain us. Let's see other possibilities, other configurations of how buildings may be framed and stabilised.

And interruptions to 'sameness' do not mean heavy penalties. A specific framing with angularities, inclinations or whatever, may be cheaper. A considered unique path of structure is often more valid than the unquestioned assumption of a distributed solution, subdivided equally through a cross-section or plan.

regular

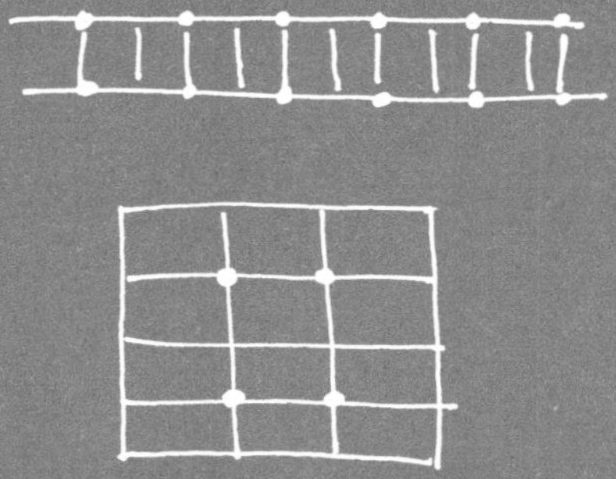

informal

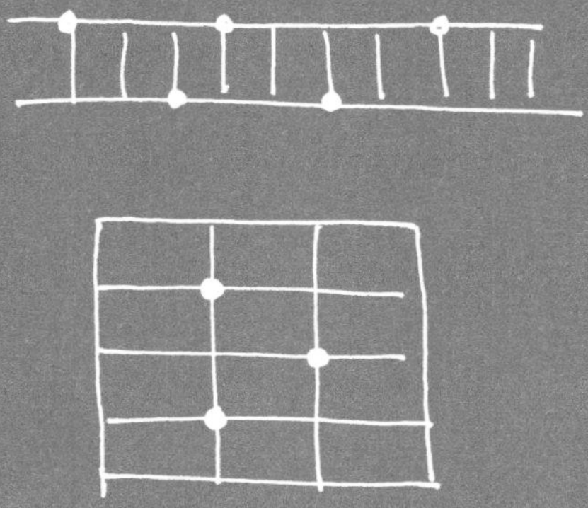

In Hall 2 of the Kunsthal a thin red line runs through the roof space. It is a small structural tube that follows, in plan, the path of an arch; and the curve intersects the roof beams to pick up lateral loads being delivered along those lines. Two pairs of ties reach out to prevent the arch from buckling in its plane of action.

As the lines of the structural system of arch and tie become interrupted by the beams, it is not clear what the thin red line means.

Is it structure?
Is it pattern?
Or, is it architectural device?
The answer is; all three.

Structure need not be comprehensible and explicit. There is no creed or absolute that dictates structure must be recognised as a basic functional skeleton or the manifest of a high-tech machine. It can be subtle and more revealing. It is a richer experience to my mind if a puzzle is set or a layer of ambiguity lies over the reading of 'structure'.

ar. penck

525I

When the thin red line is interrupted the connections are not celebrated; only the trajectory is propelled.

The mind's eye jumps over the gaps and stitches together a serial projection – a new kind of flying buttress is put together through the roof plane. Had the connections been exposed, with the brace fixed to the underside of the beams in an explicit way, the result would not have been as interesting. Instead the gaps in the thin red line cause an acceleration.

The *informal* has *speed* wrapped into it.

Slip and *jump* have varying notions of time and distance embedded in them. Ratios of distance to time lead to ideas of velocity, pulse, and rates of change. In tectonic terms this sense of motion is either arrested or frozen or just about to be launched. By contrast, reductionist thinking assumes structure to be a static, steady-state, baseline. Not much is asked of it but to serve and be 'honest'. Surprisingly, this guise of honesty often comes out as 'dumb'.

Why not structure as an animation that provokes synthesis?

Dedication to the limited language of high-tech mast and cable, or subservience to orthogonal post and beam, needs questioning. Such configurations say explicitly: 'I am machine, I am reduced skeleton'. To probe beyond this, into areas where structure is neither naked aggression nor dumb skeleton, is a quest that assumes technology yet moves on to higher and more complex levels of form. Better to claim: 'I am the thread propelling a story' and have structure as a generating path, rather than lay an unthinking grid map of column and beams over the subdivision of space. New configurations must be investigated.

Altogether there are four proposals to be made in the Kunsthal:

I: Brace

II: Slip

III: Frame

IV: Juxtaposition

Each time the expected answer is left behind and the *informal* delivers a surprise. Strange as it is exciting, raising questions about a bigger adventure, structure *talks* in the Kunsthal. The dialogue is with architecture; one discipline provokes the other.

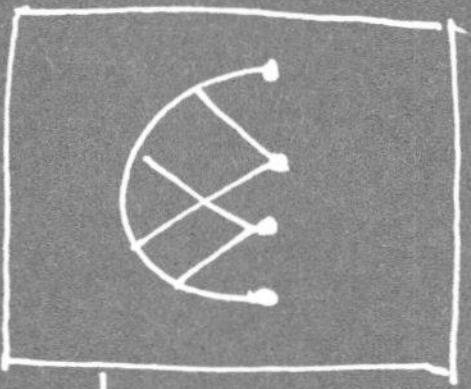

brace

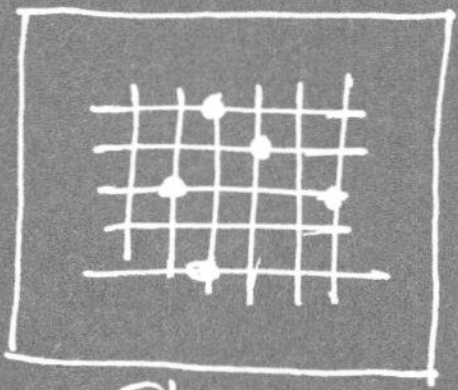

slip

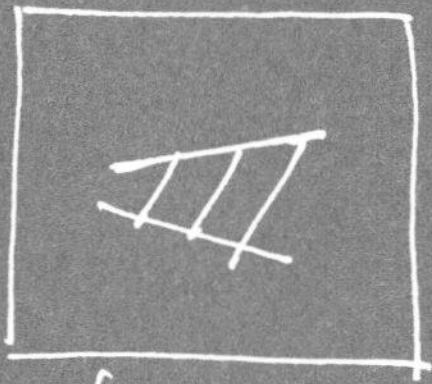

frame

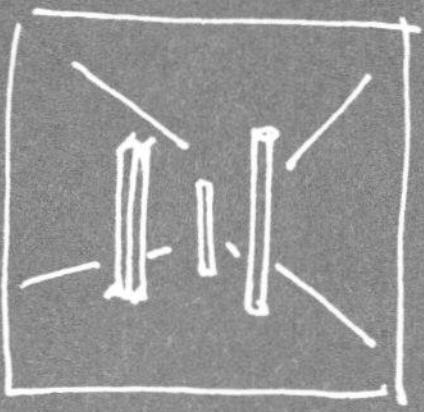

Juxtaposition

The centre image on the facing page is the traditional response to the design of a structural brace – a series of diagonals confined within two parallel lines. Such configurations run up cores to stiffen a building against wind, either explicitly in framed steel members, or implicitly in the resistance of a seamless concrete core, which has stress lines embedded in it that follow such a diagram. But instead of one universal assumption to the language of brace why not consider an alternative, a more dispersed idea?

Let the diagonals scatter across the vertical cross-section.

Care has to be taken with vertical and horizontal continuity, ensuring each diagonal connects between column points and that the load travelling along a diagonal is within an overall equilibrium – but these are the mechanics of the engineering solution.

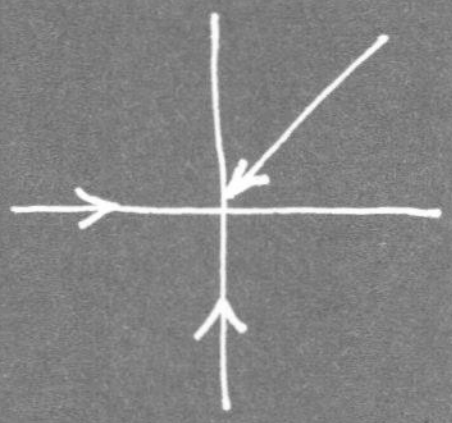

It does not take away from the greater freedom won by such a strategy.

The idea may be extended to a diagonal being considered as the abstraction for a whole zone. Plant rooms or certain program enclosures could serve as such transmission paths in a three-dimensional network of brace.

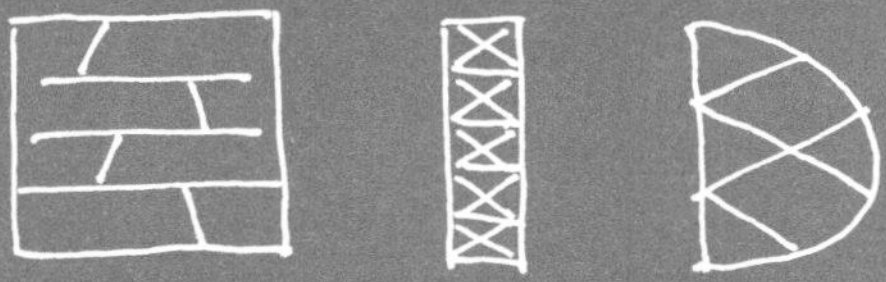

In the horizontal direction, bracing is needed also where floors and roofs of buildings serve as diaphragms passing lateral loads to vertical cores. Again, the traditional response is the figure of a truss, and one can see this in roofs of factories, warehouses, garages and large single space enclosures.

Does this have to be the only answer?

A different solution of a curving element can run right through a plan area – it works just as well, probably even with more efficiency. The thin red line of Hall 2 in the Kunsthal is such a proposal. Instead of the truss language bound in constraining parallel lines, an orbit in space releases the beautiful shape of arch; the pattern of diagonal ties juxtaposed with a thin running curvature promotes structure as evolving pattern.

Rigorous pragmatism is forgotten in a flash – the response is lighter, beyond technicalities. Architecture is freed from structural correctness and compulsive repetition.

In a large rectangular space reserved for changing exhibitions known as Hall 1, columns 'slip' past each other. Not squared up or standing to order in a formal subdivision of space, here, a local condition – a single out-of-phase movement – influences and informs the whole space.

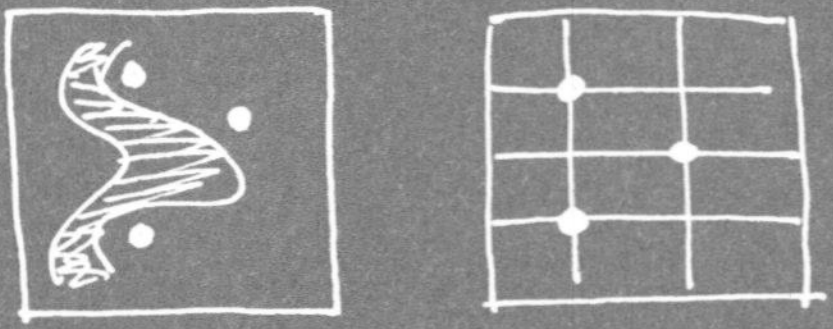

The floor plate design for this area began with columns on plan, concentric and four square. Typically, a steel framing plan was developed. (The alternative of a deep concrete coffer slab, with solid areas adjacent to the columns, was also considered; but stitching in the mechanical services led to headroom problems. Concrete was abandoned and the steel solution advanced instead.)

Despite the aim at the outset of being opportunist with structure, in one key area of the building the starting idea was along habitual lines – a symmetric and four-square partitioning of space and column support. Compared with the other rhythms of the building, Hall 1 looked dull and uninspired. Sketches show it stayed like that for some time, long after other elements leaned over or jumped or came together in odd juxtapositions.

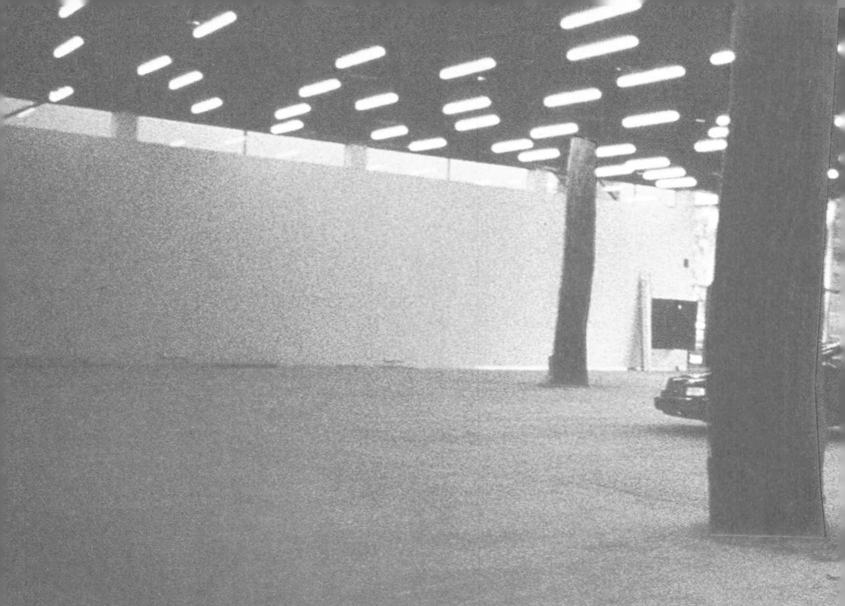

Then came the idea, simple and child-like, to assume the columns were two marching lines and to allow them to travel independently. I moved one row past the other.

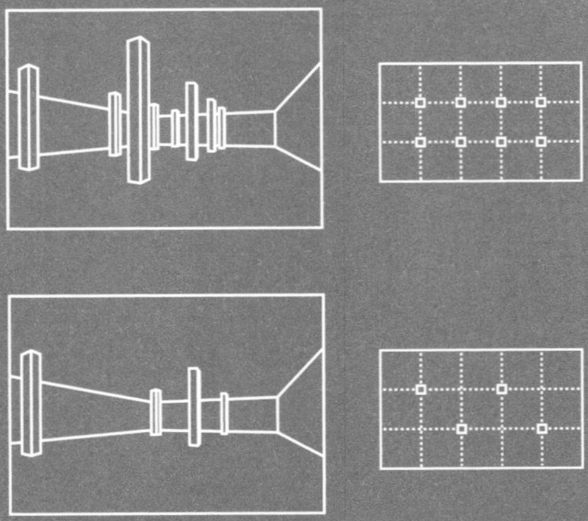

A small out-of-phase shift, but it worked. Suddenly the room was liberated. Diagonals opened up the floor plan and the room became one space, not two ring-fenced zones, not an inner enclosure surrounded by an outer promenade which the central four columns would have dictated. The *slip* on plan undid the containment, each column having an independence.

Koolhaas metamorphosed the freedom into columns that grew trees. Hunks of timber were brought in to flesh the vertical shafts. Hall 1 of the Kunsthal was no longer a room or an enclosure, through an end glass wall its internal space travelled to join up with the park outside. Somewhere between artifice and nature the room for changing exhibitions became a twilight zone of the *informal*.

In the Lecture Theatre columns lean over at a sharp angle, as if Shakespeare's Birnam Wood were moving towards Dunsinane. Prophesising danger and fear of collapse, the raking lines pose a direct threat to stability.

When a column leans over, a force has to be mobilised in the horizontal plane to stop it from falling.

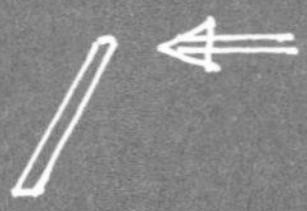

If several columns lean in the same direction, then a larger force is needed to prevent collapse.

This horizontal force in the case of the Lecture Theatre of the Kunsthal was to be resisted by the building adjacent to the *dijk* serving as a thrust block.

But the overturning force calculated put such downward pressure on the piled foundations of the block that large settlements would have occurred, relieving the very thrust which kept the columns propped in the first instance. Everything would have fallen over!

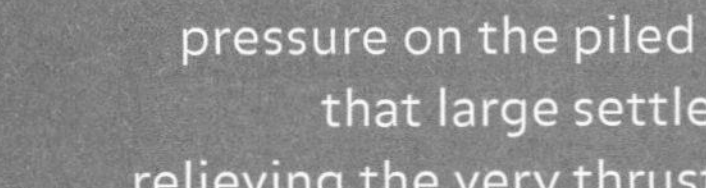

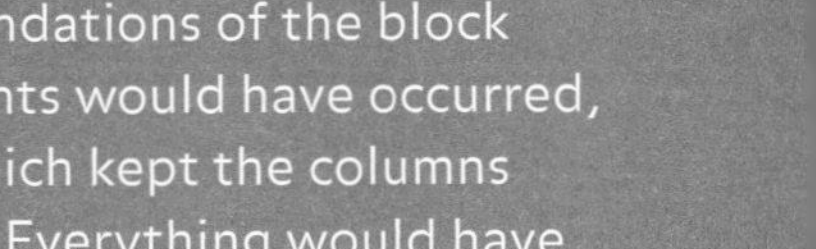

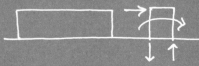

The alternative was to combine raking columns and inclined slabs in a self sustaining network of bending and direct forces which in technical terms provided a moment frame.

Due to the sloping plane of the lecture slab the frame was a strange one, with short elements stiff in resistance to bending side by side with longer flexible elements.

The frame of columns and 'beam-slabs' were made of concrete.

40 cm typical column sizes
40 cm Lecture Theatre raking slab
30 cm top horizontal slab

ROTTERDAM
De Super
Insecten Show

B

Before you enter the Kunsthal from the street you notice three columns in close proximity. They are of different shape and material, one in concrete, two in steel. The concrete column is square in section and the steel columns have different profiles. One has the appearance of a normal 'I' beam section, the other is castellated. These profiles are found regularly in many buildings but what makes this instance unusual is that the columns stand close together, their separateness being quite distinct.

They somehow 'disturb' the air. Their personalities clash.

The configuration arises due to separate roof loads being supported directly and not ironed out in hidden transfer structures to give a single point of support. The ad-hoc solution gives an energy to the idea of entry, and the three distinct natures mix and interface to offer *'threshold'* as an improvisation.

Imagine the same material and form for all the columns – there would be less impact. Imagine a regular spacing to the columns, and the dynamic vanishes. Imagine further the different conflicts of plan resolved by some 'hidden' structural gymnastic, with one column coming through ultimately in a pretence of neatness – the reduction would be complete. There would be nothing left, no animation, no off-beat pulse.

The juxtaposition brings in its own drama, and the mix urges entry, to by-pass the inconsistency for more settled regions within.

These columns signal the experience of the building itself, with its schisms, its interior slips and jumps and separate materialities.

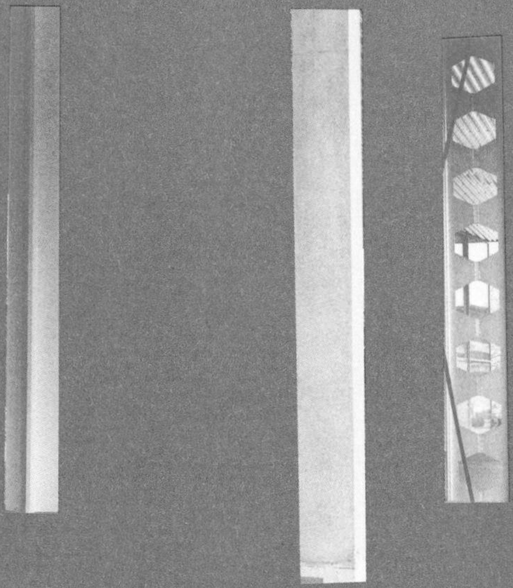

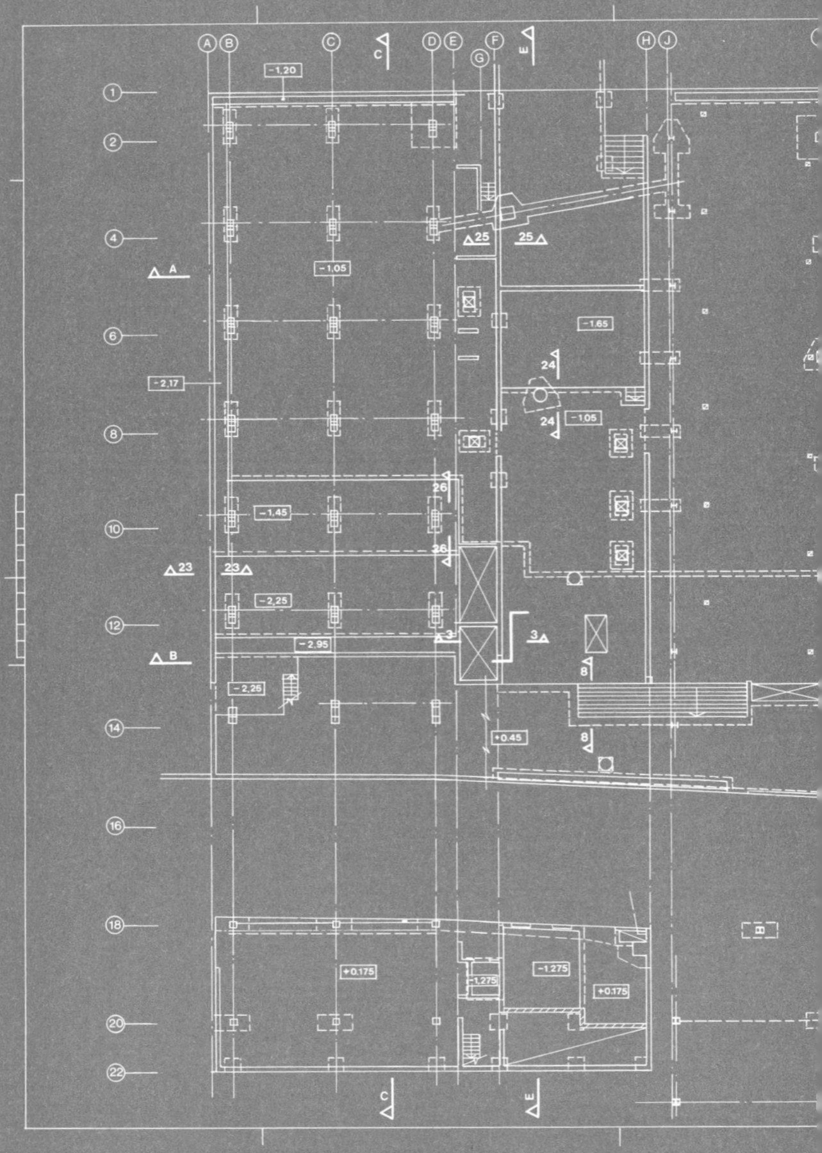

A
B
C
D
E
F
G
H
J
1
2
4
6
8
10
12
14
16
18
20
22
-1,20
-1,05
-1,65
-2,17
-1,05
-1,45
-2,25
-2,95
-2,25
+0.45
+0.175
-1.275
-1,275
+0.175
25
24
26
23
3
8

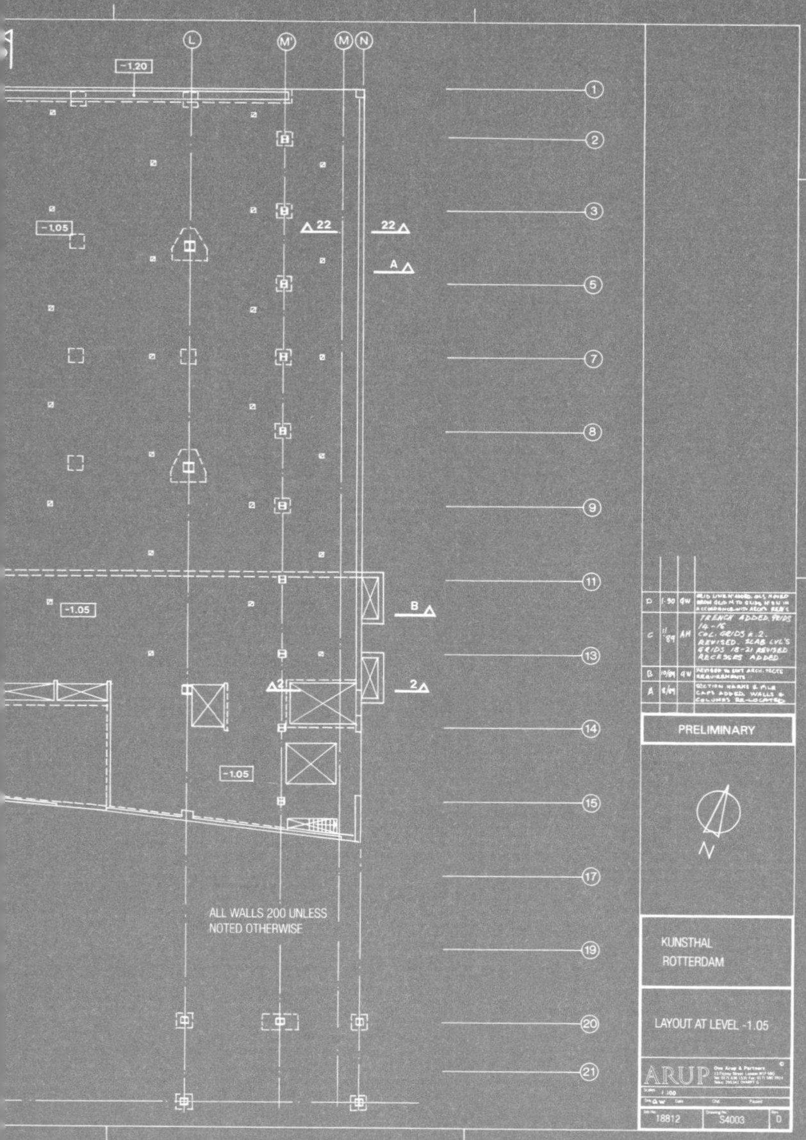

L
M'
M
N
-1.20
-1.05
-1.05
-1.05
22
22
A
B
2
2
1
2
3
5
7
8
9
11
13
14
15
17
19
20
21
ALL WALLS 200 UNLESS
NOTED OTHERWISE
D 1.90 GW
C 11/89 AH TRENCH ADDED. GRIDS 14-16
COL. GRIDS K.2. REVISED. SLAB LVL'S
GRIDS 18-21 REVISED
RECESSES ADDED
B 10/89 GW
A
PRELIMINARY
N
KUNSTHAL
ROTTERDAM
LAYOUT AT LEVEL -1.05
ARUP
Ove Arup & Partners
Scales 1:100
GW
Date
Chd
Passed
18812
S4003
D

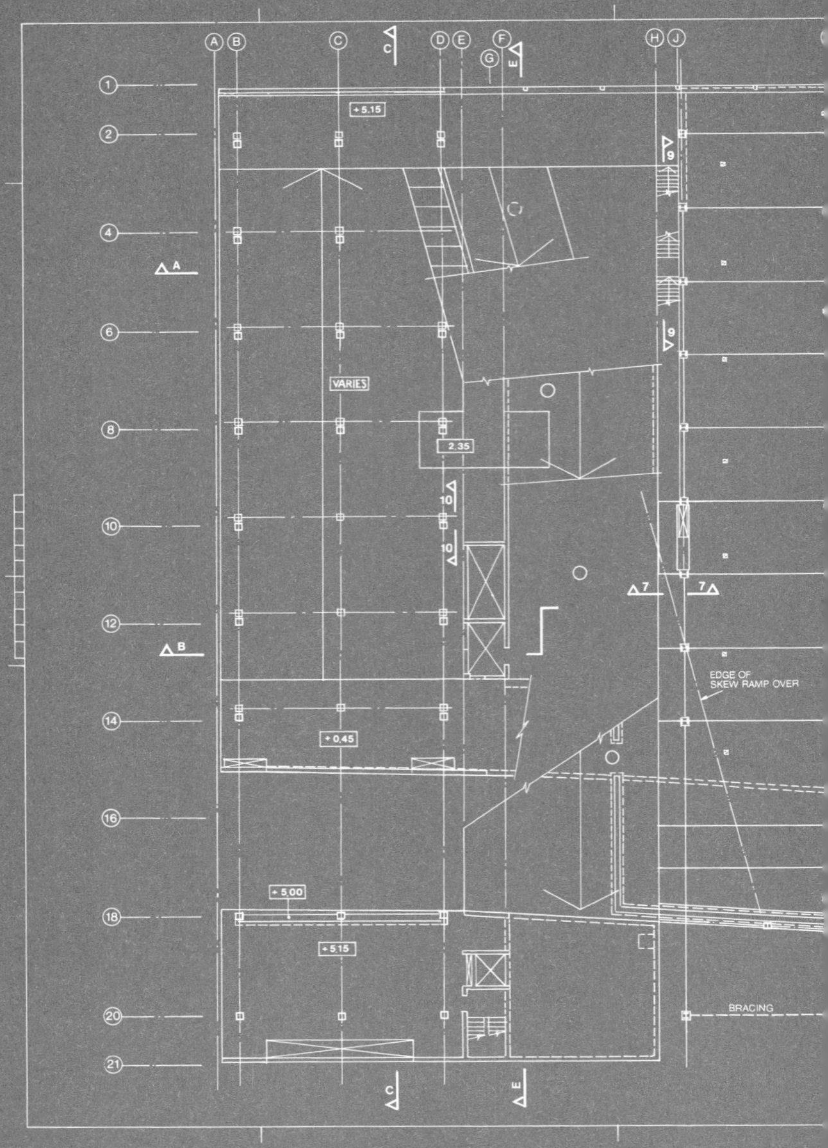
A
B
C
D
E
F
G
H
J
1
2
4
6
8
10
12
14
16
18
20
21
+5.15
VARIES
2.35
+0.45
+5.00
+5.15
EDGE OF
SKEW RAMP OVER
BRACING

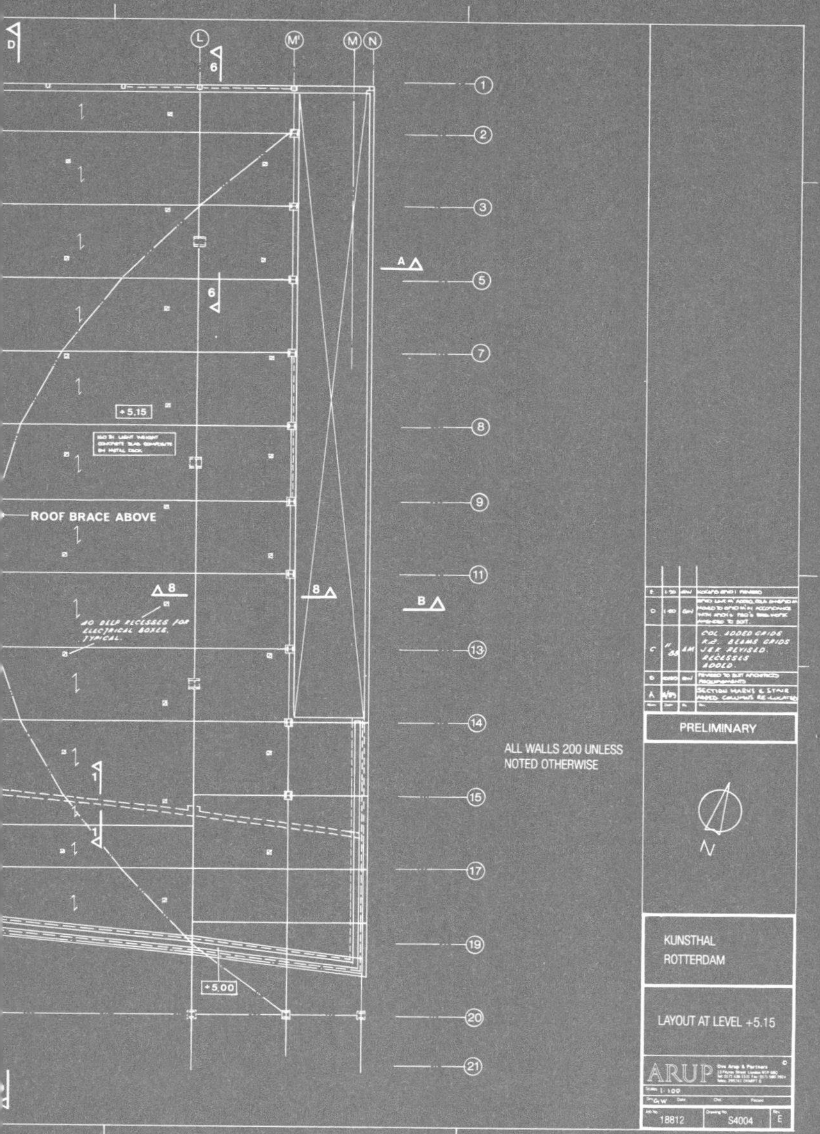

ROOF BRACE ABOVE
+5.15
+5.00
ALL WALLS 200 UNLESS NOTED OTHERWISE
PRELIMINARY
KUNSTHAL ROTTERDAM
LAYOUT AT LEVEL +5.15
ARUP
1:100
18812
S4004
E

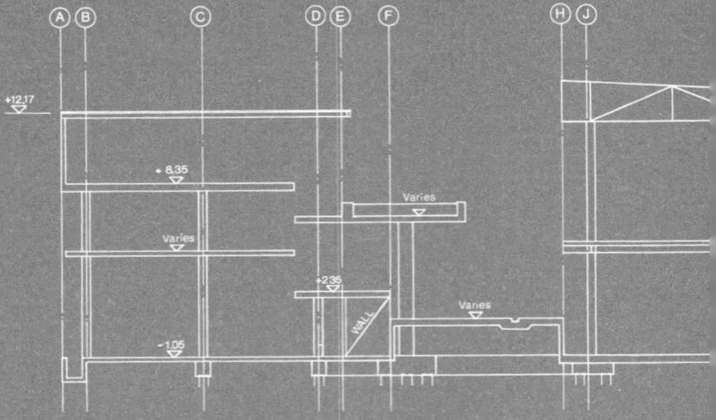
A
B
C
D
E
F
H
J
+12.17
+ 8.35
Varies
Varies
+2.35
WALL
Varies
-1.05

A–A

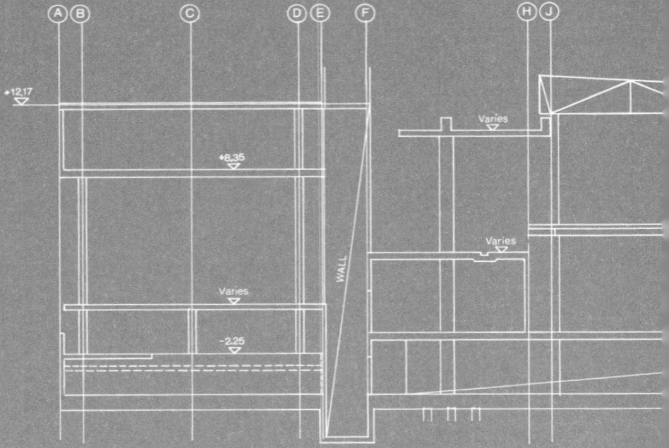
A
B
C
D
E
F
H
J
+12.17
Varies
+8.35
Varies
WALL
Varies
-2.25

B–B

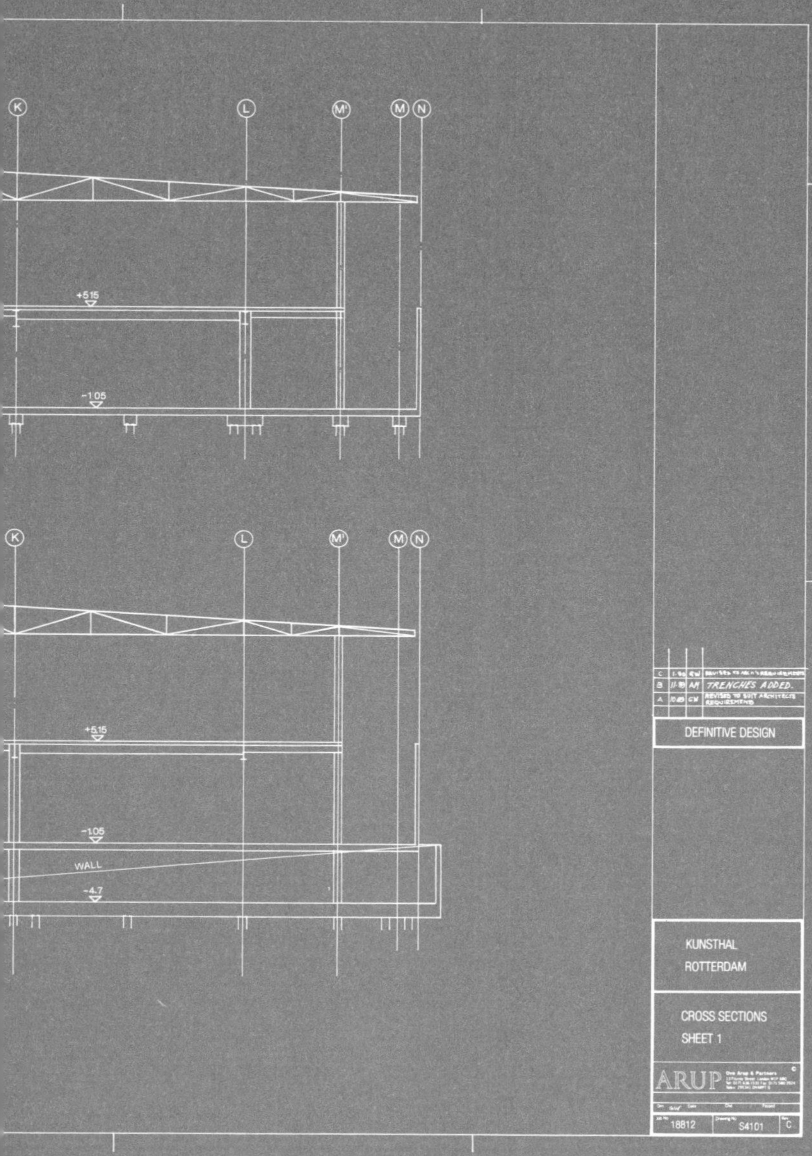
K
L
M'
M
N
+5.15
-1.05
K
L
M'
M
N
+5.15
-1.05
WALL
-4.7
B 11-89 AM TRENCHES ADDED.
A REVISED TO SUIT ARCHITECTS REQUIREMENTS
DEFINITIVE DESIGN
KUNSTHAL
ROTTERDAM
CROSS SECTIONS
SHEET 1
ARUP
Ove Arup & Partners
Job No 18812
Drawing No S4101
Rev C

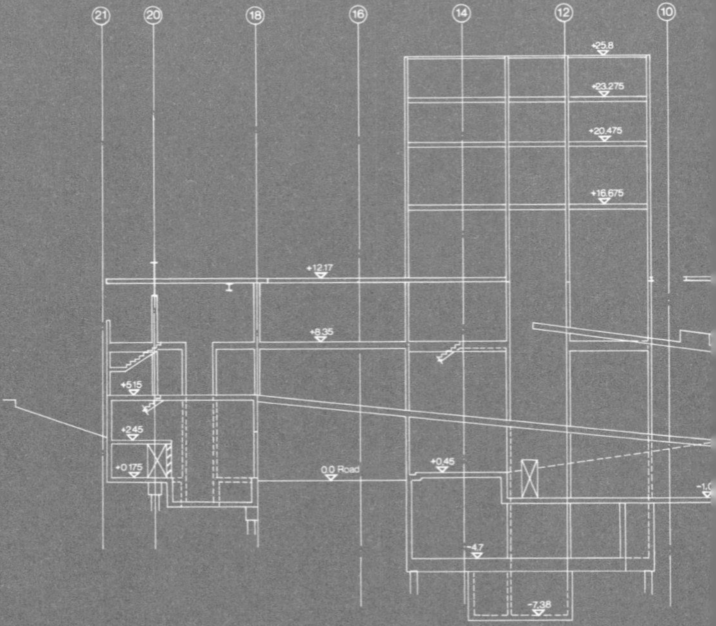
21
20
18
16
14
12
10
+25.8
+23.275
+20.475
+16.675
+12.17
+8.35
+5.15
+2.45
+0.175
0.0 Road
+0.45
-4.7
-7.38

E—E

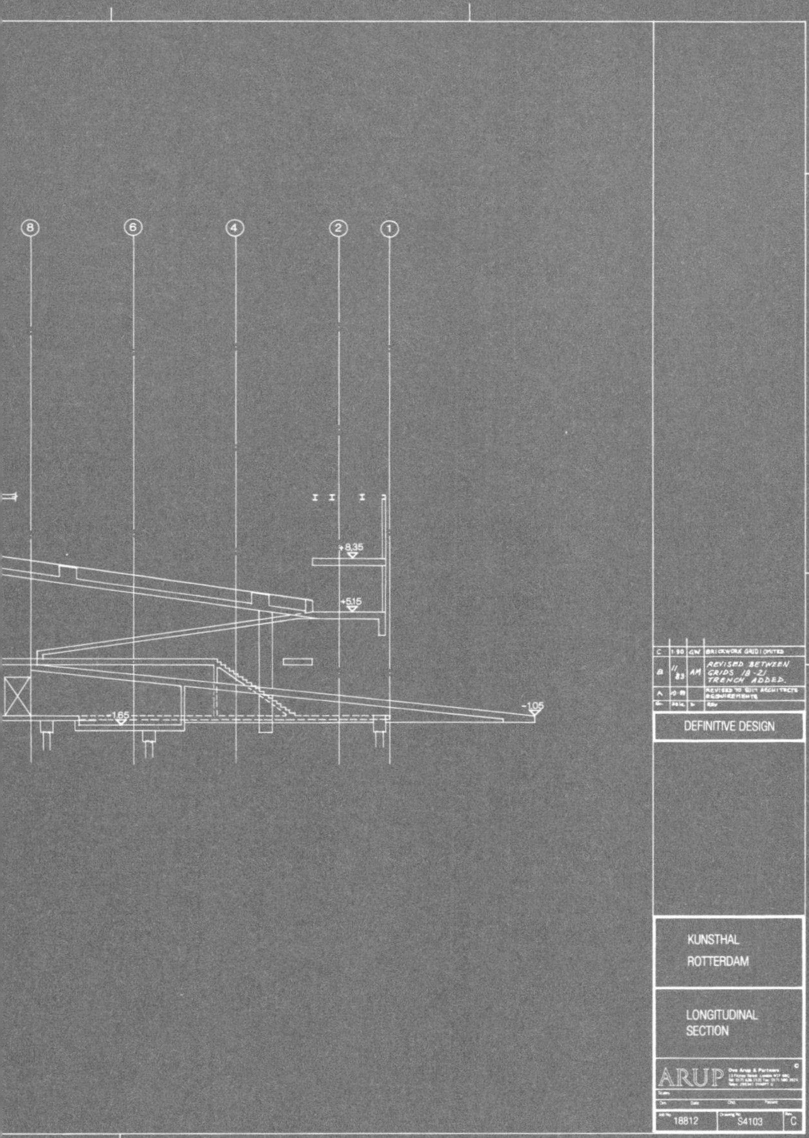
8
6
4
2
1
+8,35
+5,15
-1,65
-1,05
C 1-90 GW BRICKWORK GRID I OMITTED
B 11/83 AM REVISED BETWEEN GRIDS 18-21 TRENCH ADDED.
A REVISED TO SUIT ARCHITECTS REQUIREMENTS
DEFINITIVE DESIGN
KUNSTHAL
ROTTERDAM
LONGITUDINAL
SECTION
ARUP
One Arup & Partners
Scales
Drn. Date Chd. Passed
18812
S4103
C

A ramp is a luxury. It travels through time, collecting moments of arrival and departure, its line through space touching all parts and mixing adjacencies.

By nature it is an open vessel that defies containment. The horizon always shifts; a structure for a ramp must not seek to trap the metaphor but allow its release.

Columns placed obliquely to the line of travel of a ramp provide such release, giving a continuous mode of instability to the section. What happens in the ramp of the Kunsthal from 1st floor level to the roof is exactly this.

In section it may look hopelessly out of balance. But the structure is designed as a double cantilever.

On plan, on each side of the diagonal, an equal amount of load restores equilibrium to give overall balance. A grillage of strong upstand beams supports the ramp slab, evening out the distortions and twists due to the asymmetry.

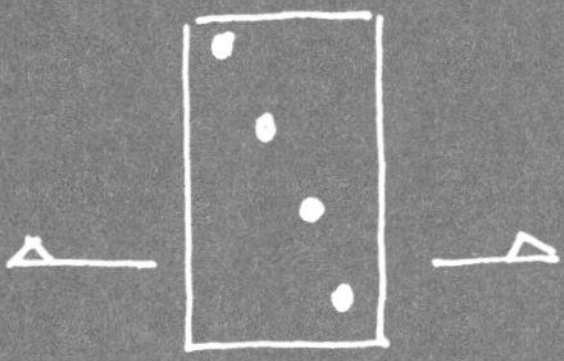

True to the nature of 'ramp' as 'mix', the column path is a sampling of Proposals 2, 3 and 4, incorporating *Slip, Frame* and *Juxtaposition*.

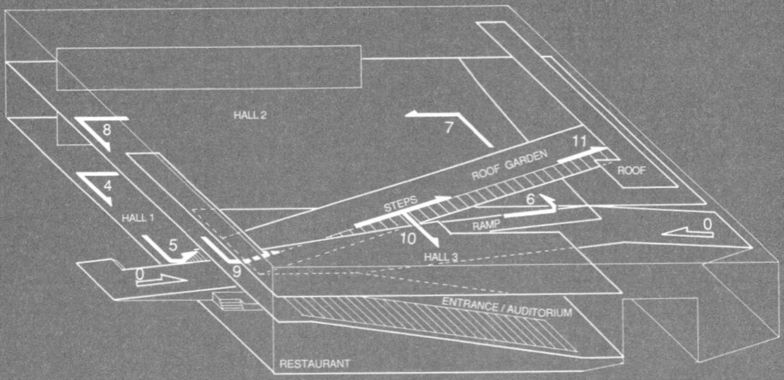

SYNCOPATION

Columns in Hall 1 emphasise a shifting beat, a syncopation. It is the difference between active network or deadening framework. The shift away from the norm is wilful, but it makes a difference – in the Kunsthal there is a liveliness and rhythm.

Other configurations extend this animation:

a gigantic beam on the roof stands up and serves as the fascia;

a plant room is stacked up as a wafer-thin slice on top of the building, serving as a vertical counterpoint and advertising screen;

the floor of a gallery loses its substance spectacularly in the form of a metal grille over the void, giving the visitor a scary passage;

ramp columns impede or encourage the journey below, as one dodges or meets a changing perspective of the building in relation to the park;

the inventory continues: of architecture and structure in dialogue, producing a range of events that go to make the Kunsthal an experiment in progress.

SPLIT IDENTITY

As one journeys through the building, structure reveals itself not as mute skeleton but as a series of provocations; sometimes explicit, at other times ambiguous. Structure emerges with different styles, in some locations graceful and flying, elsewhere awkward and stolid and rooted to the spot as at the back of high level Hall 3, in short chunky columns stuck to the roof and floor. The varying rhythms and ad-hoc strategies yield a hybridisation that wraps around the visitor.

As designed by Koolhaas the building catches tectonic transition brilliantly, yielding a sensation of anxiety / surprise / delight. Separate from its art content or complementing it, the building develops its own personality of split identities.

As with a person there are several readings.

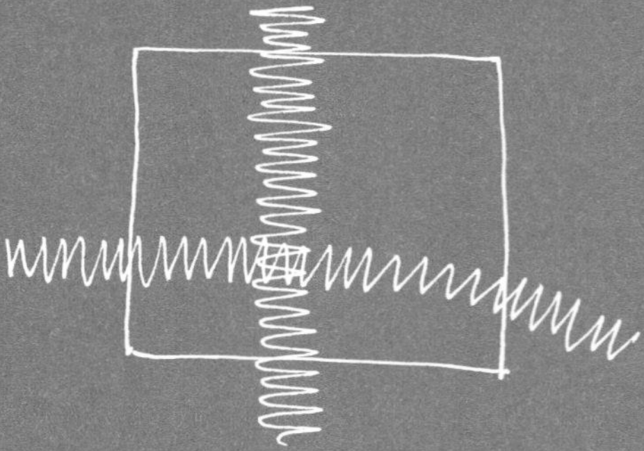

CONCLUSION

In the Kunsthal structure provokes its archetypes.

The thin red line in the roof of the Exhibition Hall traces a natural curve to 'brace' promoting structure as 'arch' and trajectory, more than conventional truss language can.

The gathering of different types of columns at the entrance emphasises support more than a particular isolated column might, however immaculately detailed or proportioned to show off its 'engineering'. In the Lecture Theatre, raking verticals lead to an intuition of frame more than straight-up-and-down post and beam. The inherent instability, that leaning over, calls out for strapping and holding down more than any 'correct' upright framing does.

The approach poses a puzzle, for not being obvious is a virtue of the *informal*: as there is no endorsement of the familiar or fashionable, there is no one-statement structure either.

The consequence is an architecture full of surprise. Now you see it, now you don't. *Informal* is that chameleon, a change-artist; and the Kunsthal in Rotterdam a crucible of such elusive bad behaviour.

109

... the *informal* steps in easily, a sudden twist or turn, a branching, and the unexpected happens – the edge of chance shows its face.

Delight, surprise, ambiguity are typical responses; ideas clash in the *informal* and strange juxtapositions take place. Overlaps occur. Instead of regular, formally controlled measures, there are varying rhythms and wayward impulses.

Uniformity is broken and balance is interrupted. The demand for Order! in the regimental sense is ignored: the big picture is something else.

Algorithm: A geometric or arithmetic rule that is repeated.

Chaos: A mathematically determinate state of turbulence. (The same start point, subjected to the same mathematical method, produces an identical result to the same extent of calculation, however unpredictable the process.)

Probability: A structure governed by chance. Its diagrams, in the manner of trees, are serial bifurcations.

Dimension: A measure of space in whole integers. In our perception there are the 3 dimensions of line, area and volume. In design space and mathematics there are n-dimensions.

Fractal: A non-integer dimension of pattern. The coastline is of a fractal geometry. A fractal has infinite range of scale.

Geometry: A mathematical description of space – a local concept.

Topology: The study of continuity – a forensic of connectivity.

Sequence: An array of independent entities.

Series: A progression of related entities.

Matrix: An arrangement in rows and columns of events or values that act simultaneously.

Equilibrium: A stable relationship of forces about a point of symmetry.

Coherence: The connecting of separate equilibriums.

Emergence: The internal will of chaotic systems to reach coherence.

Dynamic symmetry: Instantaneous balance about a moving point.

Static symmetry: The balance of shape or force about a fixed point or line.

Complex number: The number (a + ib) that has a real part (a) and an imaginary part (ib). a and b are integer values, i is the square root of –1 which is virtual, but, $i^2 = -1$.

The Argand plane: A plane of complex numbers with the horizontal axis as real numbers and the vertical axis as imaginary numbers.

Irrational numbers: Numbers like $\sqrt{2}$ that have no end to their decimal expansion. The golden ratio $(1 + \sqrt{5})/2$ is an irrational number.

Transcendental numbers: Numbers, like π, that have no pattern or end to their decimal expansion. Unlike irrational numbers, no repeating sequence of integers is found in these decimal expansions. Such numbers are tributaries of the random.

Primes: Numbers that cannot be divided by any number other than the number itself . . . 11 · 13 · 17 · 19 · 23 · 29 · 31 · 37 · 41 · 43 . . . Primes have no predictable sequence as they unfold, and remain one of the great mysteries.

Linear: The assumption of adjacency as a direct causal route.

Non-linear: The assumption of adjacency as an unpredictable process. The expression $y = x - 1/x$ is predictable, we know where the line is coming from and where it is going. Whatever value of x we begin with the identical line would be obtained. But if the equates sign is replaced by an arrow $x \rightarrow x - 1/x$ where the value of the right-hand side is fed back into the expression to calculate the next answer, the plot is unpredictable. Small shifts in the starting value of x, yield startlingly different plots for y.

Pattern: A set of marks that have abstract powers.

Network: The joining up of pattern, with function – a star map – a road map – a molecule.

Scale: Measure that gives meaning to both network and pattern.

Formal: Platonic ideal reduced to a set of rules.

informal: The non-linear characteristics of design.

The twisting-turning inside out of a Moebius strip belongs to the *informal*. A roof that turns to wall, a floor that moves into column, a skin that is structure, where boundary is not border, is part of it. Columns out of step, of different shape or material, side by side, also belong.

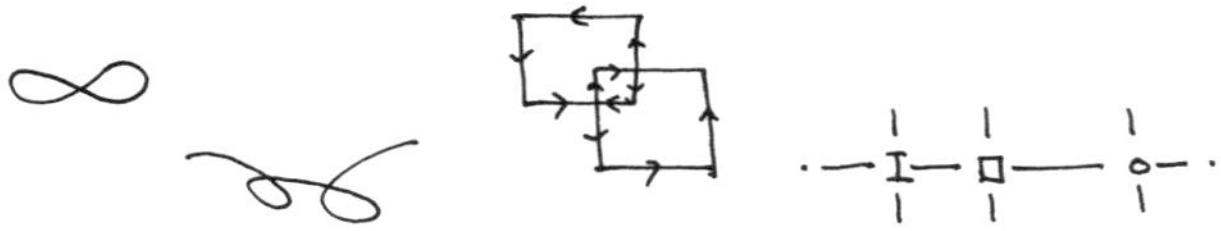

Opportunity seems to give chance a chance.

The difference between the *informal* and the Formal may be compared in the description of force. Newton offered the classical definition: force as action at a distance in a straight line.

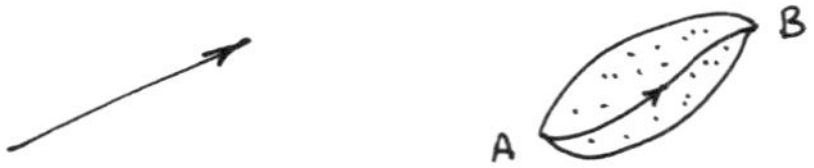

Determinism pictured force as an arrow, straight and true, bridging the void with unwavering objective linearity – the rigid link of an absolute logic chain. Now we see differently; the modern view is that between A and B there is a field of potential and a minimum path sought. Dependent on local conditions that path may vary. Subjective and relative, the informal view is based on instants of mutual cooperation, side by side differences charting the least resistance.

In the *informal* there are no distinct rules, no fixed patterns, to be copied blindly. If there is a rhythm it is in the hidden connections that are inferred and implied, and not necessarily made obvious. Order, in a hierarchical and fixed sense, is taken as furthest removed from the natural state of things.

Answers begin on a small and intimate scale, these local actions multiply, spreading outwards to inform the whole. Overlaps occur, a mixing of ideas – nothing is 'pure' about the method.

Quite the opposite is the Formal, rigid, hierarchical. Its chief characteristic is analysis which needs reference, as the past comes with close grids of argument. Sub-analysis, pictured here as a closed mesh of reference, leads to greater density. It is a reductionist process.

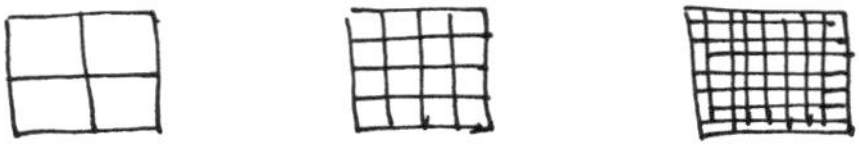

In the Formal, space is viewed as container, empty, but partitioned. One point to the other has no revelation. Working from the concept of external fixed boundary and going inwards, ever smaller until the smallest part is derived, is a safe option. The process takes no risk. Because we plan everything, working from outside to inside, the solutions are predictable and deemed to be efficient. That is why we are comfortable with it and that is why we are so easily bored.

We want to trap the idea.

The creative impulse jumping out of nowhere is scary. Control and containment are sought. Rigid boundaries are set, chopping up the idea into smaller bits. As a basis of organisation we seek an isolated repeating motif as if this reflects an irreducible unit of the continuum; we want to believe in forever and forever. It is hard to believe in singularities or gaps or folds in the thinking, as random start points create fault planes in the belief of homogeneity. In the face of such turbulence, order is endorsed as the safe fortress. But it misses the point: that the nature of reality is chance and that 'order' may only be a small, local, steady state of a much larger random.

Consider a startling opposite: a freeze-melt scenario!

ice to water to mist

Molecules of H_2O change their face and surprise us. Depending on local conditions the atoms take up different positions to alter their structure, yet it is all the same thing – H_2O. The composition remains unaltered, the fixed idea of two H and one O remains though the forms are variable. H_2O is generic. And water / ice / gas are emerging stabilities, specific to the moment of temperature.

The informal is generic in its algorithms of evolution but specific to the extent to which the algorithm runs. Interpretation is the best we can do.

THREE PRINCIPAL CHARACTERISTICS

LOCAL: The initial action that works outwards to spread its influence. An action that has its own nature; a circle a cross a column the vanishing at a corner or the containment of an angle a fold in space or any such event that sustains itself locally. In terms of music, local is a single note or sound. But just as a single note is not one dimensional, a local event radiates overtones.

JUXTAPOSITION: Two actions, side by side, clashing and influencing each other to give a new entity by virtue of adjacency. The close relation of one event to another. Agitation by proximity. The circle next to a cross two column sections next to each other or one prime number next to another.

Different adjacencies give different speeds. Time is an essential component in juxtaposition, not sequential as we know it, but a tectonic space-time of arrested moments.

HYBRID: One action overlapping the other, a co-sharing of separate natures. Two or more local natures bound within each other, the cross within the circle, the same grid duplicated and rotated, or the direct overlap of similar natures.

If juxtaposition is tempo, hybrid is chordal, a mix of separate notes sounding together. 

The characteristics of the informal are not isolated and separate but have degrees of interdependence. Juxtaposition in its extreme condition becomes two contingent natures or hybrid. Hybrid, the direct overlap of two or more local concerns, is also a local condition. Informal characteristics are initiation points for design.

EXAMPLE I

The Chemnitz Stadium roof solution came about by an external restraint – a back span was not possible in three places – resulting in an arc being drawn into space in these locations. This was a *local* impetus.

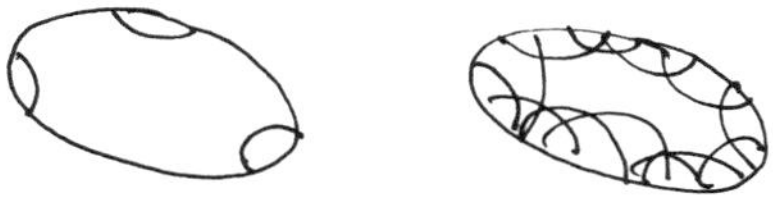

The unit idea multiplied to form a net.

EXAMPLE II

In the Expo canopy at Lisbon, the character of lightness and appearance of vanishing is due to a cut in the substance of the roof's curvature. Absence is part of the trajectory and the local de-materialisation travels through, denying mass its weight.

EXAMPLE III

In Lille, the roof beams over the exhibition hall are *hybrid* timber / re-bar / and rolled steel section,  making an unusual mix in tension, shear and compression respectively. Columns that support this roof are an overlap of cruciform cross section  and hollow tube. The roof geometry in turn is a mix of two different curvatures – one longitudinal, one transversal.

The building itself, Lille Grand Palais as it is called, is a further hybridisation of three separate programs, Concert / Conference / and Exhibition, bound within one overall schematic. Rem Koolhaas announced it memorably as *bigness*. We may call it *informal*.

EXAMPLE IV

On the walls of the V & A Spiral tiling is an intricate interlocking of three distinct shapes. Each tile embeds other shapes along with a reduced version of itself. The three tiles in a variety of juxtapositions yield an infinite *hybrid*.

EXAMPLE V

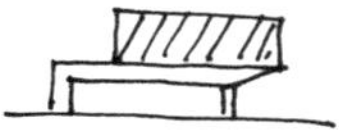

The Bordeaux Villa 'flies' due to its skewed and interdependent nature of support.

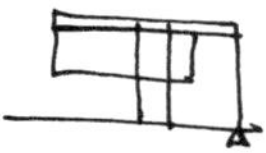

In section, one beam line acts as the bottom cradle, contrasting with a jump in space at the other end, to a top hung support.

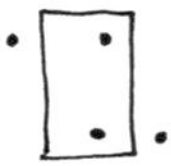

On plan, the step out of sequence is another *juxtaposition*. Asymmetry and contrary shifts provide momentum.

EXAMPLE VI

In the Kunsthal, columns near the entrance, cluster; each has a different shape and material.

Standing close to one another they provide *juxtaposition*, making 'entry' an almost tangible force field to negotiate.

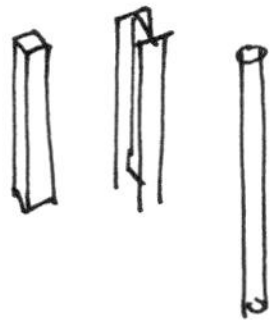

GENERIC FOLD

A line or system that folds  develops characteristics of the *informal*. Hybrid situations and juxtapositions arise propelled by the local, overlapping nature of the algorithm.

Some physicists believe that 'superstrings' vibrate or fold in unknown ways to yield the world of matter as we know it. If the atomic unit of proton, neutron and electron is *hybrid*, then *juxtaposition* produces molecules and *local* are the hidden valency bonds that configure connection. Extensions of the same characteristics lead to the chemical elements and more complex compounds.

Nature builds its huge diversity out of such aggregations. And substance may be seen as an unfolding cross-over event of interactive opportunities.

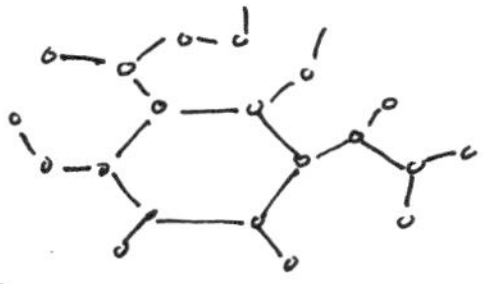

Substance is *generic fold*.

INVADING SYSTEMS

How the *informal* relates to the Formal may be seen by taking two ordered systems and allowing one to invade the other. Imagine a system of crosses running into a system of circles, immediately all the conditions of the *informal* are produced.

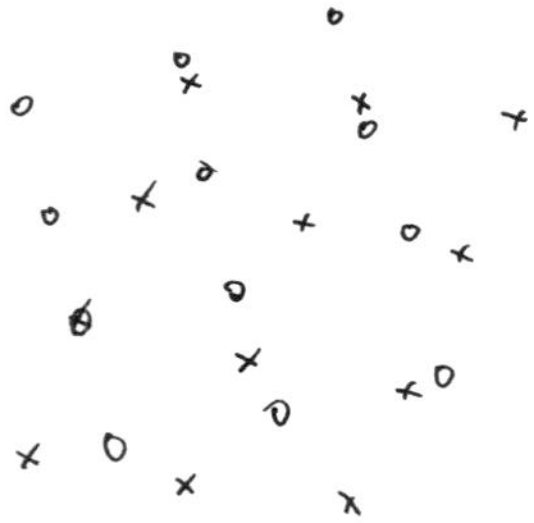

This is backing into the *informal* as it were and a reductionist way to explain its component make up; the other way, to begin with the ingredients of *local*, *hybrid* and *juxtaposition* and work outwards towards a result, cannot be similarly mapped or explained. Instead the *informal* has to be entered into and experienced as an act of faith in bandwidths of shifting certainties. A single move, a local action, is all that is needed to get started. Surprisingly the haphazard begins to 'shake-down' into pattern and, the open and unconfined leads to network and coherence.

ACTION OF ONE

The local event has special powers. I call it the 'action of one'. The methodology is *emergent*, a gradual layering of several successes.

EXAMPLE I

Consider the chess move of a knight which jumps over the board in a dog-leg movement, one across and two up or down, or two up or down and one across.

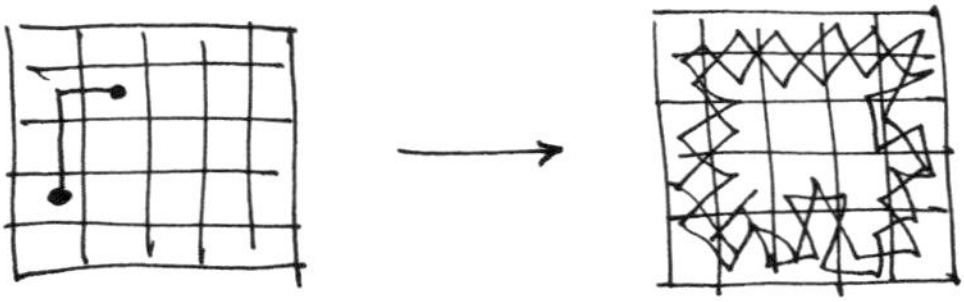

If the piece is moved continually around a chessboard an intricate design of overlap takes place, never quite closing. Depending on the start point, different patterns arise.

EXAMPLE II

If a particular tile shape is taken and turned and flipped over as necessary, a 'crazy' network unfolds. The chaos is not random but a direct result of the starting angles of the distorted polygon chosen.

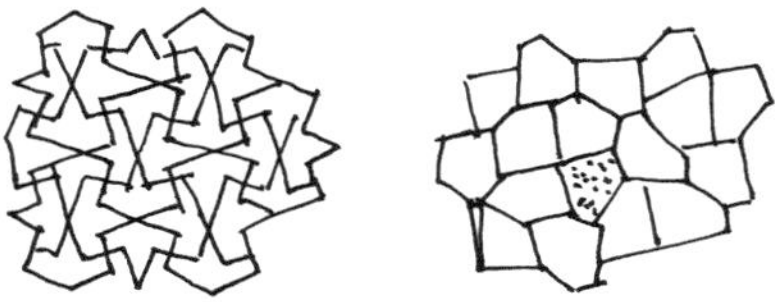

COMPOSITION FIELDS

A column is part of a larger sequence. If columns support a load they are accompanied by an 'unseen' column field; the interruption to the progression is the moment of realisation.

A beam is a sudden contraction in a force field.

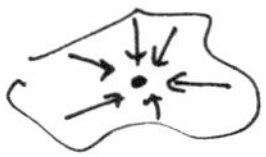

A column is a point of vortex, drawing down pools of load into itself.

Walls become extended columns, a longitudinal wave of absorption. Walls and columns act as gravity short cuts. Beams are trampoline lines and slabs act as reservoirs for hidden patterns in the flow of load.

Even the word composition loses its fixity in the *informal*, it comes back as a compilation of transients. The greater the interdependence the richer the confluences. 'Meaning' and 'understanding' grow out of the typologies of the several interferences.

DEVIL IN THE DETAIL

Placing columns side by side, skewing beams, putting grids to clash, may look like an incentive to chaos. But there is a difference between ambiguity and plain confusion. If structure is distributed evenly and decomposed into identical parts, one part has no value relative to another. The smaller the unit of repeat, as in a module of a space frame when the parts are put together, the more a singular definition is lost. Density accrues. There is confusion. Many a high-tech solution when drawn in section has a clear image of cable and mast efficiency but when viewed in totality, a different and fussy picture emerges. Wonderful to look at with its machine-like brilliance in section, when assembled, the solution turns into an accident of wires and cables. When structural elements have even distribution, the imagination has nothing to hold on to but the connection.

Much effort is expended to fashion the joint between elements, but ultimately the ambition degenerates into a fetish.

In the *informal* compiling an interval is better than spacing the gap. Building the interval up from an inner logic is better than calculating what space should go between elements.

The *informal* does not take sections, only freeze-frame pictures of a three dimensional unravelling. The snap shots are ambiguous and provoke interpretation. Composition is holistic and multi-dimensional from the start.

Space is taken as infinitely dense, with all possibilities embedded there. It is a black hole, the ultimate positive. To realise a design one has to map or unravel a trace from out of that hole.

Each thread has its own story – we could leave it or stretch it out or fold it into our creativity. Whatever we do, the thread will carry its complex mystery, we imagine its irrational character as a constant intrigue. And the thread is a negative, being withdrawn from that total positive matrix.

The proposal here is that design is tentative and fragile lasting only for a while, the white inspiration soon fading towards the black conjecture of what might have been. It is a perpetual irony that the much prized product never looks complete, so much else seems possible. The solution soon becomes a victim to its own creativity.

But a building cannot simply be put away, we encounter it for years as a sentinel, mocking past hypotheses and aspirations. So we keep entering that black hole, looking for the threads to bring back. If there is a method to the search, it lies somewhere in improvising, and *informal* pathways back out of the labyrinth.

125

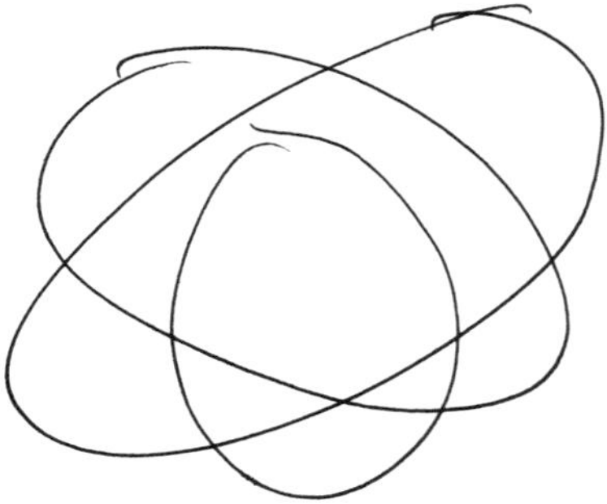

We began with Clouds and Forest and
Earth – pagan forces set against the backdrop
of urban Chemnitz.

To have chased tradition would have been to
turn around in formal circles, recreating the
fixed groove in which stadium follows track, in
concentric laps. We wanted something
different, eccentric orbits, a release of the
wild energies that Nature seems so easily
to control.

Should a stadium in cross-section be a composite
building of dependant attachments; why
not try different layers that
are independent?

The basic idea was to fix the track in the landscape, then have a floating object in the seating tiers and a cloud (roof) that hovered over. In between air and heaven and ground and sweat and energy the vertical lines of connection would need to be random, opportunist, serving different needs.

There would be no coherent, uniform Cartesian logic to the solution.

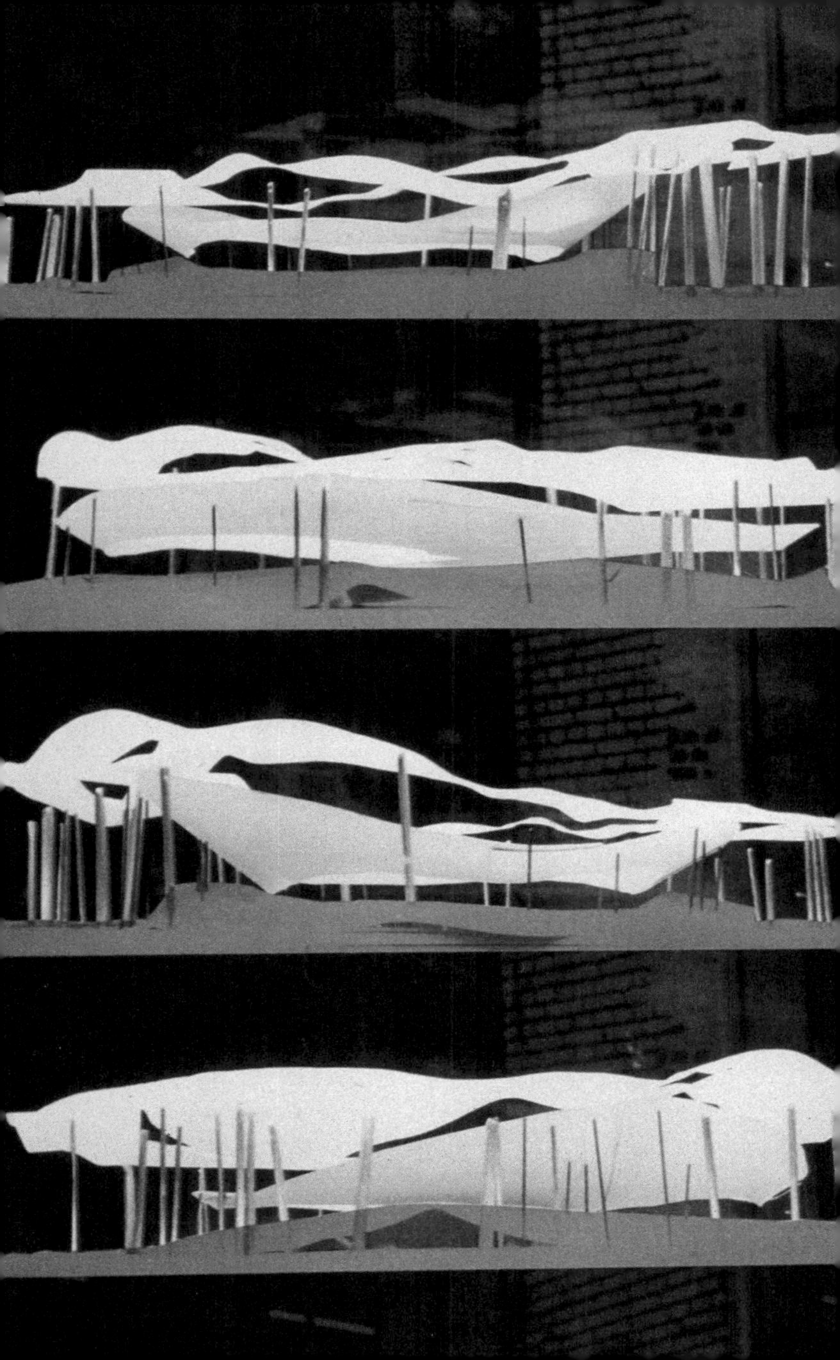

With Nature inspiring a chaotic impulse the architects Peter Kulka with Ulrich Königs' initial design set out to interpret or mimic sources of random energy. There was a declaration for the stadium to be a non building; they wanted to break with Order and create a new typology of separate orbits spinning in different ways. Each ring was to have a different function attached to a metaphor; the roof a Cloud, the main tier a 'floating object' and the lower seating a base oval of Earth. In between the layers a random series of columns were to grow as Forest.

A paper model, deliberate in its extremes, was prepared.

The model released new energies.

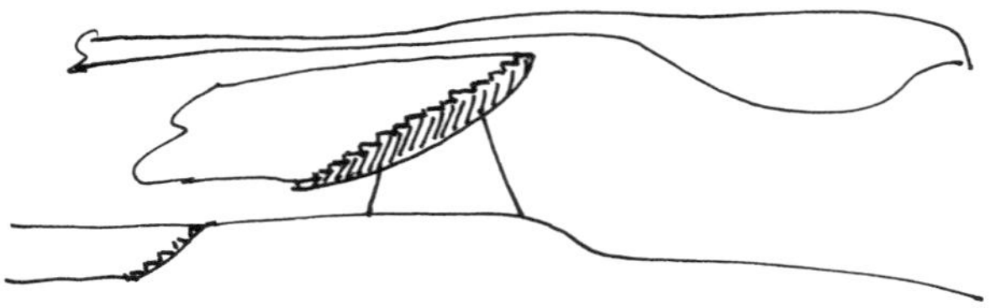

The roof layer, decoupled from the seating, spread in a waveform over the site; columns in arbitrary positions inclined upwards to support it.

In between ground and roof in an undulating orbit a yellow warped disc holding the main grandstand rose and fell.

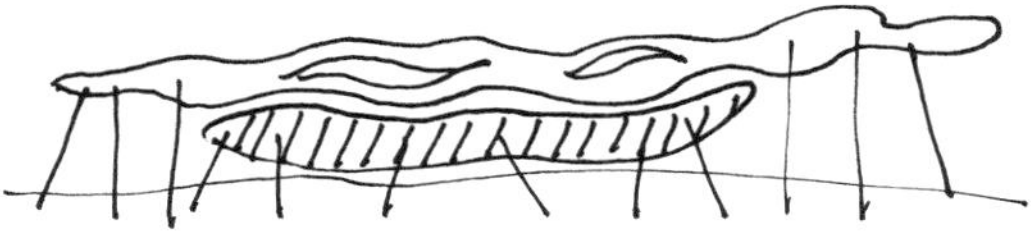

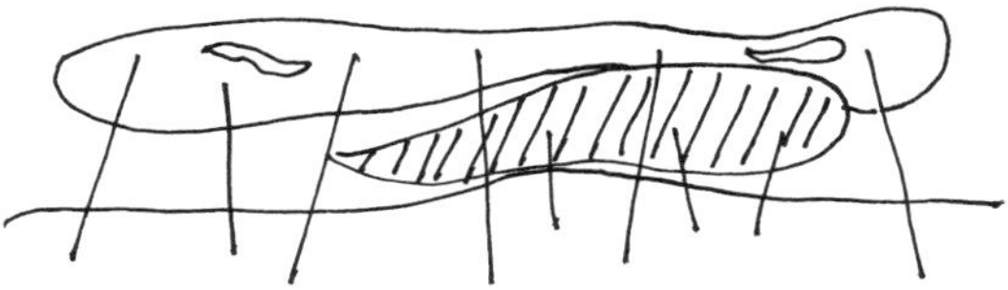

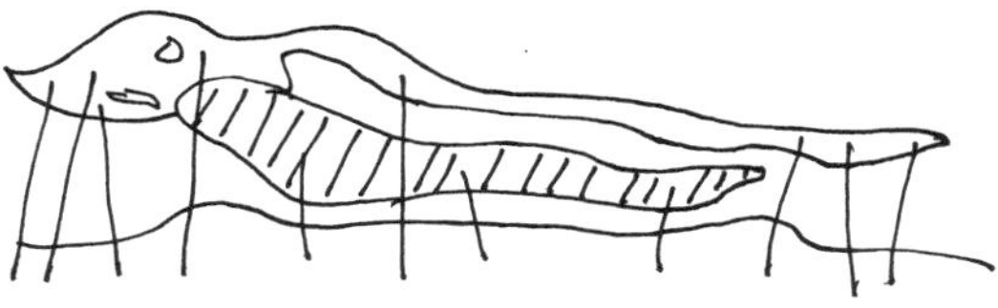

And the earth mound bordering the track reminded us of the original dilemma – the fixed orbit that contained the unpredictable nature of the games, winning or losing.

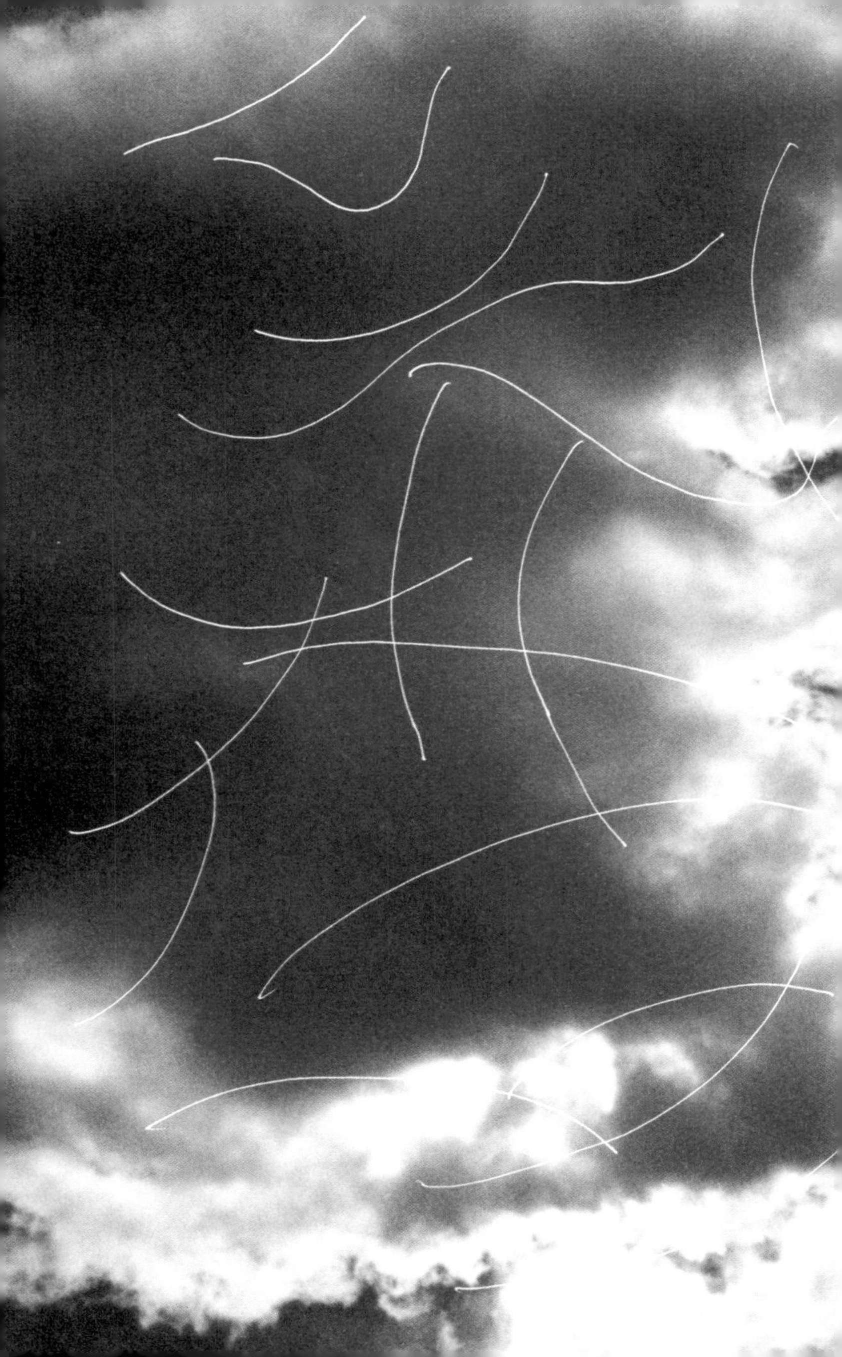

Overlapping arcs weave
a steel net, fractal-like
and cloud-like

COPY OR MIME?

To copy an improvised paper model into a hard tectonic needs questioning. Is it worth recreating every crease and fold? The transformation of the paper cloud into a gravity defying roof needs a different kind of translation. Not so much a direct copy of the free-form surface but a strategy that can generate a similarly complex typology.

My concern was to look for the simile, possible algorithms from which ideas would grow for Cloud and Forest. How not to copy but build towards an ideal by reinventing. What was the spirit in the metaphors? What of their essence?

CLOUD – LOOPS, WHORLS, TURNING, TUMBLING

We drew oblique marks, scatter effects. It was easy to talk about but hard to describe on paper. There seemed to be no miracle at hand, and we drifted slowly into a false start. We drew a roof layout that appeared in semi-random style with straight cantilevers over seating areas, in a conventional manner, then bifurcating on the back span into an arbitrariness which allowed a scatter of support columns mimicking a forest. We had a result but not one as provocative as we might have expected. The initial model spoke of more radical solutions.

We broke for lunch. And we talked of other things: Professor Kulka's building in Dresden; German unification; football; etc.

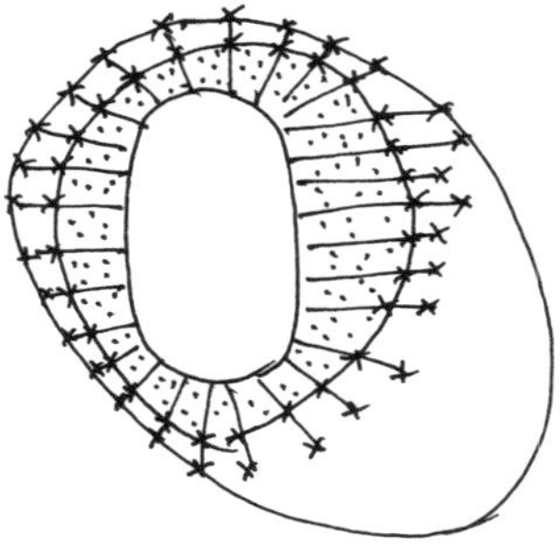

When we got back to the studio we concentrated on the other elements, the principal tier of seating, lines of sight, and the coordination of entrance tunnels below to align with the supporting columns. We decided that each suspended layer of structure should be independent, making it possible to optimise the column support for the 'floating' object without worrying about the roof above. The undulation of the warped tier itself was not excessive and options in steel and concrete developed quite easily. We had answers for the organisation and planning of the stadium as a whole – then we went back to the roof.

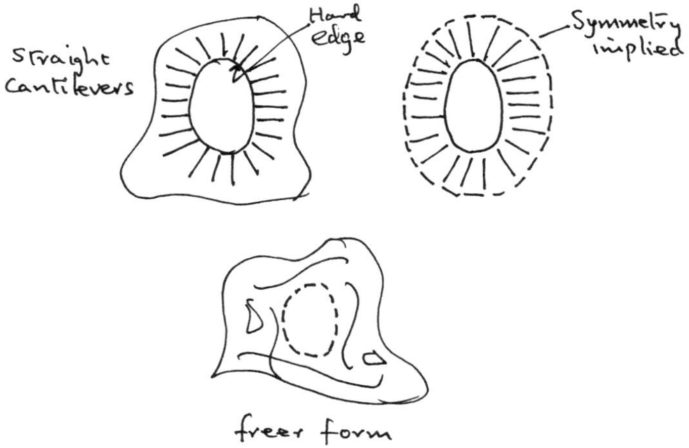

All the drawing we had done that morning seemed contrived. Cantilever sections travelling towards the inner edge, if anything, reinforced the formality of a ring – the idea in the model of a free definition was not there. Straight cantilevers did not easily allow the longitudinal waveform either, though there were ways to split the beam profiles in elevation to mimic the undulation. But to what point?

The stage we had reached did not really speak of any of the freedoms we had set for ourselves. And I did not want just to copy the model.

a grid duplicated
and rotated produces
node points of 'scatter'

The answer lay in abandoning metaphors for Cloud and Forest and going back to first principles. If we were to find the random solution we must not assume a picture of an outcome; I believed the answer lay in the data – and that we only had to look for it. My starting point was a sketch investigating the site conditions.

At three places along the roof orbit which followed the site boundary the back of the seating and roof line coincided. There was no room for a cantilever to be tied down.

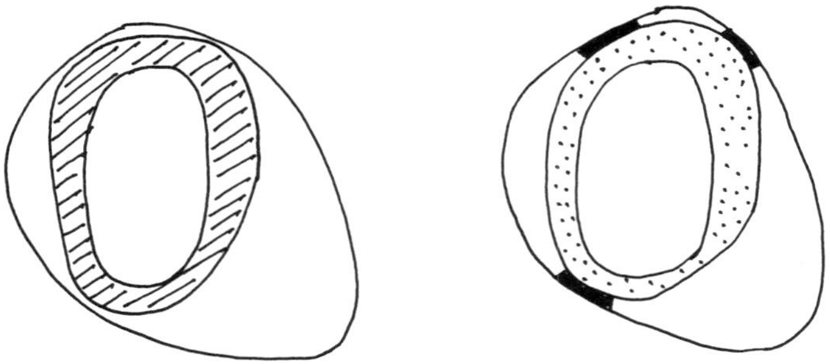

At these locations I drew an arc into space.

The arc would behave as a beam with high bending and torsion. To prevent it from collapsing, another arc followed in support of the first. The strategy was one of mutual self-help, each ring supporting and interacting with the other. As the arcs grew, from out of the three isolated original impulses a steel net began to emerge.

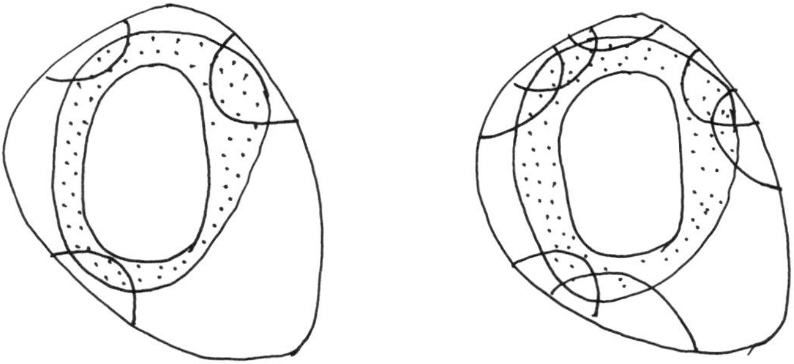

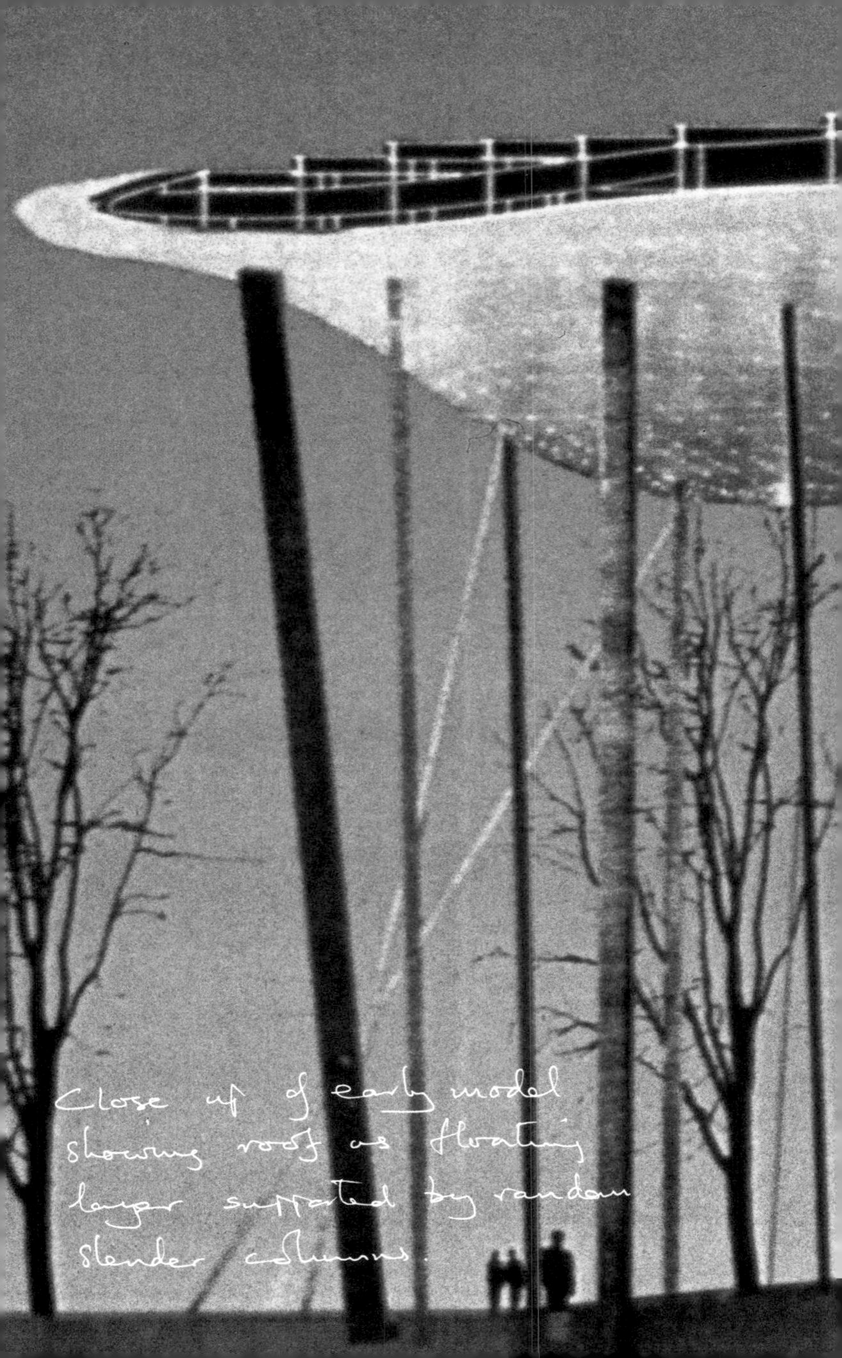
Close up of early model
showing roof as floating
layer supported by random
slender columns.

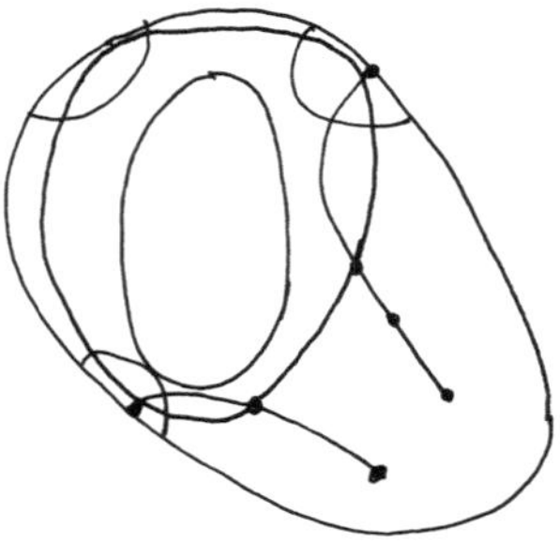

Since the roof covered a larger area than the main tier of seats, some of these arcs extended beyond the 'floating object' acting as continuous beams over several supports.

The idea of 'turning' inherent in the overlapping arcs gave the roof a textural homogeneity that was absent from the cantilever solution, for straight lines converging in serial fashion to an edge did not have the natural power of an interlocking web or net. The orbits gave a high energy trace

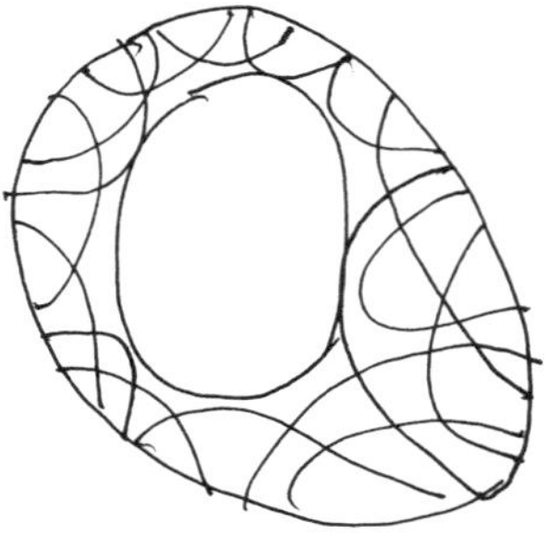

If we wanted a metaphor on a constructive basis, here was a good one: is not a cloud a bundle of turnings?

When the roof net was generated it was conceived as flat, just patterns of intersection. But there had to be undulations, a rising and falling, both local and over a larger reach of longitudinal section. Instead of shaping the roof in elevation by eye, its internal connectiveness was used to give shape.

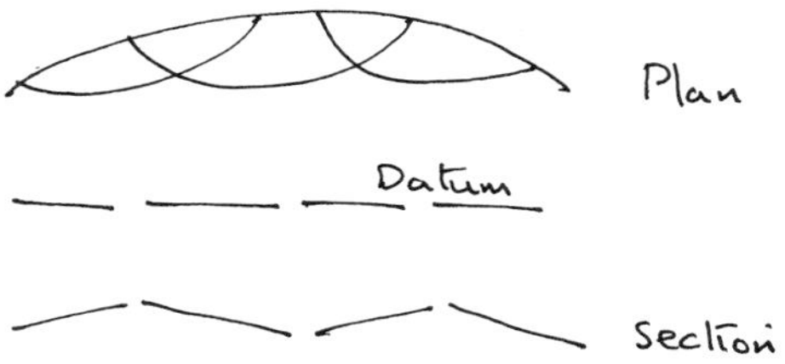

The orbits were ascribed their self-weight, and gravity allowed to work on one half of the plan. A reverse gravity was applied then to the other half. The frequency of connection and stiffness of the rings led directly to the controlled curvatures. Positive / negative, push / pull, yielded the wave form.

This self-calibration was then taken as the geometry of the structure. Subsequent analysis of roof loads and structural performance was monitored from this datum.

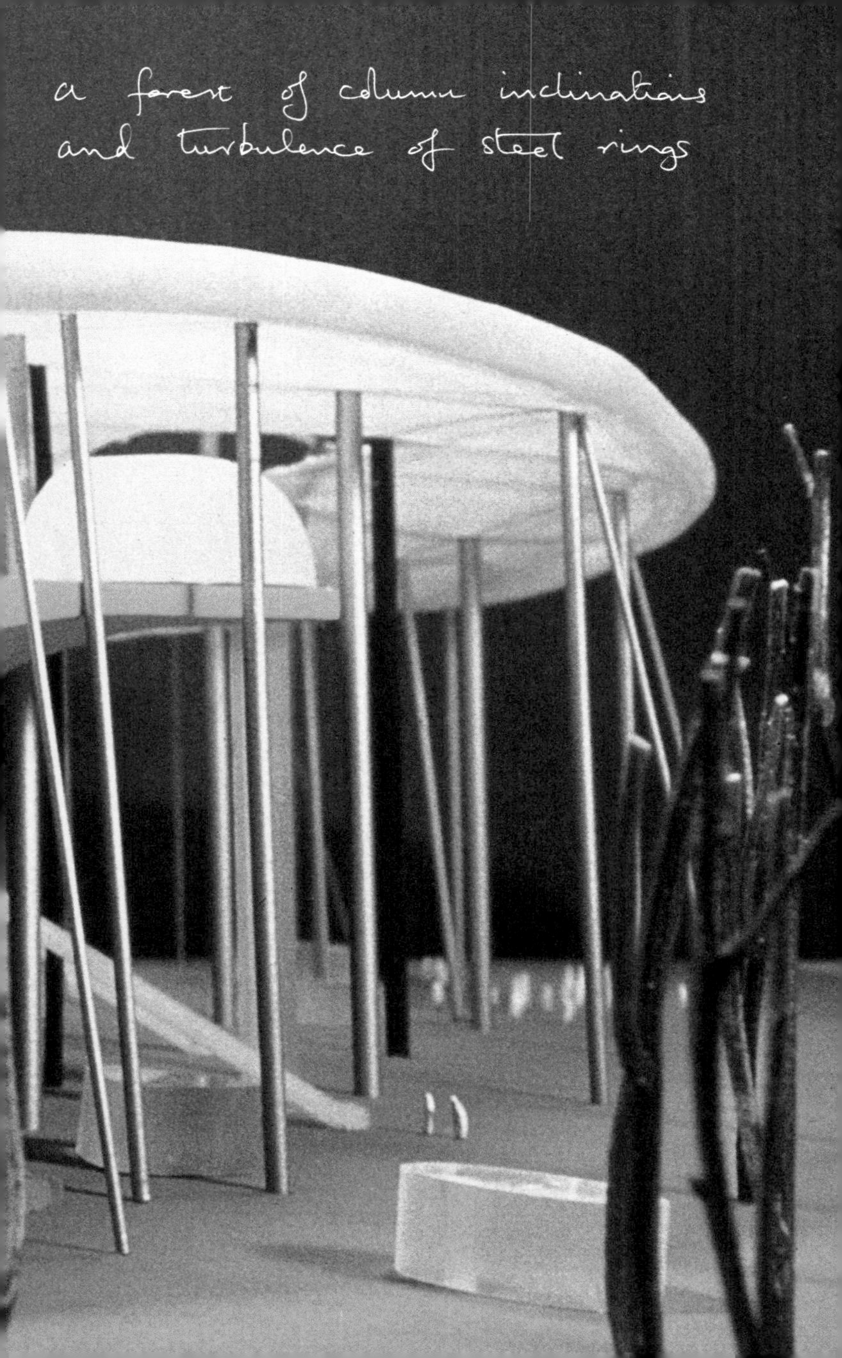
a forest of column inclinations
and turbulence of steel rings

Ulrich Königs saw that the segments between loops could be filled in different ways allowing for various sub-grids in support of a roof cover. He sketched out the possibilities, some areas between arcs even being left void – the roof could be of fabric or metal, depending on the nature of the sub-grid. These were exciting options but for the competition there was no time to work out the detail of the sub-grids, and a translucent sheet was attached just under the rings, to simulate transparency.

The principle trajectories of the beam elements could be structured in different ways as well.

Simple tube elements could be used, good in torsion, or the arc made up as a hybrid cruciform of horizontal and vertical trusses connected by inclined planes of diagonal bracing. This was more complicated and possibly more interesting than tubes – rigging like – with a spidery effect, adding to the tracery idea; but for the competition, we chose the simple tube option. And a connection principle was worked out to allow structural continuity at intersections.

FOREST, TREES, INCLINATIONS, SCATTER

In the model, columns were inserted 'randomly' by eye. Independent of the seating tier they were freely located, to give the effect of scattering. This was to mime the idea of Forest as an externalisation. I was more interested in an internal strategy that would provide a similar effect, something that worked according to a simple rule.

As an investigation of the *informal* I had studied a series of ideas or templates generating 'randomness', backing into it as it were from formal and ordered arrangements. Though the placements seemed random in these experiments, the scatter was easily mapped. Order transformed into dispersion.

TRANSFORMING GRID

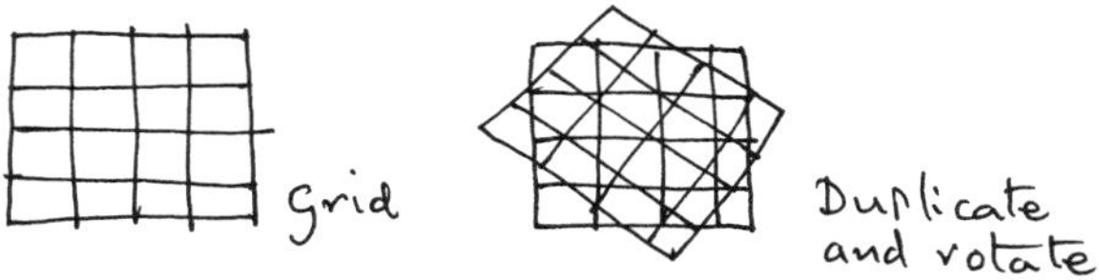

If a grid is duplicated and then rotated over the first diagram, a scatter of points comes into play.

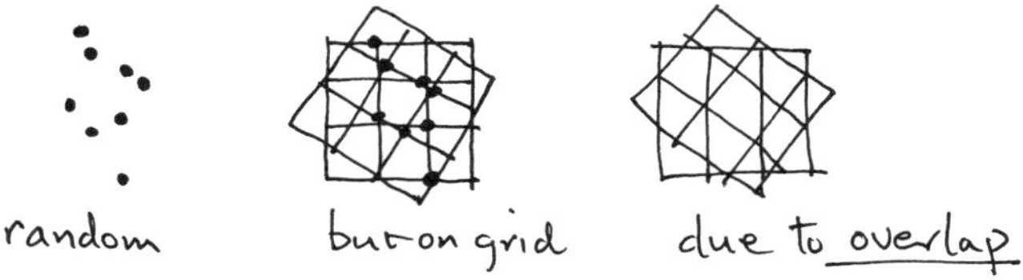

Since the grid geometry and the degree of rotation is known, the setting out of any point is straightforward. If the roof is superimposed over such a map of points, where columns are necessary to support a particular node on the roof, a line is dropped from that intersection to a convenient grid point on the ground.

In this manner, a variety of inclinations and random placings is generated. The Forest grows, not an external mapping of Nature but an interiorisation; transformation and translation rather than copy or mime.

Undulating roof line over
the main seating tier and
fixed orbit of ground seating

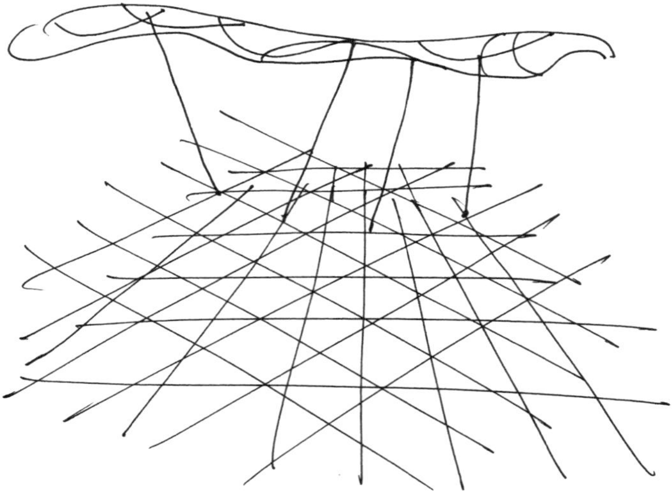

THE CHEMNITZ SOLUTION

A heavy ring at the bottom, dense, made of earth, serving as a fixed orbit,
followed the track. Above, another ring orbiting, this time with more
energy expanding and contracting in plan and moving in the vertical
plane as a slow wave. This was the floating object, a disc sweeping
intermediacy between earth and sky.

And higher up, a steel net that turned on itself, hovering, like
a cloud.

From dark to light, from closed to open, the encircling spoke of different complexities and separate freedoms; and a surrounding zone of serial plantings pushed columns upwards into the roof net, in clusters or singly. Metaphors for Cloud, Forest and Earth were needed no more. The Chemnitz solution had given us what we wanted, a new language for Stadium.

In the event we won the competition.

And the vagaries of chance hit the project immediately, politics related to public funding stopped the realisation going forward. The project has been on hold since. Whether it will be built – we don't know. We wait in hope.

INFLUENCE NETS

Ideas have their own fields of discovery – some local and quickly confined to a small area of influence, others seem capable of spreading. Something about the Chemnitz solution suggests an open question rather than a closed answer.

The rings could be anything – a basket of weave, a piece of coral, or a roof when the scale happens to be 200 metres across and the arcs are made of large structural tubes. At microscale the rings could be networks around a bone or the map of a matrix that gives plants and leaves their stiffness.

The roof projects itself as an assembly of cells, and connectivity dominates. Pattern becomes *a priori* structure. 'Meaning' comes only with scale.

At whatever magnification, structure acts as a network of information exchange, either for biological barter or stress interaction.

the final competition model presented by Kulka & Konings to the jury

I went back after the competition to ask further questions.

I wanted to know if a set of arcs similar to the orbits of the stadium roof could be generated by a mathematical rule; did the intuition for rings have a hidden, even approximate, basis in numbered functions? Could an arithmetic be found that turned into circling geometries?

I began with a single ring – duplicated it and rotated it past the first.

As one orbit passed the other a series of intersections came into view. I freeze-framed the motion.

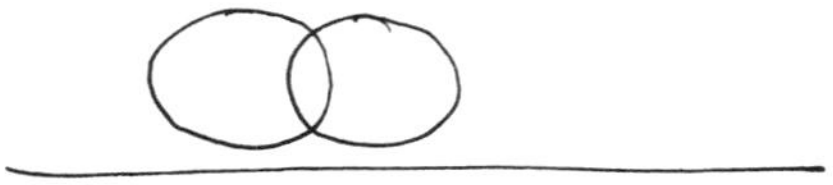

Upon duplication, the new ring may shrink or expand and a fresh new configuration could repeat the same process, copying its image and rotating further.

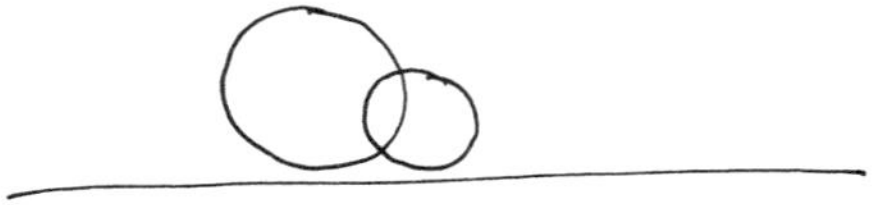

By multiplying the unit idea, the complexity grows.

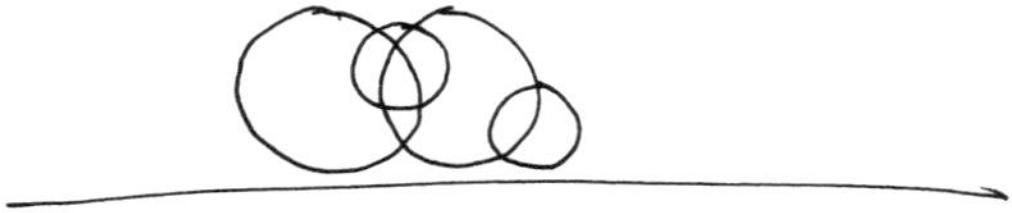

Studying the resulting networks was interesting but did it head towards a solution? The answers seemed too limiting, the information for a powerful algorithm was lacking – was it the nature of 'ring', such a closed and rigorous starting shape that restricted the outcome? What if instead of 'ring', we were to take the locus of a point, a moving spot that had its own energies?

I began again.

I used a solid disc and a dot marked on it. As the disc rotated the dot recorded a series of 'bouncing' arcs.

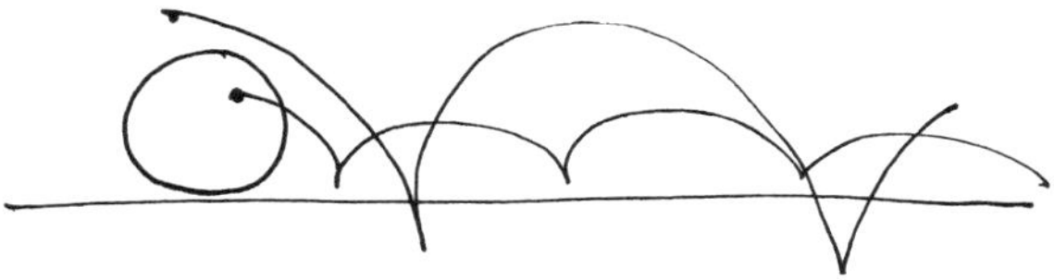

These are called cycloids.

Visualise the moving point as a source of light – imagine a dark room and a black disc being rolled along a table.

The disc turns and the rotating point of light traces flying arcs.

With two holes drilled in the disc the light draws a series of intersecting curves.

Imagine a dot rotating on a disc – different start points will lead to different answers – some chaotic, others symmetric.

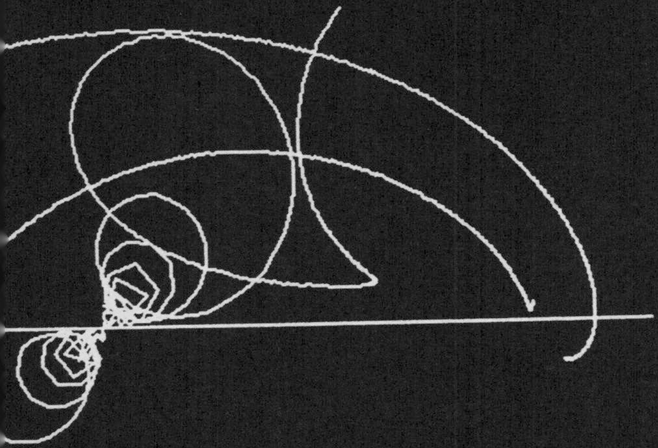

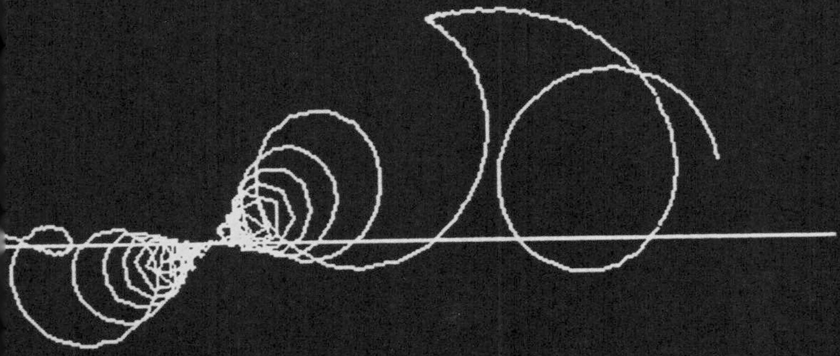

Depending on the location of the holes, different traces occur. Some are symmetrical and regular, others erratic. If the light source is external to the disc but attached to it, then wild possibilities arise.

The trace becomes highly erratic.

Such entangled behaviour may not be appropriate for structure but the result is fascinating. It gives an insight into the non-linear.

Varying start points yield different answers, each unpredictable in outcome. Some traces are ordered, others tracking into total chaos. Both states are mathematically determinate. Behind the seemingly random there is a rule at work, the exact distances of the dots in their rotations are computable. Behind the apparent free will to self-organise or self-destruct there is this precise calculation.

The moving point leads to a much richer idea for an algorithm, as the locus of a point has more freedom than a prescribed circle that turns. The closed ring, that already presumed shape, has too much definition applied to it at the moment of starting, hence there is less potential for diverging options. It is the principle of entropy at work – the less internal discipline and rigour in the particular initial state, the more choices in the final state.

Now imagine the disc moving away from the straight line, around the edge of the site boundary.

Overlapping arcs of different radii materialise, but the centre aperture does not get defined.

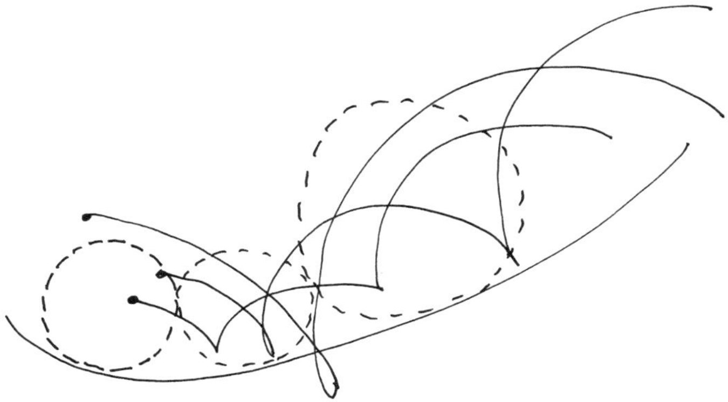

Other traces of the rotating disc
on other geometries

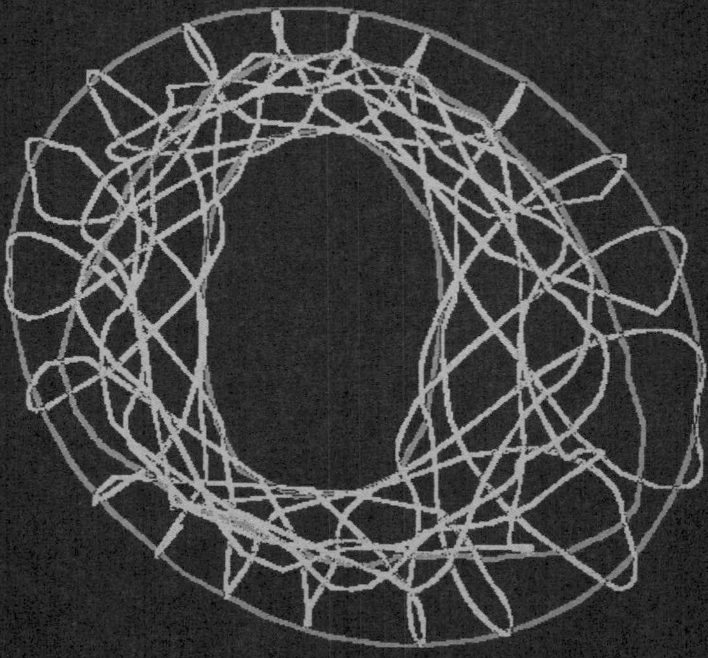

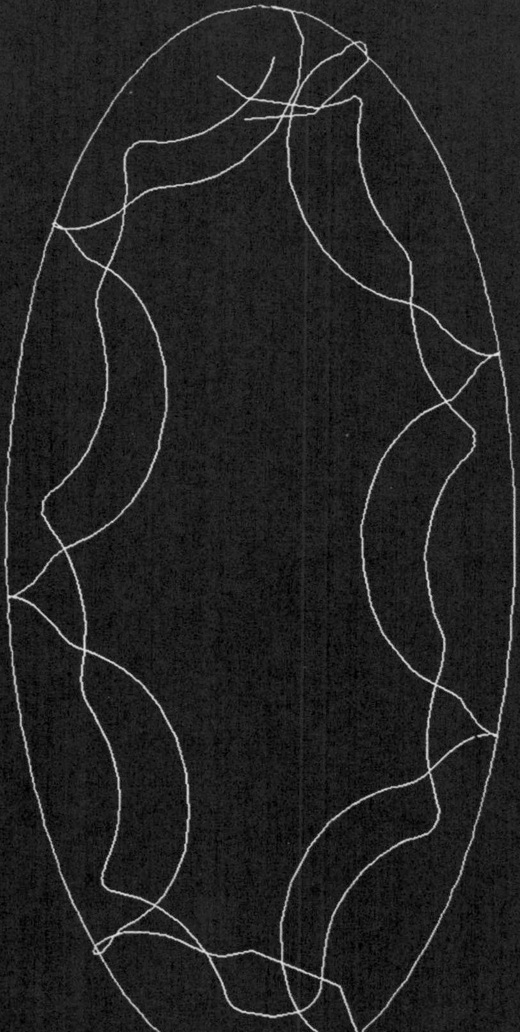

I liked this lack of definition to the inner edge and thought it in keeping with the generality of random energies; the architects thought otherwise, they preferred the inner edge to be defined as an unbroken rim.

That restriction was put in as another boundary condition and this gave impetus to the final strategy.

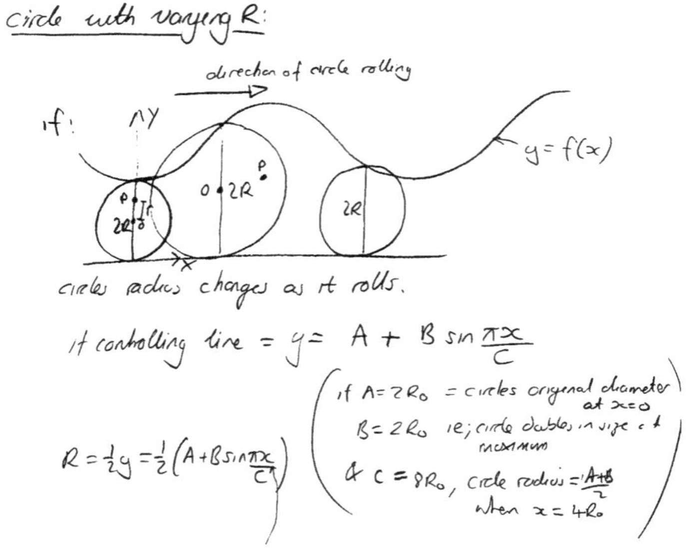
circle with varying R:
direction of circle rolling
if:
Y
y = f(x)
2R
X
circles radius changes as it rolls.
if controlling line = y = A + B sin πx/C
if A = 2R₀ = circles original diameter at x=0
B = 2R₀ ie; circle doubles in size at maximum
& C = 8R₀, circle radius = (A+B)/2 when x = 4R₀
R = ½y = ½(A + B sin πx/C)

What if the disc runs between two fixed boundaries?

Each boundary can be defined mathematically and at all moments the disc or any dot in relation to its centre may still be tracked and plotted. The assumption is that the disc shrinks and expands as it runs between the inner and outer orbits of the roof.

In other words, a 'breathing' disc!

If the dots in the disc are as threads through the eyes of needles, the rotating disc begins to 'stitch' and 'weave' structure. A single thread may have properties assigned to it, of area and stiffness.

An embroidery or network grows, seeded with intelligence.

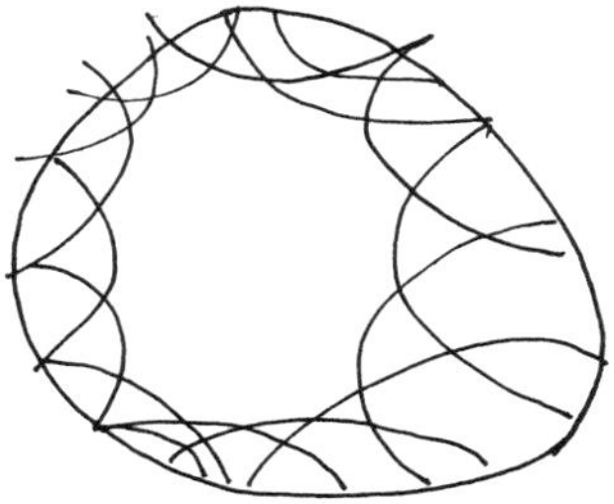

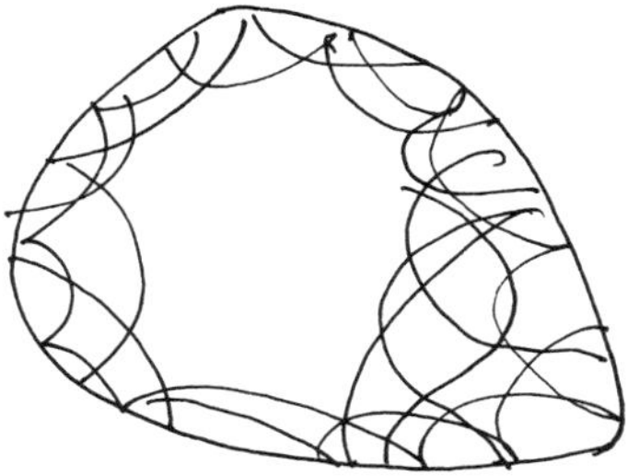

With certain default values given to an analysis package, a roof-net structure could evolve by reacting to specific failure criteria. Edge deflection or maximum stress in a member could force a readjusting of the dots to begin a stronger and better weave. This is the ultimate scenario – a structure that can stitch itself together, the seemingly random start points being turned into a rigorous synthesis.

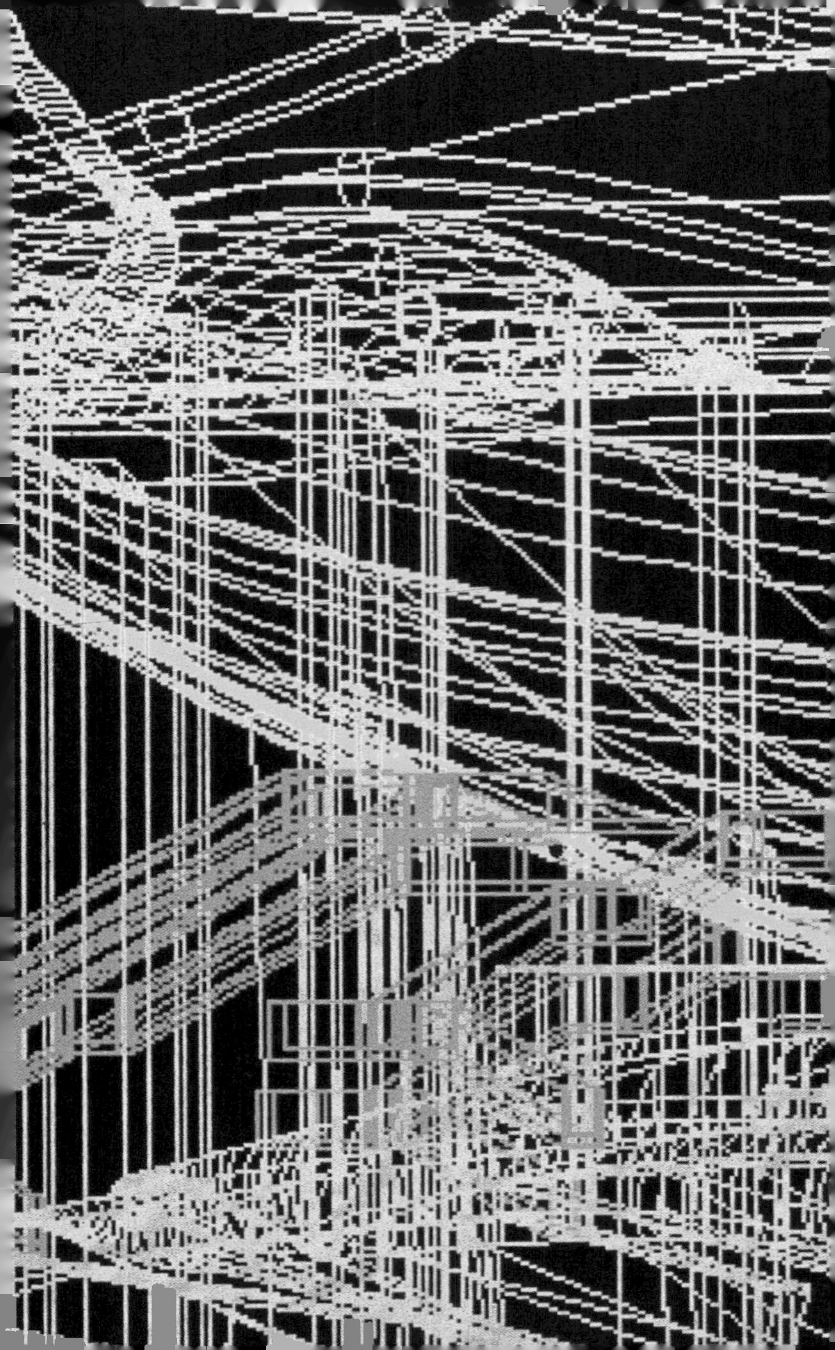

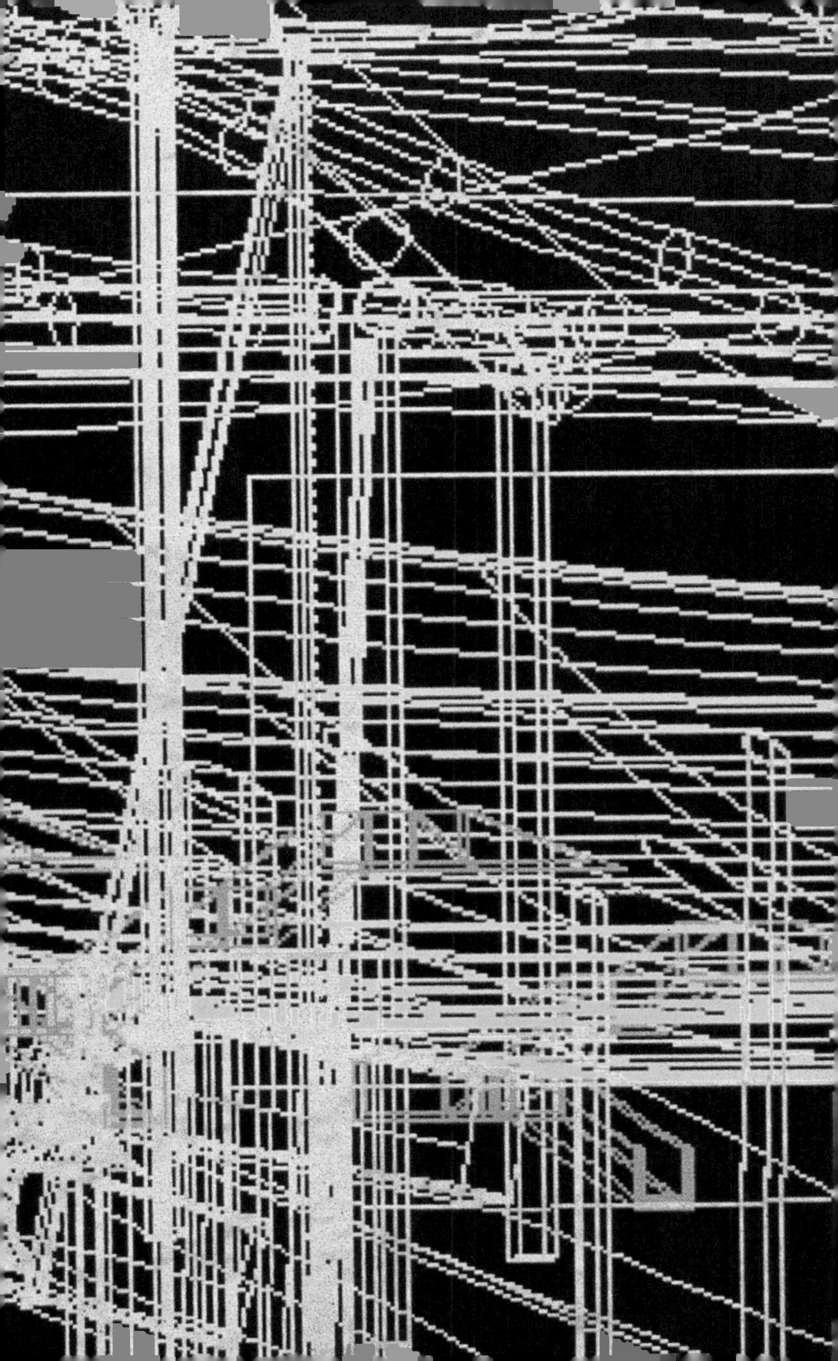

THE UNIT AND THE MULTIPLIER

The Chemnitz solution took individual ideas and extrapolated them by duplication and rotations. The concept is of the unit and the multiplier. Nature seems to work in similar ways in its internalisations.

TWO FACED

Nature is venerated, courted and romanticised. And there is the other side to it, an impersonal template of strategies that connect and assemble layers of data and pattern – Nature as a mosaic of shifting number and changing geometry that best fits endurance and survival.

The face of such a Nature is implacable. In its colossal inhumanity yet infinite success we find fear and attraction, the enticement of the impossible being made possible holding for us an echo of the sublime. Sheer multiplicity and invention claim our fascination, but behind the inextricably chaotic, where is the logic?

If sentimentality and a cosy Mother Nature are put aside, we look into the core of a prodigious information sampler. We discover a pattern-maker of infinite skill. The pictures weave interdependence in a fine mesh of invention. Here, the simple and the complex inform each other. Nature becomes a collective exchange and loses its capital letter for hierarchy. This is not a stripped out minimalist world of 'less is more' or a reduction moving to stand-alone categories, but the richer thought of a cross-feed, multiplex world, where 'more-is-less-is-more'.

It is an ultimate loop.

In the infinitesimal we find the realm of the all possible. (The single cell which harbours the entire map of the organism allows cloning.) There are several infinities.

Magnification of nature's patterns provides self-similar pictures. From the interstellar gases to the phantom inhabitations of sub-atomic vanishings there is a consistency and a conceptual culture at work. A framework of four energies (nuclear – strong and weak, gravity and electromagnetic) driven by a compulsion to overlap through feedback, produces complex forms out of successive evolutions.

If we see the constructions of mineral, vegetable or animal as discrete, the continuum is in the virtual networks of their hidden energies, for nothing really touches in nature.

But everything is felt.

The livelier and more complex the organism the higher the speed of data sampling and exchange.

Life is information: its algorithms a mysterious combination of random electronic circuit and an internal self-will for coherence. We cannot trap such a nature for we are not distinct from it. We should attempt to divine it.

SHAPE SHIFTING

Nature has no fixed symmetry. An electron is not a precise orbit around an impenetrable nucleus but a fuzzy cloud in and out of adjacent orbits. Between centrifugal force and charge, balance is kept somehow by the changing dynamic.

When chemical reactions swap ions, equilibrium is reached by a recounting of the numbers. Hydrogen and oxygen yield water as $2H_2 + O_2 = 2H_2O$, giving an equal amount of O + H on each side. Salt is made by precipitation from solution to crystal: $2Na + Cl_2 = 2Na\,Cl$ does the counting and structuring from liquid to solid. Somewhere between phase shifts the balance point is hidden. In the transition of matter, from one state into another, the symmetry is in the changing numbers.

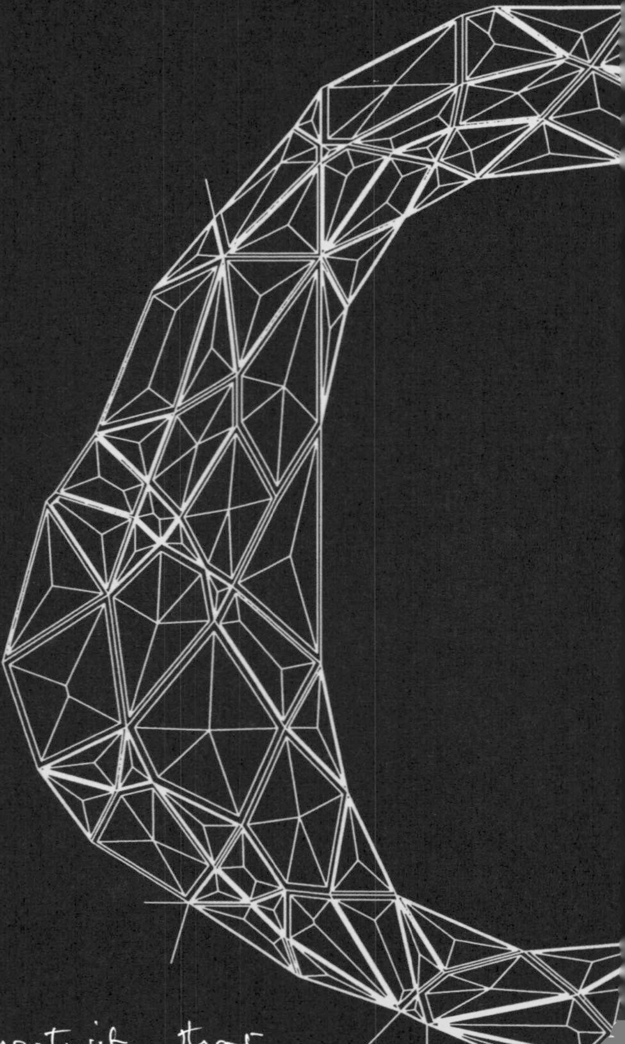

a connectivity that
speaks of something
more than stadium roof

The ideas that nature builds on are local concepts which multiply, mix and overlap. Even a single idea, like branch 'Y', repeated incessantly, turns into the pattern of root, branch, and leaf.

In fact *tree* is the algorithm branch!

The arteries of the lung or the river tributaries of a delta follow similar commands. As always, in the instruction of the unit is the information for the whole.

If the unit is composition, the multiplier is the algorithm that leads to pattern. The end product is the extent run of the algorithm.

There are no pre-definitions, just covert commands. Successive linkages, according to set unit configurations, yielding either crystalline precision or amorphous liquids and gases. These are the clues for easy access to the infinite; but how impossible to know its workings. The beguiling mysticism is in the mantra which makes it all possible – the impromptu sketch evolving geometries and number shifts and paths that somehow overlap and come together to yield earth, air, fire and water.

To mimic nature from the outside by externalising and copying what the eye sees is limiting. Better to look inside and find the interior motif that builds outwards again.

What we would view then are the structures of the knotted and the irregular, of cross-breeding and overlap, that lie seemingly at the heart of nature's secret ambitions. In special instances, like in the crystalline lattice structures of regularity, such fragile moments of stability may be read in ordered Cartesian terms: but to see them as fixed and part of an eternal hierarchy is to misunderstand. The crystal is a snapshot. So is a structural framework. Regimental order is transient, a fleeting glimpse only.

Nature's unit and multiplier inspires a much richer mix, a generic typology, of fluid and fractional geometries.

Such seemingly random but structured patterns strike a resonance within us, for our 'internalisations' may be built on similar ideas – a kind of haunting, of interior space being made external, of buried archetype surfacing.

The whispers we hear will sharpen our intuition.

173

The fantasy always compels, the thought of a new plan is exciting.

In contrast, hard reality, the end result of what we do in the name of that quest, is less interesting. Once we're done with design the next adventure begins opening up new horizons. The concentration is on start-up rather than finish. But when the ambition is huge and way beyond the normal scope of a project, then the sheer scale and presumption needs its own incredulity questioned. Did it work? Was the ambition right? When that plan is to supersede the old with the new and redefine a whole city centre then the project and its theory are worthy of interrogation, repeatedly.

It was with this in mind that I revisited Lille, to return as a visitor and walk the streets, to view the construction and to partake of the vision it offered. In the process I hoped to learn something new about the project again.

Lille was to be catapulted into the year 2000 and beyond in a conurbation that linked London, Paris, and Brussels – in a catchment of 50 million people. City councillors talked of *Bralille* – Brussels stretched out to join Lille economically and financially in a new hub for Europe. We were flown round the site in a helicopter.

The first surprise is the people – all sorts – travellers en route to somewhere. They swarm around, walking the streets or standing idle, waiting for the next train:

Paris – Brussels – London.

They are not tourists who have come to look at the old Lille but a new breed of transients who occupy it for a while, two hours or two days, and move on. The fast train does that, bringing them to Lille – but also the designer shops, restaurants, and hotels refurbished out of the old fabric.

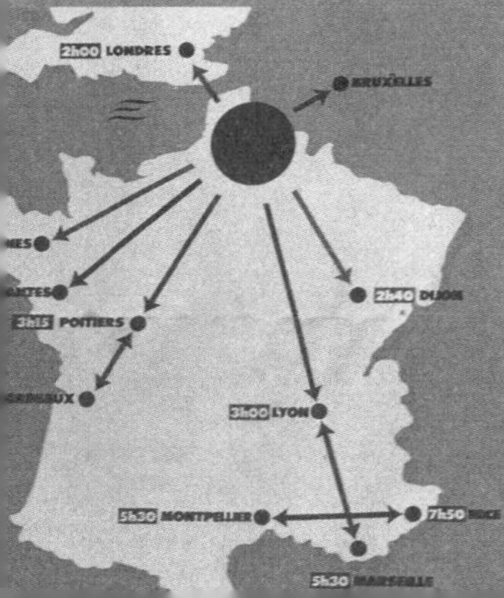

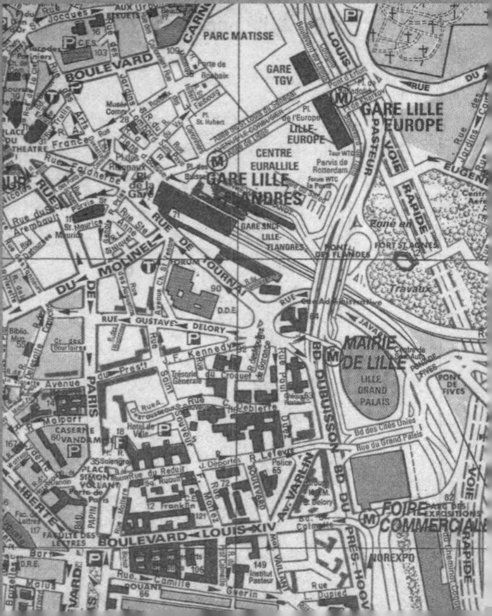

The scale was vast and daunting. So were the city's dreams; a 200,000 m^2 development on a 70 hectare site that would attract investors, raise ground rents and be the great architectural statement of a new Lille – 100,000 m^2 of office, 700 housing units, 3 hotels, 6,000 parking places, 50,000 m^2 of exhibition centre and a 10 hectare urban park.

I walk along the aptly named Rue Nueve and pass Disney, Etam, Minelli, The Body Shop, Kookai, New Look, Quicksilver... Within a hundred paces of one another the trend setting labels compete. English is spoken everywhere – in the shops and on the streets – the Brits seem to be here in strength.

At the intersection of Rue du Sec Arembautl, one of the towers of Euralille in the distance marks the skyline, its stark green glass angle in sharp contrast to the low pitched tiled roofs of the street. Much has changed.

I remember these streets empty with the reserve of an old town meeting the first glance of a foreigner. But the mood has changed; the new crowd is young and mixed, the look open.

I ask shop owners when they opened their stores. Many said around 1997, three years after the project was complete – these were the UK and American designer labels. More recently in 1999, the French labels also moved in, building on the first wave of commercial success.

One hour from Brussels or Paris, two hours from London – why not stop and work and shop and conference and concert in Lille – that was the vision and ambition of André Maurois, the Mayor of Lille. In two words: 'Think Big!'

Rem Koolhaas was invited to develop the master plan, and Ove Arup and Partners were appointed to join OMA, to advise on strategic issues relating to infrastructure and the logistics of building. The total investment was estimated in billions of francs.

Design began in 1988.

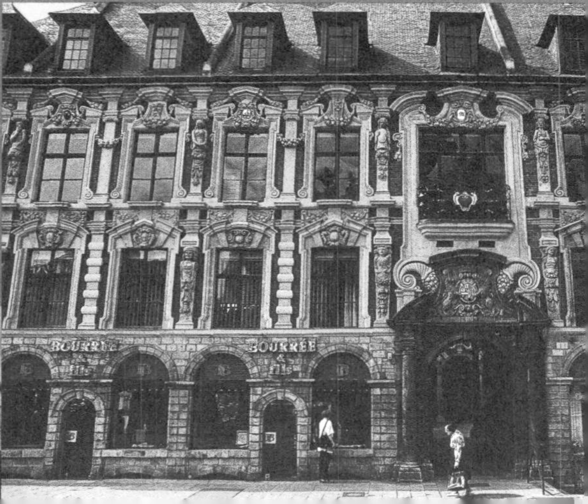

I went on walking the length of Rue du Molinel, towards the old station. Gare de Lille Flanders still wears its stone façade in neoclassical style; and in front of it there is a small plaza where crowds gather. Some people use the old station for the local trains, others pause *en-route* to the TGV located a hundred metres away. The new and the old cross over here; it is an ideal place for people watching.

Koolhaas held a *cherette* in Rotterdam with people from a variety of disciplines, and we brainstormed for six days. At the end there were two options for consideration; a master plan of isolated parts held together by avenues and roads, a patchwork scenario allowing sequential financing, or its opposite one of consolidation, in an all or nothing plan. Euralille was born out of no compromise. It was like an alien landing in the midst of a sleepy urban fabric, the towers, glass and overlayers of density not remembering the polite manners of context or convention.

Lille needed a future of arrival to be trapped in the nervous tension of a high energy tectonic and Koolhaas' plan did just that.

Office towers straddled the tracks signalling the energy line of the bullet train. A huge triangular plaza tipped from the heart of the old centre towards an edge 400 metres away to catch the fast projectile within the confines of a new station. A basement was to be dug to accommodate subterranean levels.

A little boy is rubbing his hands over his bare chest trying to get rid of an itch, he stretches out his arms and contorts with karate poses and dips his hand into water. A fountain rears up, breaks and washes down, filling a pool that stretches the length of the square. A group of African kids sits on the edge of the parapet and poses for photographs – on the ground their pile of soft canvas holdalls. Another young dark-skinned girl presses a phone to her ear, one of her fingers in the other ear to plug out the sounds of traffic and passers by. The Station Square is busy – blue sky and slight haze. Sunlight glistens off the metal seams of the buildings above the station roof. Backpackers are everywhere. It is 4.30 pm.

Underground subways were diverted. The line of the périphérique was planned to be altered; endless quantities of earth, 1150 million cubic metres of basement excavation were to be piled up into a new park. Etcetera.

Construction began in 1990.

One man puts his foot in the water, shoe and all. He walks off, one shoe squishing wet, the other hot and dry, towards the main commercial centre a few metres away. Crowds push through those long shopping malls in hectic rites of consumerism. Along the shop fronts, columns lined with a reflecting material shoot up coloured lights; the mood is festive, and eating areas offer a variety of international foods. I get tired looking and not buying, and make my escape.

Soon the outlandish and gargantuan took shape. What was initially speculative and fanciful materialised into hard measurement and cost plans. The impossible suddenly looked possible. Word got out. The public endorsed the scheme, the media featured the story.

I walk towards the old quarter a few hundred metres away, situated behind the Opera. Here the buildings are ancient, many refurbished. The newness continues. A museum shop sells memories of lost Egyptians and Hittites along with designer scarves and ties inspired by Monet and Klee. A man with slicked down hair in a wine red suit takes his female partner into Gucci – she's in red too. One of the great restaurants of Northern France is around the corner with a wonderful seafood stall in its shop front. It is full. So are the other restaurants.

Is my memory playing tricks? It was not like this when I first came here. The town was then fading slowly into its past; no colour, no vitality, no coach parties. Who would have gone to work, shop, conference and concert in Lille a few years ago?

As the modern Leviathan raised itself from out of the ground, Euralille provided full time guides to take people around the site, the visits becoming an industry. Coach loads arrived daily. Architectural wannabes and urbanists and railway people from around the world trekked through the kilometres of walkways, photographing the site, trying to capture the size of it all. After what was more than four million hours of design and a construction force of up to 2000 people the project was complete.

The TGV stopped in Lille in November 1993.

Visitors arrived; and the huge shopping centre was an immediate success. There was a spin-off to the high street as designer labels opened shops.

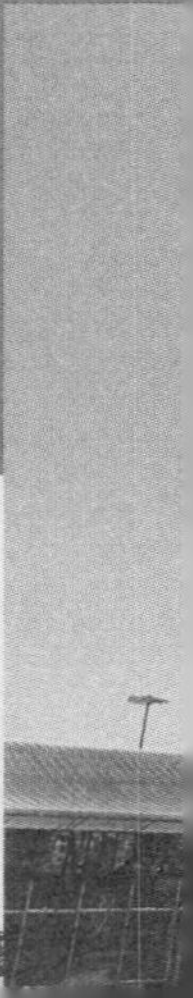

To end the day I make my way to the Musée des Beaux-Arts situated in the Place de la République. (During my trips to Lille I had no time to visit it, always in a rush to catch the evening plane back – but not today. I luxuriate in my re-visit, and indulge in the past.) In the basement of the museum are the magnificent maquettes of the northern cities' defences built in the 18th century, some 9 metres in length and 5 metres wide. They are huge and fantastic.

But not all the office space let as fast as promoters wanted. Phase II of the master plan was dropped. This was a pity, it would have diverted a major highway and given better access to the scheme as a whole including the Exhibition Centre, currently ringed round with roads.

On the positive side I cannot doubt the increased buzz the project seems to have brought to Lille. People throng the streets. There is a *busyness*, everywhere.

I am informed Euralille employs 6000 people, there is also ancillary support which creates further jobs. The commercial activity prospers and the tourists come.

Euralille is the trigger. Like a spacecraft out of nowhere the project lands on hectares of vacancy, eating up the waste grounds of drug dealers and prostitutes.

Every house and tree-lined avenue of Gravelines, Lille, Avesnes, Aire-sur-la-Lys, Tournai, Namur, and many other cities are shown in great detail, down to the chimney pots on the houses. And I find out that Vauban, a military engineer of genius, planned a new Lille in the 17th century.

After the successful siege of the city by Louis IV in 1667 Vauban was invited by the King to design and implement new fortifications. These took place from 1668 to 1670 with 1800 people involved in their construction; his work extended the town and the innovative construction was labelled 'La Reine des Citadels'. Vauban became Governor of Lille and ruled for 40 years.

In abandoned spaces between the Périphérique and the edge of the old town Euralille fills up the gaps. A hundred metres away from the neoclassical station building and the main street, the Rue Faidherbe, thousands of square metres of shopping malls and office buildings now extend the town, connecting the once cut-off adjacent suburb.

In the records of history Lille first gets a mention in 1066 in the grand Charter. Later in 1369 through marriage with the powerful duchy of Burgundy, Lille joined Dijon and Brussels as a capital of importance and later prospered in the wool trade. In the 15th and 16th centuries Lille became part of the Spanish Netherlands until Louis XIV took the city for France.

Stunned by the models I wander upstairs. On the second floor of the museum are the paintings of Rubens, David and Delacroix and a host of other pictures by Flemish artists.

In one room is a particular painting by Hieronymous Bosch entitled 'Le concert dans l'oeuf'. Ten people, one nun, two other women and seven men appear in a large cracked egg. Some sit on the edge of the crack, some stand within. Some sing with earnestness. Others look anguished and reluctant. Is it a birth? Blackbird omens fly about – a supporting lutenist to the singing group and an angel with a monkey face are crushed in other cracks of the white shell.

The picture is bizarre, fascinating and crazy. Are they holding a concert taking their time in the egg having found it deposited on their shores, or are they manifestations of a fluid suddenly made whole, the potential of the egg transformed into some kind of celebration?

As one walks the length of the Megapolis large horizontal layers of buildings spread out along the road boundaries. Towers rising from this plateau align a secret axis, signalling the fast train. One tower in particular strikes a special emphasis, its odd angles and green colour invoking a strange but beautiful geometry. These towers jump 60 metres across the tunnel below to allow the TGV line to pass through. They stand as both sentinels and markers.

The tectonic is so large that it envelops individuals, the proximity of its various functions encouraging participation – the group instinct is primed. One engages with the nature of a modern labyrinth, comforting, frightening, growing in the mind with the power that dimension and hybridisation confers.

The resonances could not be better, the Master Plan of Vauban in 1671 and the fractured egg of Hieronymous Bosch.

I think of Euralille and its new Plan and I also think of Congrexpo, another strange kind of egg deposited in Lille recently, just down the road.

Juxtaposition of new with old, with no pretext at conformity, seems to work.

The speculation will surely be tested further, how Lille transforms and achieves the promise of its brave new world. To my mind the early response is good – the density confirming the city as a place of renewal. The idea could grow. Lille may be a first node.

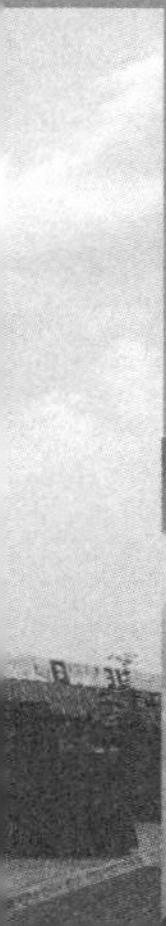

189

The Spiral challenges the concept of a museum: does space have to be container-like and neutered to house works of art? When there is much invention and fantasy in porcelain or jewellery or the lines of a fashion garment, should the space around the exhibits be inanimate; is not the real invention to present art, not as lost object in a static box container, but as vital trigger in a spatial dynamic?

Question: is art treasure to be hoarded, or fresh thought to be continually transformed?

With a shape that is formless and a façade that motivates geometry as a mathematical mosaic, the V&A Spiral designed by Daniel Libeskind opens the debate: Norm and Form would have new definitions from the year 2000 onwards.

A cherished symmetry and insistence of right-angled forms rejected, and the old paradigm of fixed centre left behind, the V&A Spiral vaults into new space. Inside is outside. Floors are denied columns, and walls offer no vertical short cuts for gravity. Structure and architecture become one immediacy.

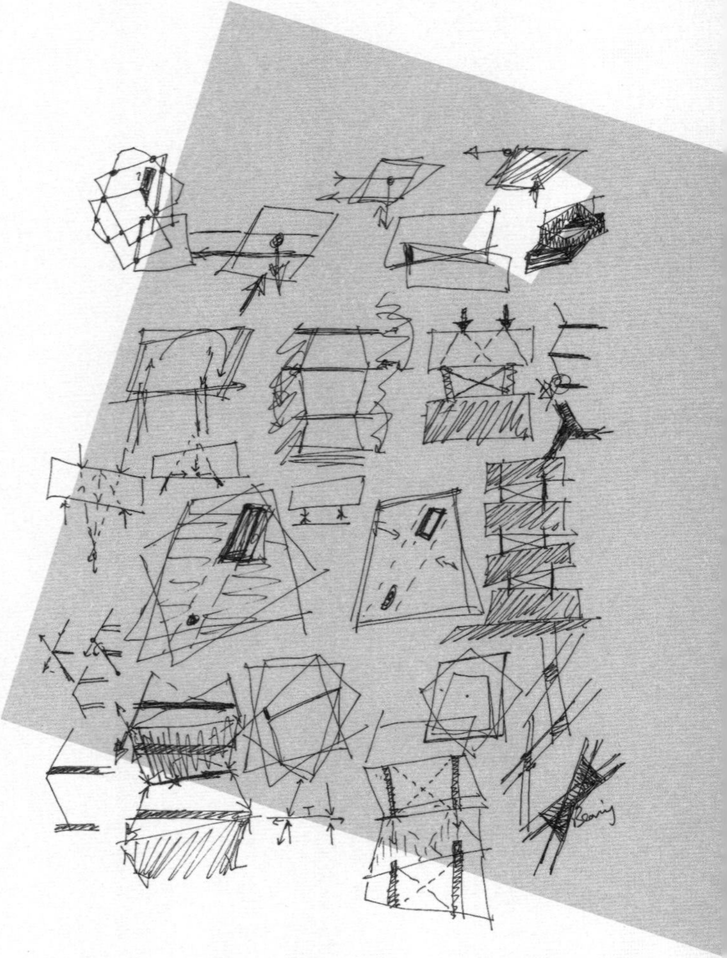

I looked into the form without really knowing it at first; I saw walls flying across space. The tilting planes climbed and cut into each other, violent, shattering any notion of building in the conventional sense.

And the dialogue began between Daniel Libeskind and myself, how could such a form be built?

Libeskind took me back to ancient times, to the Pyramids. We talked of stone and how to build a form like this from masonry – but the oblique planes and large spans would have needed huge 'strapping' with prestress or numerous tie devices. Attractive as the idea was in its primitive urges, I advocated concrete or steel to maintain the daring alignments.

There were two ways to consider the question:

implant a certain massiveness and celebrate a high redundancy in the configuration;

or trap the tilting planes in a modern rationale of discrete 'framing'.

The former would give concrete as a material of tradition, used in an extreme definition; the latter would reduce the great planes to a framing buttressed by internal stiffeners and cross bracing. One method provides density, opacity, and three-dimensional surface as structure, the other lightness and openness that is then clad and windowed. The first answer leads to a labyrinth, the second to transparency.

We exchanged metaphors.

If the form were closed, it could be a mineral deposit, or if an open transparent steel framed building, it could be a lantern or a beacon. If it were heavy, could it be hacked out of granite, or was it buildable out of special masonry? The images helped loosen the thinking and inspired us to look for the radical.

How to choose?

There was no science to it, the instinctive decision was to go for the inscrutable, the closed-in secret. As a check, I mocked up the stick model, trying to find common lines for the vertical structure, attempting to brace diagonally in between edges, but the structure looked forced and contrived. The seamless flow of planes felt inherently better. So we decided on concrete, the artesian material of sand, water and gravel, to 'pour' the form.

A sketch polarised the concept:

DEVELOPMENT

In the first model standing one metre high and built out of stiff white card, the walls leapt dramatically in a stacking of twenty-metre-deep planes, exciting and extravagant. In cut-away mode though, viewed from the inside, something else happened. At five-metre storey heights, floors interrupted the raking planes. The internal spaces became serene, uncluttered, and with no columns. Light streamed down through the overlaps on plan. A slow shifting of space occurred, around a gradual displacing sense of the vertical.

outside dramatic and violent
inside quiet and contemplative
outside theatrical and extrovert
inside reflective and introvert

Closing like a secret and opening like a drama – the Spiral caught both progressions.

The form was at the singular point of a cusp.

The Spiral.

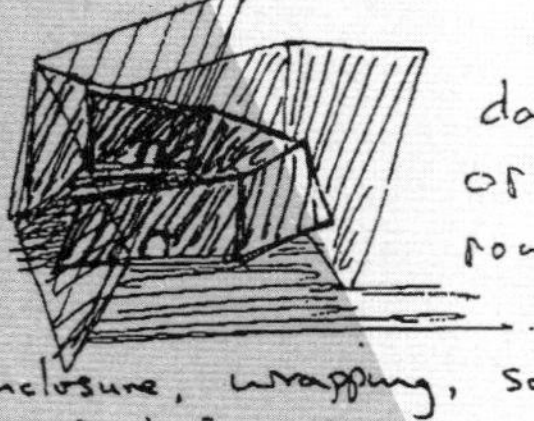

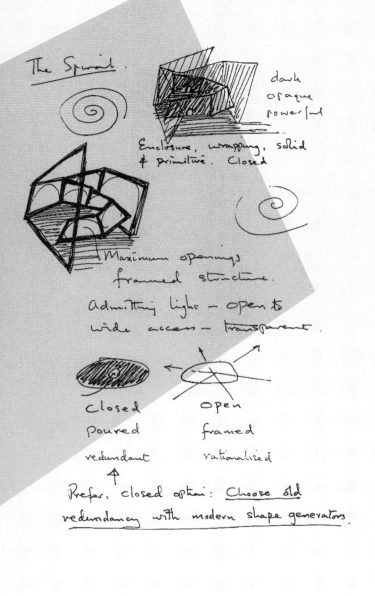

dark
opaque
powerful

Enclosure, wrapping, solid
& primitive. Closed

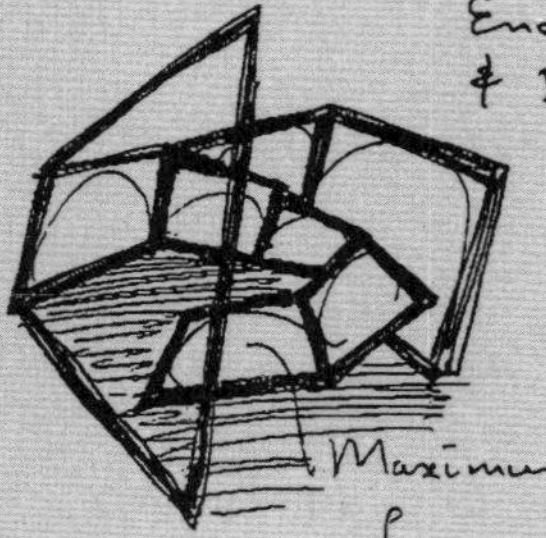

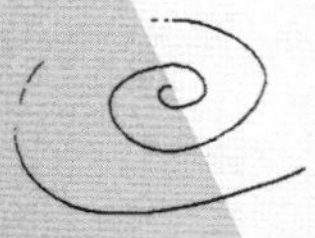

Maximum openings
framed structure.

Admitting light – open to
wide access – transparent.

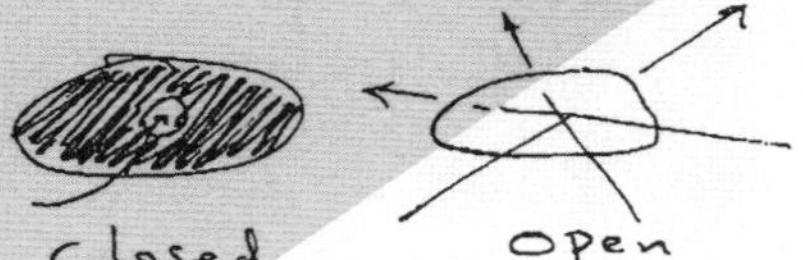

Closed	Open
poured	framed
redundant	rationalised

↑

Prefer. closed option: Choose old
redundancy with modern shape generators.

From time immemorial a winding form has caught peoples' imagination, its symbol serves as talisman and votive force, the contrary movements seeding a deep mystery and ambiguity. To adepts and magicians spirals were Guardians of the Gate and Protectors of the Centre, to ancient geometers the spiral was a 'Mirabilis'. Through tornadoes and whirlpools, in shells and in the horns of rams, in the petals of flowers, spirals frequent nature; spirals turn galaxies and braid DNA strands.

And the dialogue continued; the mind-play that surrounds and transforms a solution.

Libeskind and I talked of numbers and their power: of the Eastern legacy of number as abstract and touched with hidden algorithm; and, in the Hebraic tradition, text as number. We talked of serialisation, of music – of the Eastern inspiration for melodic lines that fold and overlay each other, of the Western tradition for harmony and modulation. How these discussions influenced what happened is impossible to tell, but it set off an enquiry with buried codes that helped forge a close partnership.

As Libeskind developed the semantics of spiral I looked at the syntax of connectivity and implied movement. It was not just architecture and engineering but a wider endeavour being moulded.

STATICS

The first thoughts I had of structure were in terms of one plane bearing on another, a piggy-back of shared loads working their way down to the ground. Each discrete wall was treated as a mini two-dimensional problem, supported on at least two points. But the model encouraged certain walls to have only one bearing point, and crank in space without support.

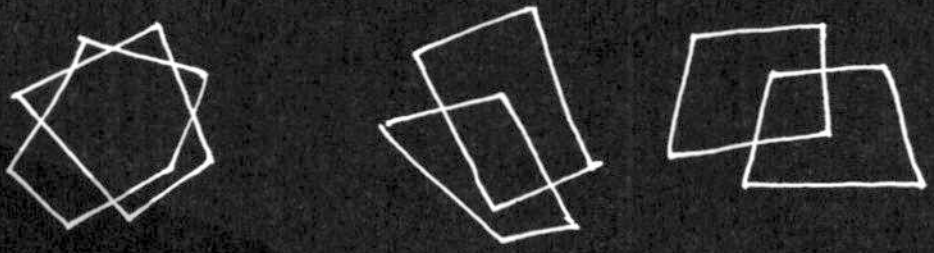

Rather than stacked planes, now zigzags came to mind. It felt as if the form wanted to lift-off. The continuity began to grow.

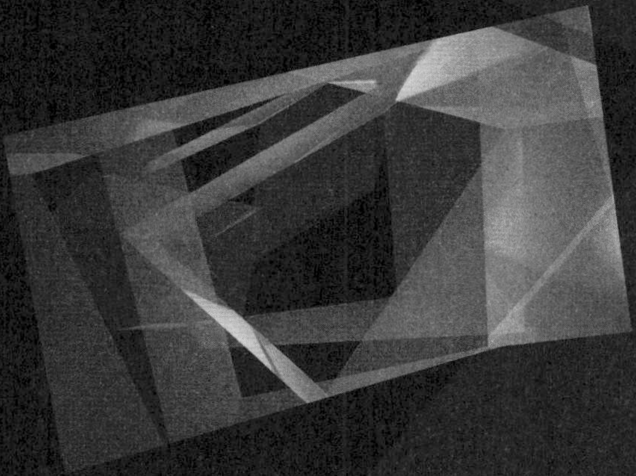

VERTIGO

On elevation the model suggested a stacking of tilting planes assembled like a pack of cards, but when looking down the vertical from the top of the form, a linked rotation took shape. A spiral of sorts took hold; something like the staircase in Hitchcock's film 'Vertigo' – a crooked and distorted trajectory.

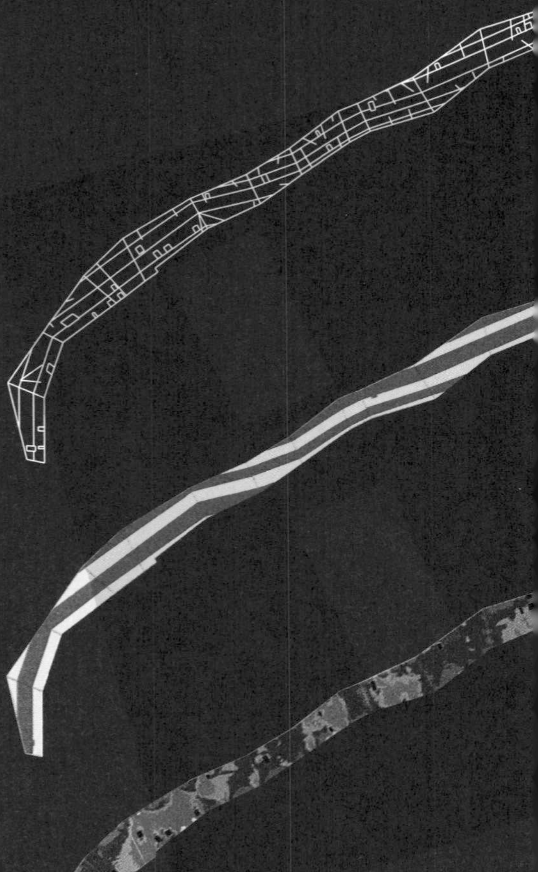

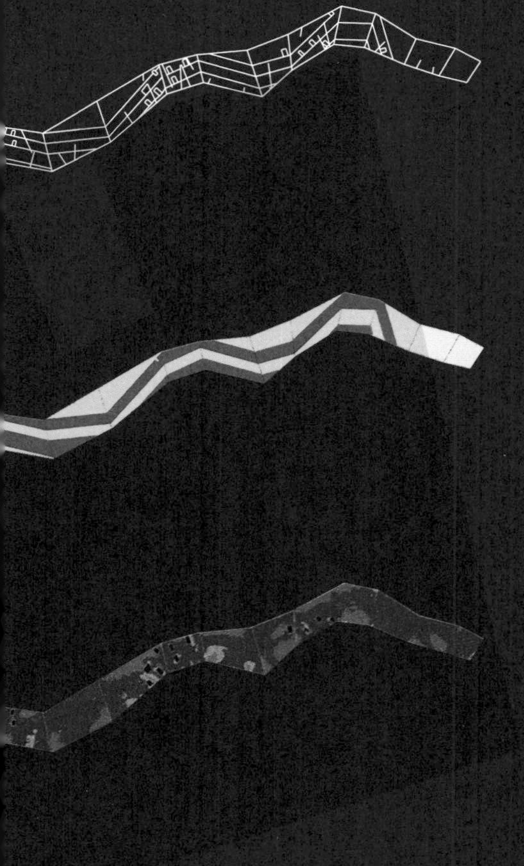

The oblique planes seemed not to be separate but capable of one gigantic turning. If it was a wrapping, then all the parts could belong to one and the same impulse. And the observation levels at the top, first thought of as a glass box and 'clamped' onto the form, could now logically be the end folds of the trajectory. The conclusion was that the whole twenty three steeply-angled planes were but one strip! Folding out the wall planes resulted in a snake-like figure. If the floors attached to the walls were drawn onto the strip, a striped and segmented snake took hold. Each stripe was the length of a floor's connection to the walls that intersected it.

Floor eight, for example, travels the furthest along the strip, attached to more walls than any other floor. That means, level eight will be the most labyrinth-like, with many entrances and exits. If cuts are made in the strip, both top and bottom, and numbered in sequence, then matching bottom numbers with top ones yields an interlocking form. Like a child's toy, the V&A entrance building is assembled by a set of numbers. In terms of scale, the length of the snake would be the length of Exhibition Road that borders the site, a full 500 metres.

What was the real geometry of such an unravelling? What were the turning patterns of this coiling? We had built the analogue in card and timber, but was there a mathematical algorithm? I was intrigued as to whether a set of simple rules could approach the complexity of the form. Was it after all a geometric strategy, albeit of a special sort? With Francis Archer of Arups, I began the search for a simple set of rules that could lead to an interlocking form, arising out of cross-overs on plan – a spiral of sorts.

Classical spirals have two models:

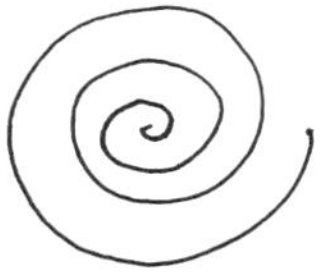

the logarithmic

and the Archimedean.

The logarithmic is exponential and is the shape Nature favours to mark growth. The Archimedean spiral, named after the famous Greek mathematician, is a constant turning, where the distance from the centre grows in equal jumps like in the windings of a spring.

Both spirals have one thing in common – a fixed centre. Classical thinking was based on such stabilisations, the logic of the rule flowing from a fixed and unmoving reference, everything being causal and linear, one spacing relating to the other.

A new spiral would be different – non-linear and unpredictable.

RULES

What is needed is a pattern of criss-cross on plan.

There can be no fixed centre.

The centre should be local to a particular level, not a global reference.

There has to be an erratic tendency which makes the distance of the orbits from the local centre vary.

The result is to be an unpredictable or *chaotic* spiral – its trace suddenly jumping and changing radius realising a locus of cross-over.

THE EXPERIMENT

The answer lies in a drawing that looks like a target.

A radius travels around the circles, changing in length and jumping, stopping at points, its origin moving. Connecting up the points produces interlock and a sideways drift.

The radius starts to swing around a circle stopping at one point; then moves and turns at similar angles about the centre to other points.

At a certain moment the radius shortens and swings around a similar angle as before. If this continues with a fixed centre we get a crooked spiral, an imprint of the distorting perspective of the 'Vertigo' stairway.

But if the centre moves, as the radius revolves changing its length, the chaotic spiral results. We have an interlocking trace.

To enter the third dimension,
the trace is lifted off the ground
in a zigzag, each leg rising successively
a certain height.

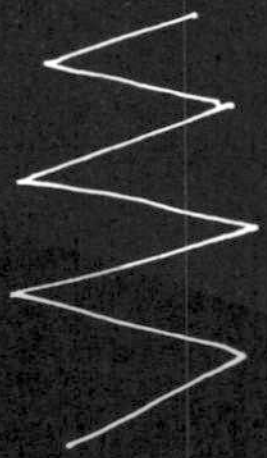

The lines become the centre
lines of the walls
in elevation.

Each centre line is now
rotated and a normal
(a line at 90° to the rotation)
projected into space. At
right angles to this normal,
an infinite plane is swept
through the line.

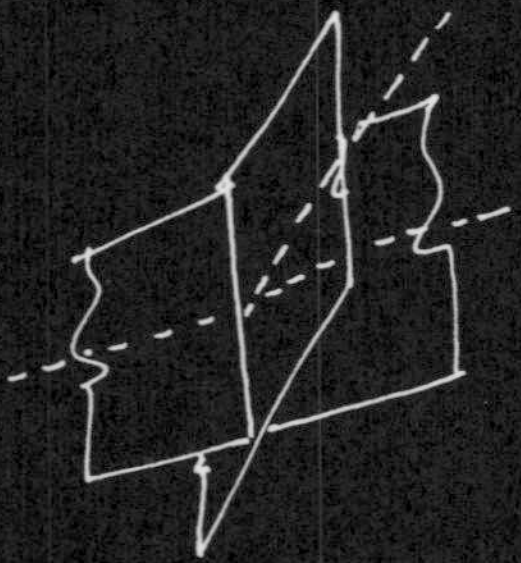

The intersections of these planes
generate corner fold lines which
have mathematical equations.
Hence, the edge of a wall and
its height can be set along
these lines of intersection.

By giving a vertical offset distance,
for both top and bottom corner
from the centre line, at each
end of a wall, a panel can be formed.

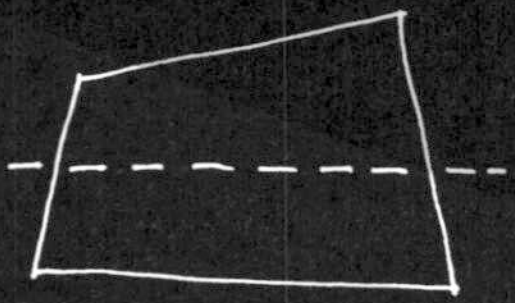

Insisting on intersection is vital,
for it gives bearing and structure.
A serial logic grows. The form
transfers loads through its skin
needing no other support. The
steps of this calculation may
be carried out on a spreadsheet.

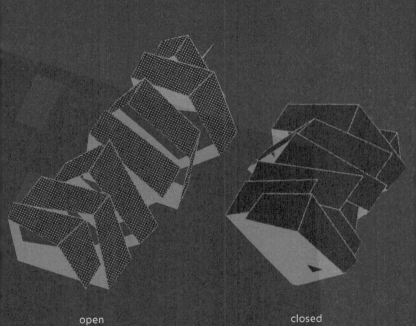

open

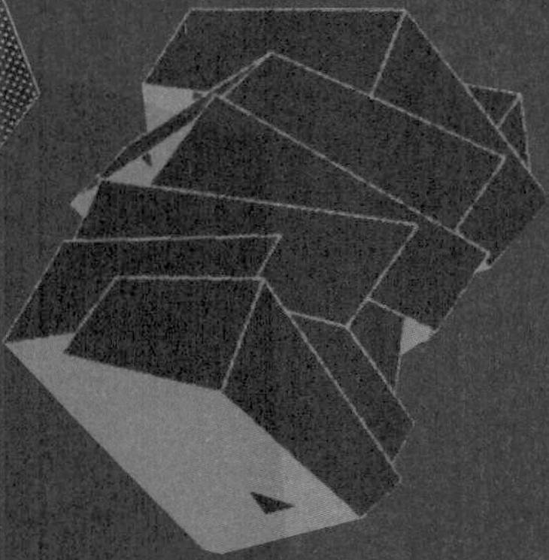

closed

Because the program is generic, depending on the start point, no two traces would be the same.

If the angle at which the radius spins around is small, then the form evolves smoothly. When the angle at which the radius swings around is large, the trace is spiky, sharp; the consequent form, a densely intersecting shape like a crystalline clump of mineral spars.

What we have is a range of interlocking shapes, all of them built out of rotations and widenings or shortenings, but all arising from a logic of the locus of a point orbiting around a centre, in stepped jumps. In other words, a spiral, but a generic one, capable of many interpretations.

large angles

small angles

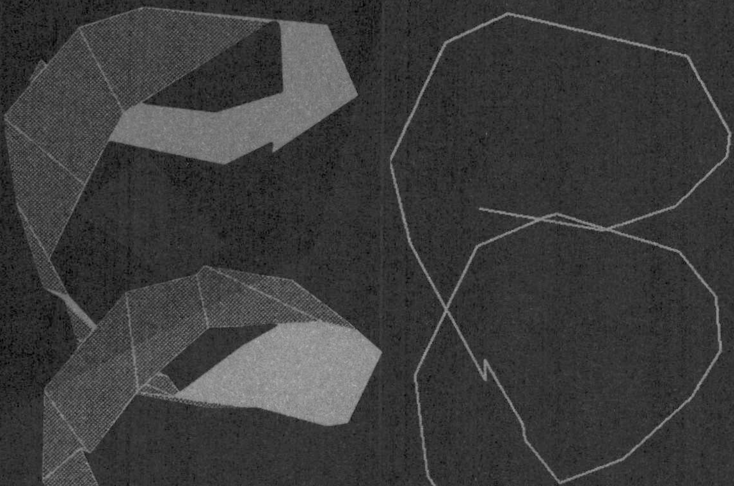

If buildings today on the High Street are proposed by generating envelopes, a strip that folds at right angles at regular intervals will produce shoe-box like enclosures. The trace is of a repeating closed loop on the horizontal plane. In this scenario a roof is 'cover', a lid.

The V&A Spiral is also a strip but one that climbs as it folds with no roof. It is finite but unbounded.

Another way to approach this coiling is to go back to the oldest method of building an analogue – with paper and scissors.

Take a strip of paper, mark it in equal measure and fold it about the vertical lines. A closed circle is obtained.

If the lines are staggered, gradually increasing in their vertical spacing, a spiral results, in plan only.

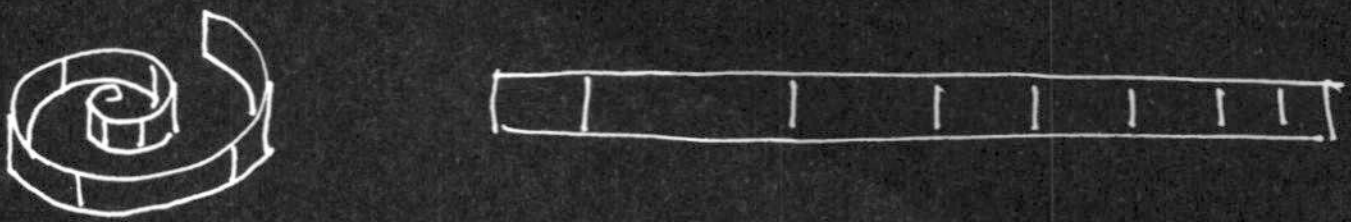

If the lines are inclined, the spiral 'climbs' into space and goes upwards or downwards, depending on the angle of the line.

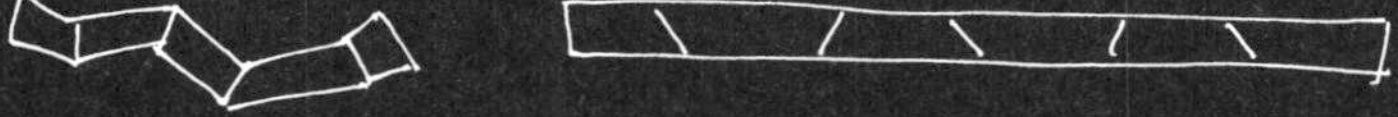

If the strip is not uniform in height and is marked with different inclinations, then a form rises that starts to intersect with itself.

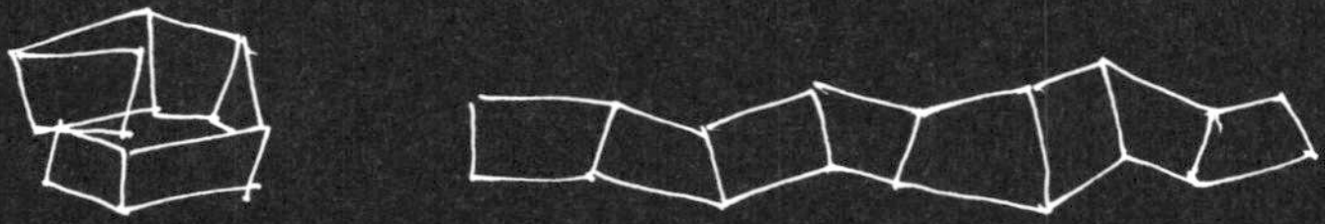

This is backing into the solution as it were – as I preconceive the outcome, I know how to get there.

With a digital medium there is no need for such restraint. The future is open.

All one has to do is choose an initial configuration that leads to the widest possible range of solutions. Though more difficult to grasp initially, because of the abstraction, the generic propels variety and is a richer path for discovery.

The experiment we carried out abandoned preconceptions – and the forms grew and wound their way into interlock, climbing into space as if with a will of their own.

209

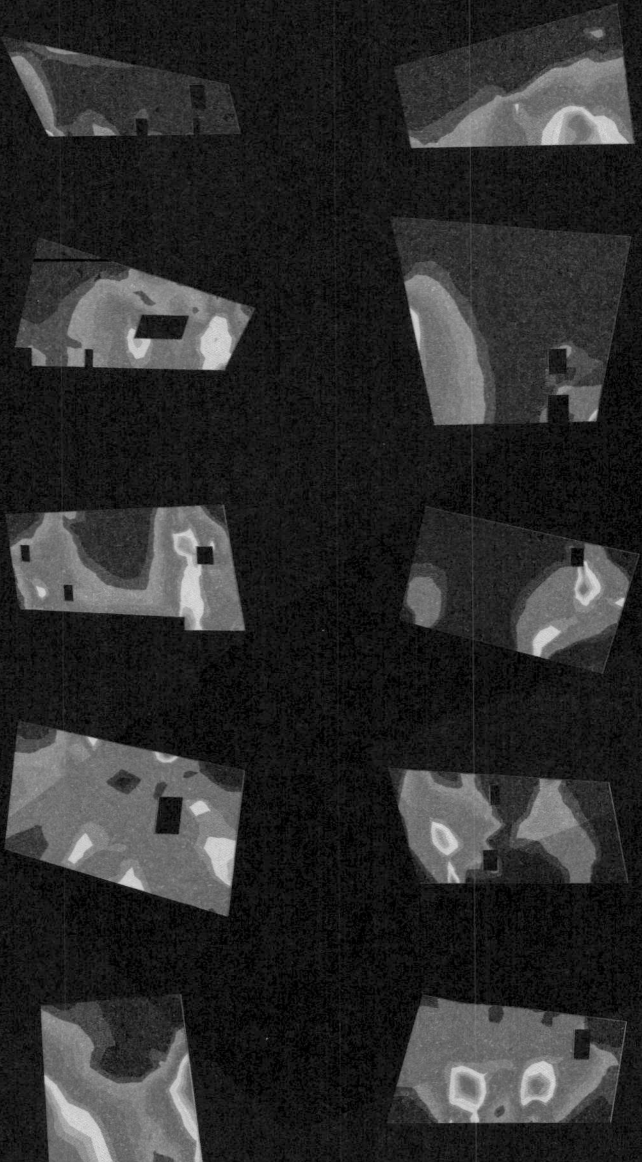

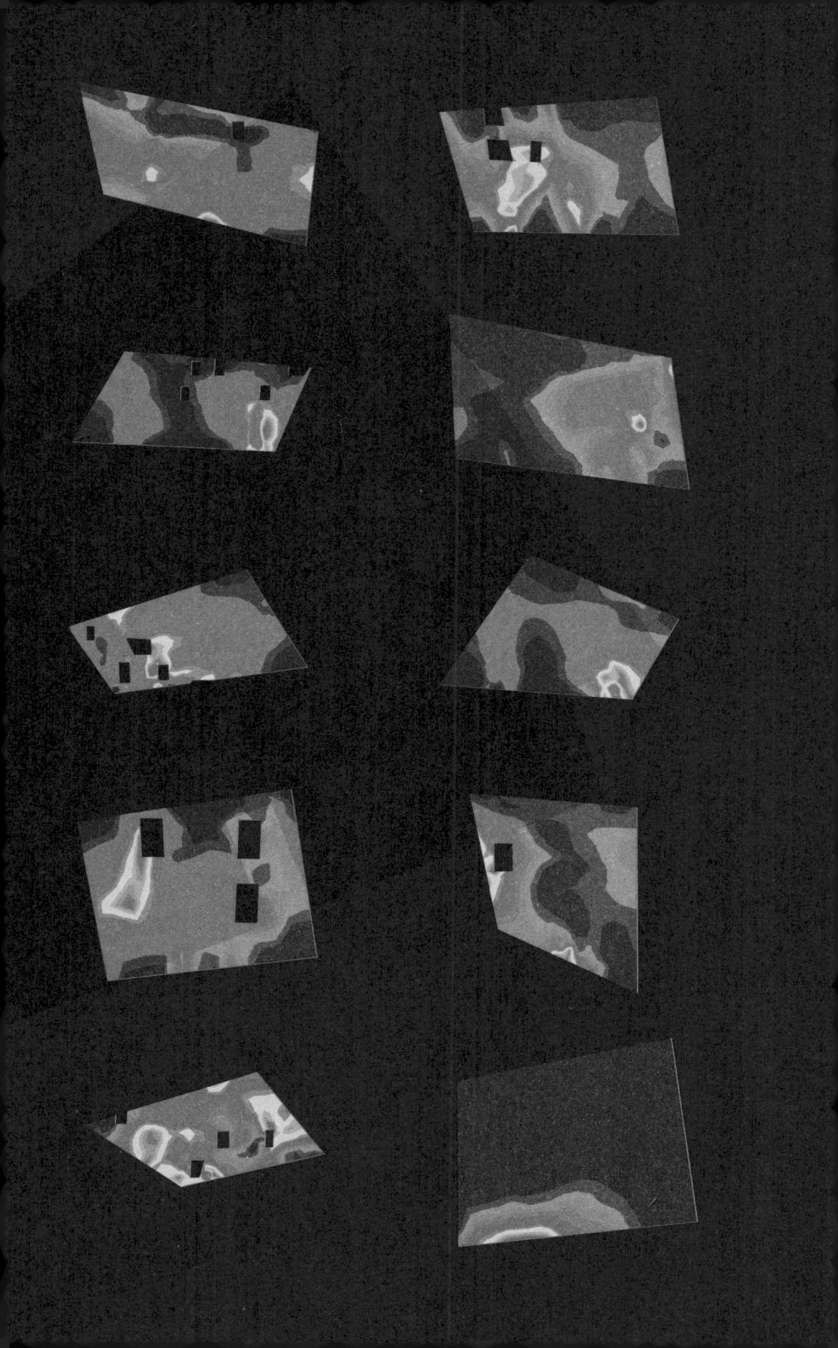

Watching the algorithm run on the computer screen is to see a mad pixel explosion growing in scattered jumps. Unknown in where it's going, the patterns and overlapped sequences inject a different intuition to the eye, of unfolding, rather than the one used to static forms. A special dynamic beguiles the mind, unfelt structures rise as shapes evolve on the monitor screen.

The digital model of course is an approximation to the first model, put in by eye, but it demonstrates how we might have 'searched' for a solution had we started with no preconception. At the heart of the matter is the question: where do the aesthetic eye and an algorithm converge? How will a computer know when to stop and how does that relate to what we like?

A sophisticated program could 'learn' and optimise mechanical concerns; like levels of stress, degrees of stability, a minimum enclosure for a given number of walls, a specified floor area within a certain volume, etc. Somewhere a 'pilot' is needed to bring the solution home; the eye will want to enter and look within.

The next generation of software and hardware will allow this, linking complex form generation to analysis, to 3D visualisations. No analogue will be needed – the search for an answer may be purely virtual.

When the generation of form is mathematical, all the necessary geometry and data is there to improve the intelligence of the model. For example, planes crucial to load transfer could have intersections, given preferred limits for bearing, and the spiral could adjust and 'grow' to accommodate structural concerns. Here the challenge lies in 'training' the feedback loop to 'learn' and converge on starting points that lead to successful outcomes. Between generating program and analysis a seamless link is needed.

The trace then becomes more intelligent; it customises itself to a prescribed code of conduct. Like DNA it can be imprinted to recognise beneficial situations.

Algorithms of structure, of travelling lines emerging into shape, open new doors to a radical reappraisal of form generation. Not confined anymore to the strictness of regimented line, non-linear typologies beckon.

But to deny a rigour to the investigation of non-linear shape would only promote architectural form as a gesture of software. That could be dangerous, because it is ultimately meaningless. Our brains, random as they are, do not act without interior connections – there are rules – albeit ones hidden to us.

Perhaps intuition has an internal mapping of its own, of non-linear algorithms. Testing this further is a task of the *informal*.

217

The temptation is to say nothing and let the work speak for itself – who wants to theorise? But in the method of design, of small differences in start points leading only to the unpredictable, I looked into the non-linear and its special character, and was intrigued.

Its complex nature was hard to pin down. I tried to articulate and classify. And what began in 1991 turned by 1995 into a working manifesto, delivered at a lecture in Berlin. The reaction was encouraging.

The investigation continues today into the approach and its intimate interdependencies. I call it *informal*.

The *informal* is
approach to
moment and

Ignoring
layering and
informal keeps
not based on
hierarchy but
of the

opportunistic, an
design that seizes a local
makes something of it.

preconception or formal
repetitive rhythm, the
one guessing. Ideas are
principles of rigid
on an intense exploration
immediate.

It is not ad
but a
start points
creates its own

When we
convert it to
Order!
effort. We try
We try hard but
dullness and

hocism, which is collage,
methodology of evolving
that, by emergence,
series of orders.

attempt to trap chaos and
our preconceptions,
becomes an enormous
to eliminate fault or error.
the effort turns to
the heavy Formal.

The more
the notion that
states of order.
in fact a kernel
sets sequences

Several
Simultaneity

subtle approach is to seek
chaos is a mix of several
What is an improvisation is
of stability, which in turn
that reach equilibrium.

equilibriums coexist.
matters; not hierarchy.

The *informal*
characteristics:
juxtaposition.
ingredients of
embraces the
Cartesian
geometry are

The *informal*
This means
experiment as a

has three principal
local, hybrid and
They are active
an animate geometry that
linear and non-linear. Both
and post Einsteinian
encompassed by it.

gives rise to ambiguity.
interpretation and
natural course of events.

Berlin, June 1995

229

241

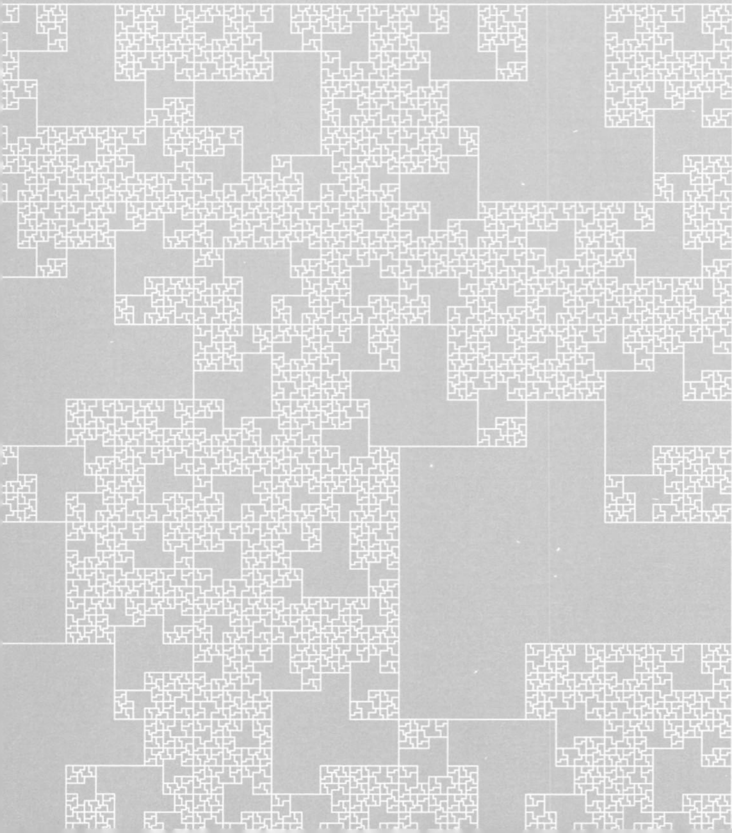

Daniel Libeskind and I had been talking of tiling.

Victorian patterns and William Morris, the intricacies of the Alhambra and other past poetics of ornament came to mind; but a different instinct took hold for the Spiral.

We felt the great planes had a movement in space that needed not just 'cover' but augmentation; a vibration of sorts across the walls. It could not be traditional tiling, it had to be something else. I saw a 'shiver' running up the form.

External tiling normally completes the object, refines it, and gives the building an ultimate blessing; yet covering the Spiral pointed to another strategy, a kind of mobility that would never complete the building but keep it unfinished, always evolving.

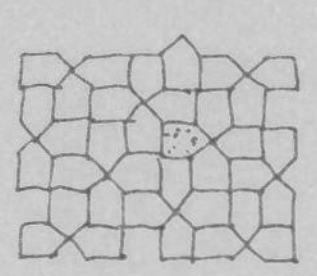

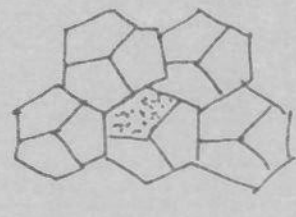

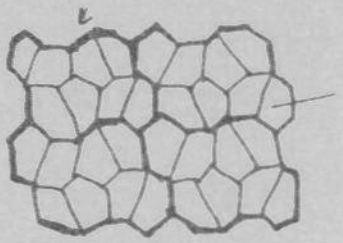

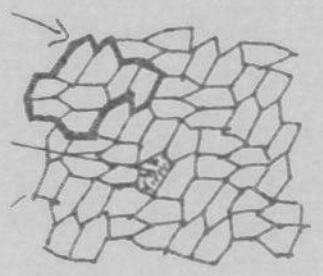

The idea starts with finding a unit of pattern and using it over and over again in different interlocking adjacencies. What appears to be random will grow to cover the plane. If we know the unit and understand all its flip-overs and rotations, as a 'fit' is generated, the notion of 'random' disappears. Serialisation takes over. Instead of static repeating motifs we have movement, a 'charged up' liveliness. Sequence becomes important. Governed by certain rules of organisation tiling turns into the dynamic of tessellation.

Patterns within patterns may be sought, even the thought of tiling at one scale turning into structure at another.

To keep the feeling of sameness and have the potential to be different, I wanted to seed a self-similarity of pattern, necessary to realise these ideas, replicating 'network', and not fixed pattern.

The first shapes that came to mind were distorted pentagons, setting up craggy and spiked patterns, but they seemed too violent and 'one dimensional', not quite in resonance with the Spiral itself.

As the research continued the patterns became more intricate; the answers seemed to lie in a mathematical mosaic.

We came across a fascinating idea from an American mathematician called Robert Ammann. He discovered a 'unit' of tiling, of three different interlocking but related shapes – the tiles had a special and subtle property, each one made up of the other two shapes along with a reduced version of itself. They fitted according to a set of exact rules.

Though the pattern produced by these tiles looks similar, the pattern never repeats: it is *aperiodic*.

Let us label the shapes P, Q and R.

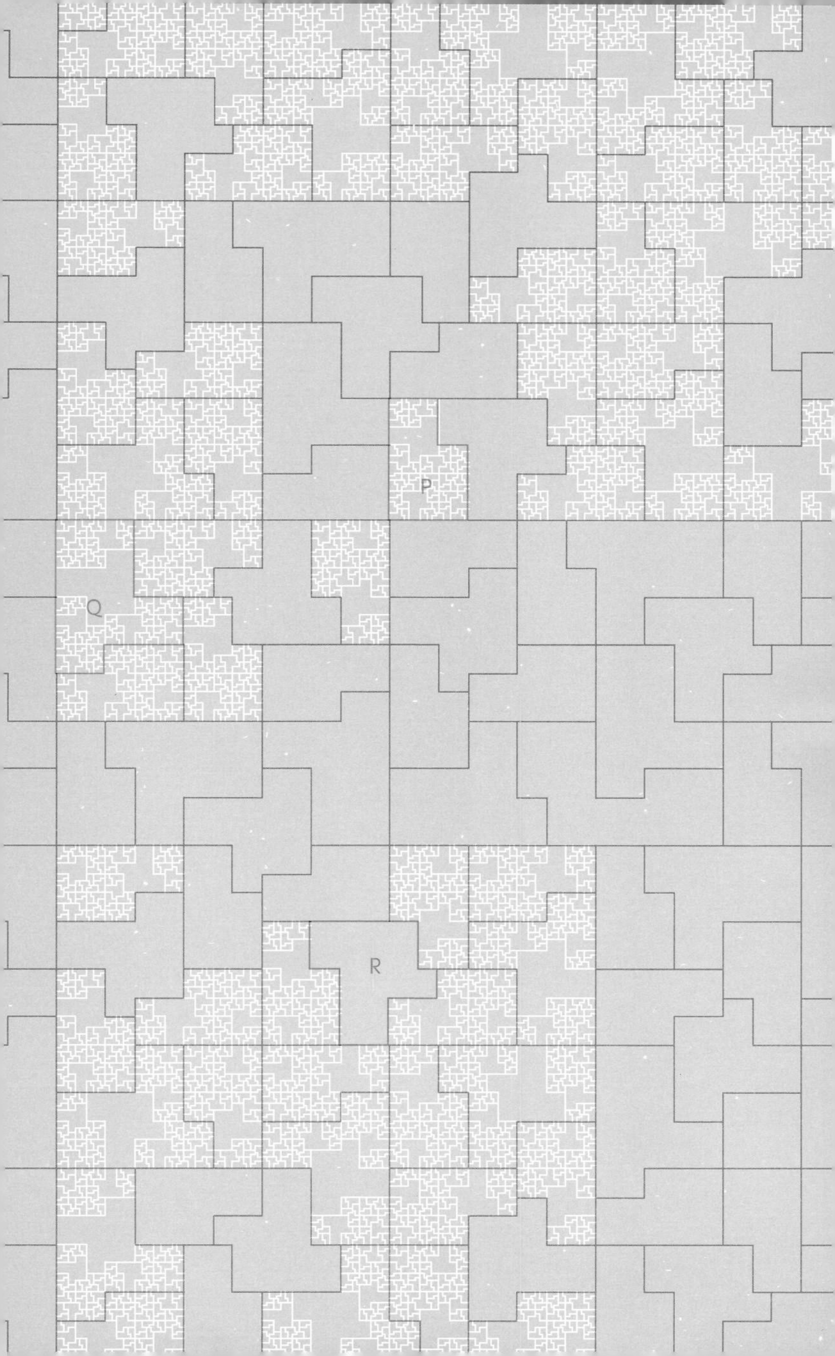
P
Q
R

Dimensions for the Ammann tiles are derived from a hidden set of meshing grids that run diagonal to the tiles, beneath the surface of the pattern. The surprise is that these hidden lines form rectangles of length to breadth ratio equal to that of the golden section. One of the grids is orthogonal, but inclined at 45° to the vertical. The other grid is at an angle governed by powers of the golden ratio.

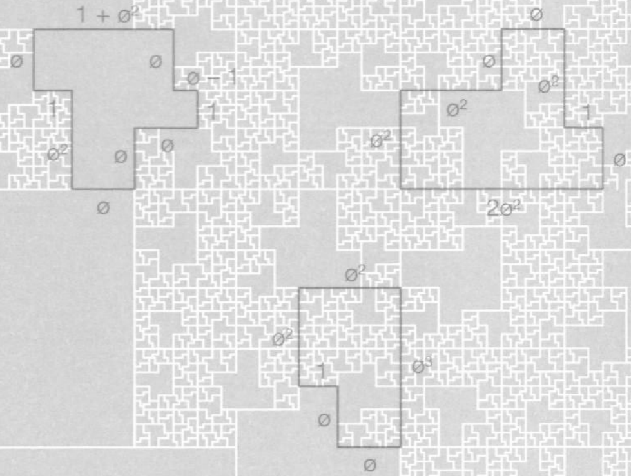

The unique property the golden rectangle has of removing a square from it to leave behind a smaller rectangle that has the same proportions of the original rectangle, is relevant to the idea of self-similarity. It is also the root property of aperiodicity, a fundamental quality of the more complex behaviour of fractal patterns.

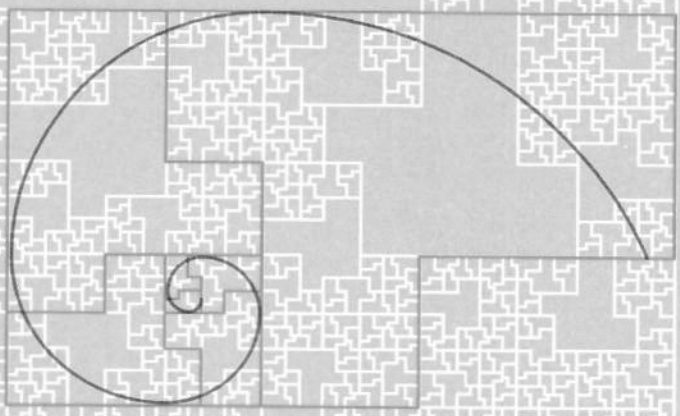

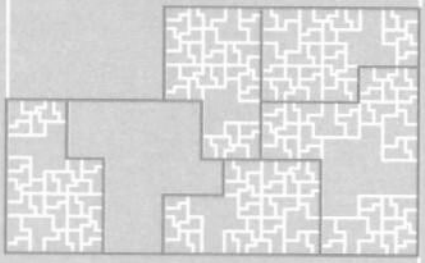

Each P tile contains a mix of P, Q & R.

The same thing could be done with shapes Q & R: each tile is a hybrid of itself and the other two shapes.

The tiling discovered by Ammann covers the plane completely; there are no gaps. The pattern is two-dimensional – it has a bounded 'flat' area, measured by length and breadth. In dimensional terms, it is the same as the Alhambra tiling or any other traditional tiling of repeating motif.

I wanted to develop this further and let the pattern grow a set of 'holes'. Since the geometry of the pattern is based on recursive mathematical principles, such a 'hole' will occur at various scales. All one has to do is stop a part of the pattern from evolving.

In the decomposition of the P & Q tiles, for example, if the R shape is stopped every time it occurs, then gaps open up. As P & Q shapes keep forming through the range of scales, the R shapes keep being stopped. A tapestry of holes appears at all levels. There is incompleteness to the two dimensionality, although there is self-similarity.

The pattern does not completely envelope an area, there is always an absent part, like a travelling margin that never quite closes on itself.

The result is a fractal.

Its dimension is 1.77.

(Not dimension 1 which is the straight line, and not dimension 2, which is a closed and bounded area, but in between.)

The fractal dimension may be viewed as a measure of the meandering and density of a pattern, along an infinite range of scale.

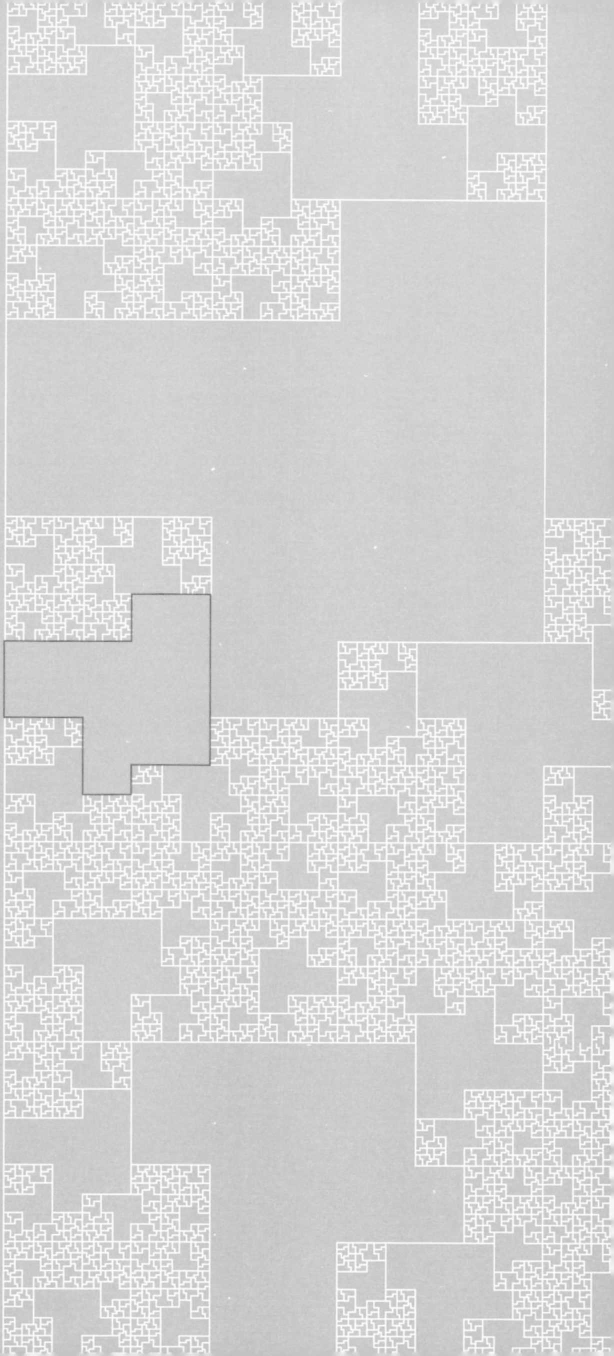

Where the pattern is most dense, an inclined set of intersecting orthogonal lines seem to appear. These are shadows of the Ammann lines, traces of the golden section revealing itself as the hidden organiser. Computer animations show the pattern erupting out of these regions. As the algorithm runs; the eye travels into infinity...

In fact, they are not lines at all but deep crevasses, out of which the pattern keeps being born. These dense concentrations are at angles that mirror one of the hidden Ammann grids.

Note: As the pattern decomposes – if P or Q shapes are suppressed – then a different fractal is obtained. Because there are many P & Q shapes in relation to R shapes, as the pattern gets smaller the fractal would be harder to view. The Ps and Qs tend towards a 'dust'. It is not as distinctive a pattern as the one obtained by stopping the R tile.

Since a fractal is scaleless, the folded-out strip of the V&A Spiral walls may be superimposed over the derived pattern.

The strip can then be pulled away 'picking' up the part of the fractal it has contact with and be folded back on itself.

The walls are now tiled.

We used the word *fractile* to combine the mathematics of a fractal pattern and the concept of tiling.

REALISATION

Since the fractal is scaleless a decision had to be taken on the optimum size of a tile. In relation to the aesthetic of the walls and practical considerations for handling the tiles, a typical size was agreed at 80 cm wide and 40 cm high.

A ceramic was chosen for the tiles; the colour, just off-white, a kind of ivory.

To emphasise the fractal pattern Libeskind proposed that the P & Q shapes be raised out of the plane slightly in contrast to the R shapes, which are the 'holes' in the pattern.

The tiles are air gapped and shadow lines will form a network of the P, Q, R shapes, as light plays over the surface. The deeper edges of the fractal will come into view, moving the eye over the wall planes, pausing at one scale only to jump to another.

Enlarging or compressing, the same idea repeats and yet is never the same: here was the dynamic we wanted.

FROM DECORATION TO SUBSTANCE

An early idea was to use the tiling pattern as a template that could multiply in size, from small scale at the bottom of the form to a larger one at the top where the pattern could become structure.

The form was viewed as going from heavy and opaque, to light and transparent.

The 'hidden' pattern of the Ammann grids provides ready cross-bracing lines which, in conjunction with the tiling, could be made to work as an in-plane load bearing structure. (As the tiling is developed in detail this will be looked into further.)

In a simpler manner the Ammann grid may be expressed to provide orthogonal framing in the areas left open by the overlapping trajectories. In particular, the last rotation of the structure at the top of the form leaves a large opening needing closure. Here, the Ammann grids will be both structure and ornament, as primary and secondary rhythms are utilised in the framing.

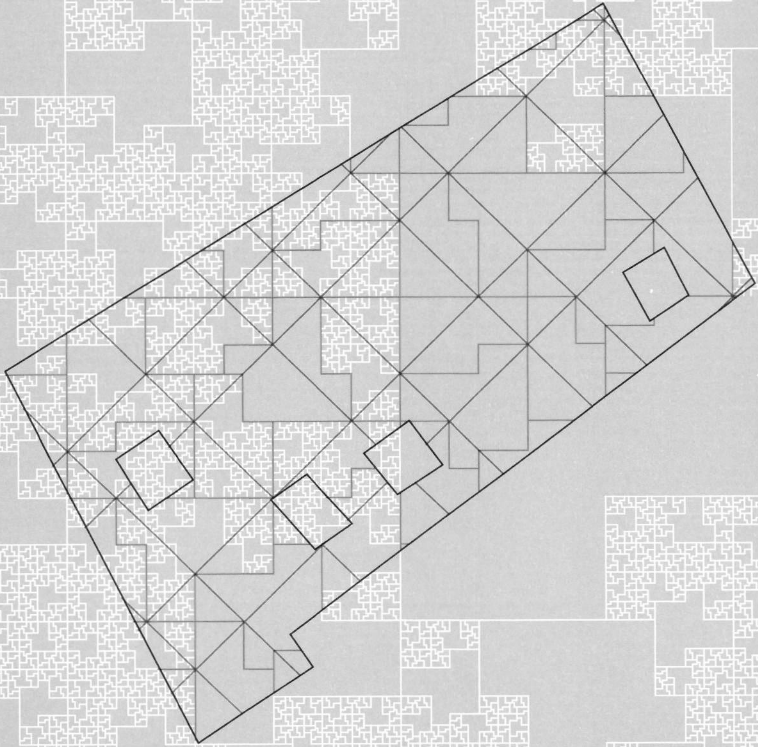

Instead of the abstract mathematics that prescribe the tiling, there is another approach to develop an understanding of how the pattern is created.

We may construct the interlocking shapes through an arithmetical progression of simple numbers.

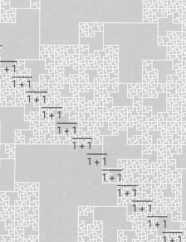

$$1+\cfrac{1}{1+\cfrac{1}{1+\cfrac{1}{1+\cfrac{1}{1+\cfrac{1}{1+\cfrac{1}{1+\cfrac{1}{1+\cfrac{1}{1+\cfrac{1}{1+\cfrac{1}{1+\cfrac{1}{1+\cfrac{1}{1+\cfrac{1}{1+\cfrac{1}{1+\cfrac{1}{1+\cfrac{1}{1+1\ \text{etc...}}}}}}}}}}}}}}}}}$$

The pattern above is a continuous fraction. At successive stages or 'cuts' in the cascade, the following fractions arise.

$$1+\frac{1}{1}=\frac{2}{1} \qquad 1+\cfrac{1}{1+\cfrac{1}{1}}=\frac{3}{2} \qquad 1+\cfrac{1}{1+\cfrac{1}{1+\cfrac{1}{1}}}=\frac{5}{3} \quad \text{etc...}$$

The values are:

$$\frac{2}{1} \quad \frac{3}{2} \quad \frac{5}{3} \quad \frac{8}{5} \quad \frac{13}{8} \quad \frac{21}{13} \quad \frac{34}{21} \quad \frac{55}{34}$$

Values of these fractions rapidly approach the golden ratio which approximates to 1.618.

$$\frac{13}{8}=1.613 \qquad \frac{21}{13}=1.616 \qquad \frac{34}{21}=1.619 \qquad \frac{55}{34}=1.618 \text{ etc...}$$

Rectangles with length to breadth ratios of

$$\frac{13}{8} \quad \frac{21}{13} \quad \frac{34}{21} \quad \frac{55}{34} \quad \text{etc...}$$

are said to be golden rectangles.

The numbers

1
1
2
3
5
8
13
21
34
55...

are called the Fibonacci series.

Each number in the series is produced by adding the previous two numbers. This seemingly innocuous array provides a rich lode of information, so much so that a current mathematical journal is devoted entirely to its magical properties.

In controlled moves, going backwards only to jump ahead, the Fibonacci series gives insight into growth by accumulation. It seems to be a secret method that nature responds to in many ways. Patterns of natural growth, from snail shells to spirals in sunflowers or pineapple skins, can be counted by Fibonacci numbers.

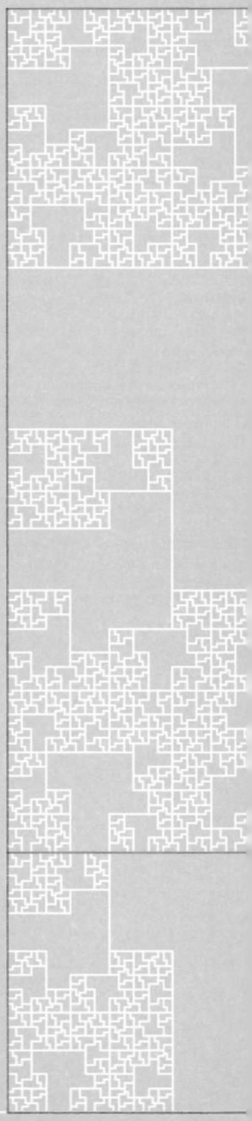

34

The V&A tiling can also be counted by the same Fibonacci numbers.

If the form of the V&A is a new kind of spiral – a chaotic one – then on its walls, hidden behind the tiling pattern, is a special diagram.

The ancient geometers called it a 'Mirabilis', a strategy for perfection as they saw it.

Based on the movement of a point on a line the theory behind the golden section asks:

'At which point does a line divide so that the greater to the lesser part is the same as the whole is to the greater part?'

Where is point C so that $\frac{AC}{BC} = \frac{AB}{AC}$?

If AC is equal to a, and BC is equal to b, then

$$\frac{a}{b} = \frac{a+b}{a}$$

$$\text{or } a^2 = ab + b^2$$

$$\text{i.e. } a^2 - ab - b^2 = 0$$

This yields a quadratic equation which has a root (a/b) equal to

$\frac{1+\sqrt{5}}{2}$ = the golden ratio (approximately 1.618).

It is an irrational number which has a decimal expansion that has no limit.

The value 1.61803398874989 . . . goes on forever.

In mathematical terms the golden ratio is a first step away from the discrete world of integers. Leaving behind real numbers and moving towards a more dense and infinite packing, of irrational and transcendental numbers, this ratio points towards more complex regions of the continuum.

In the way arithmetic moves into geometry and vice versa we see continuity not as a linear process, but as a circular transformative revelation.

265

A fractal is a geometric shape of *non-integer* dimension. (Ordinary space has three dimensions: length of D=1; area of D=2; and volume where D=3.) The non-integer value relates to the degree of folding the particular pattern or shape has.

An algorithm that works on a geometric motif can lead to a fractal.

By zooming in or out a fractal looks the same. As a corollary to this, for any fixed scale, a fractal offers infinite irregularity.

The fractal dimension is given by

$$D = \lim_{a \to 0} \frac{\log Na}{\log (1/a)}$$

where 'Na' is the total number of times equal length segments 'a' of a pattern occurs, when 'a' becomes arbitrarily small.

Far away or close up in zoom, a coastline has no definite length. A fork of lightning at any scale defies being a line or an area. A cloud, if one could walk over it, would deny the three dimensions of volume, or the two of area. What shape is mist?

With a fractal we enter the space that lies between dimensions, a region of never-ending folds and bifurcations and intricate patterns that run into infinity repeating at different scales, embedding one layer upon another. In a cascade of self-similarity a fractal interlinks the finest tracery to the overall statement, like the veins of a leaf repeat the pattern of a tree, namely branching.

In a fractal world the integer dimensions 1, 2 and 3 are remote and artificial, marking only the edges of an orthogonal containment. It is as if the entanglement of space, at the moment of jumping whole dimensions, folds into set grooves. In between lies everything else.

BETWEEN DIMENSION 0 AND 1

Consider a straight line and take away a middle third. Let this repeat on each of the sections remaining and continue to infinity.

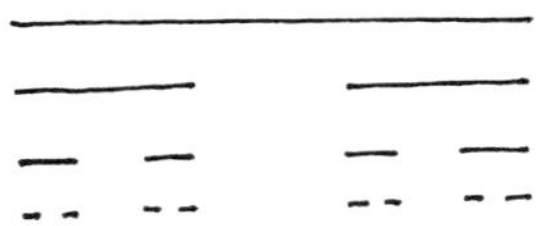

Though the eye cannot follow, the mathematics of partition continues until there are only infinitesimals left. What is left is a fine dust, a particular kind of fractional scattered existence – near the threshold of nothingness. The fractal dimension of this pattern is D = 0.66.

Suppose a line is bent into a shape that has four equal parts.

If each straight line section copies the same shape, a fractal results.

Instead of a straight line, if a triangle was taken as the start point each of its three sides indented and then the same pattern repeated, a fractal known as the Koch snowflake results.

The Koch fractal has the dimension D =1.26. Its dimension is a measure of folding away from a straight line existence.

The higher the fractional dimension, the closer the turnings and meanderings.

In the Minkowski fractal the base line is bent up and down into eight equal parts, the idea then repeats. Each straight section at any scale repeats the eight-part folding. There is more folding here than in the Koch fractal and consequently the fractal dimension is higher, at D = 1.5.

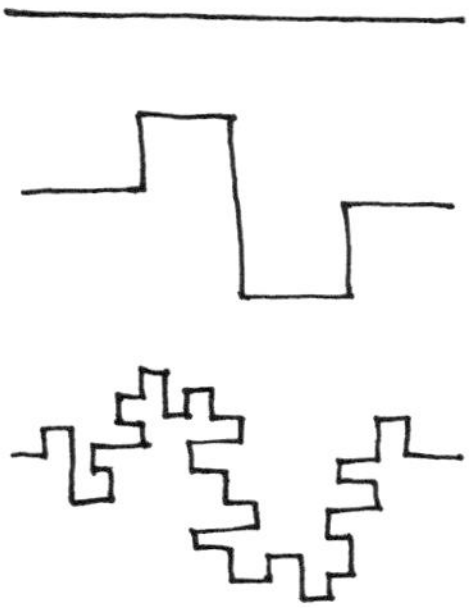

SQUARED FRACTALS?

If a square is divided into further squares the resulting pattern will have a self-similarity.

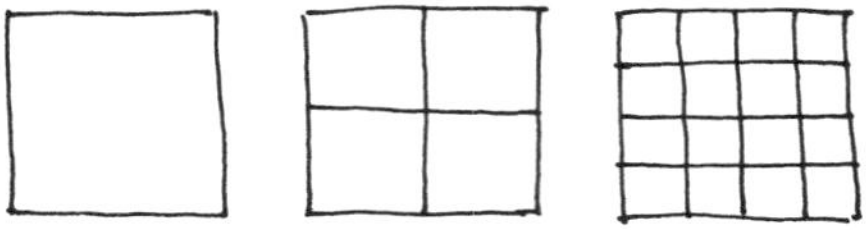

If the subdivision continues and the progression is analysed by fractal mathematics, the dimension of this pattern comes out as 2. In other words, there is no fractional dimension, the network of pattern has an integer dimension. Since we began with an assumption of closed area, the initial square, and subdivided it further, we only produce further areas, however fine the subdivision. There has been no folding or creasing that may initiate a fractal. The same thing happens with a triangle or other start diagrams of a regular closed area.

But if on subdivision of the triangle the central sub-triangle is left out, the familiar Sierpinski gasket evolves.

INFINITY

Imagine the fractals being taken deeper and deeper into their folding. As this continues, the eye cannot follow; yet the motifs repeat, ever finer.

One way of perceiving the infinite depth of a fractal is to consider the following: if one could trace its outline with an infinitely thin point, at infinite speed, it would be a task that would take infinite time!

With the Koch curve, we would also have a geometric impossibility; the curve at its infinite progression will be one that has no tangent, which means that each part of the curve is infinitely long! This is a curious state of affairs and a reflection that ordinary rules break down at infinity.

The coastline is a fractal. So is the edge of a cloud. Or, the branching of an artery or the blood vessels in the lining of the lung.

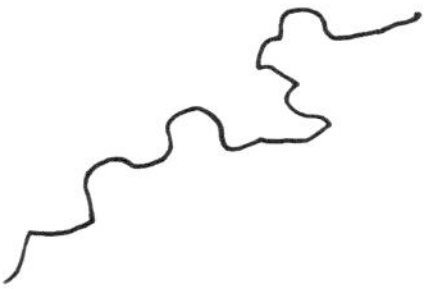

Nature folds and branches in repeating rhythms. It is a kind of packing into space that maximises the potential for exposure. This means, at its densest, a fractal has an infinite exposure. But why? Why would nature seem to favour this mode of compression and extension, both at the same time?

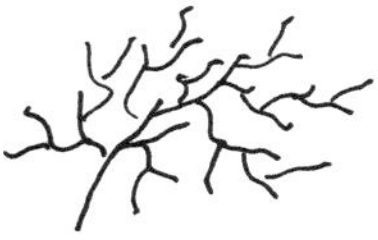

The answer must lie in information exchange. Living systems need a continuous stream of information on pressure, temperature, moisture, pH value, electrical charge, magnetic fields, and so on. The systems which have the best potential for exchanging information will have the best chance of survival. Fractal behaviour, with its finest folding and branching, is a good measure of that success.

SELF-SIMILARITY

At whatever scale one considers the Koch or Minkowski fractal, each part however small reflects the whole. This is a hallmark of the fractal, self-similarity at all scales.

The ability to self replicate at all levels seems to be a fundamental requirement of nature – witness the fact that from any one cell the whole animal or plant may be cloned; the act of memory seems to be spread throughout. Imagine a thing that remembers at all levels, even to its tiniest branching, and then the vanishing smallest pulse that has the same pattern of the greater rhythm, that set it off in the first place.

It is like a great unison of endless overlap.

The notion of 'will' is animated throughout. And it echoes through the mind. We may not forget what it is, for its basic signature is in the synapses that drive and structure our brains.

273

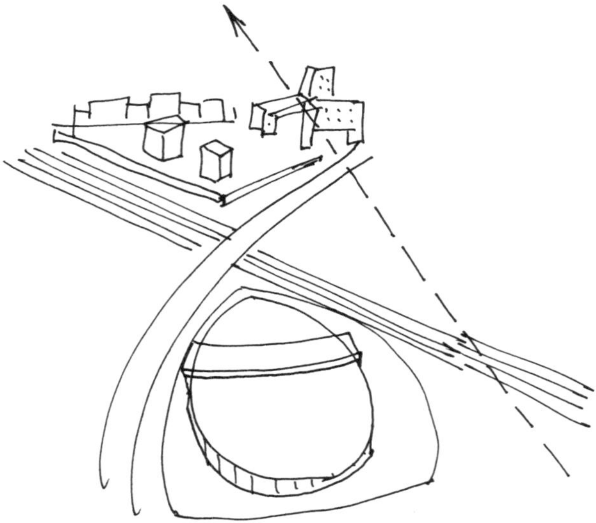

Euralille, one of the *grands projets* of France conceived and realised in just five years, celebrates the arrival of the TGV fast train to Lille, en route to London and Brussels. To mark the achievement France honoured the city in a singular way – the Tour began there in 1994.

The whole spectacle of bikes and anticipated yellow jerseys was staged in a strange looking building, an admixture of shapes and separate programs called Congrexpo. Just a short distance away is the vast complex of shops, offices and housing – Euralille.

The first idea was to launch Congrexpo over the railway lines as an introduction to the scheme, but spanning the tracks was expensive – there was insufficient height given to the building on elevation. On nearby land, surrounded by roads and railways, an island site was chosen instead to accommodate what was essentially a one storey, shed-like building. But what a shed it turned out to be.

This multi-experience, multi-character Congrexpo acts like a city within a city. It is a compendium of spaces; some partitioned and stacked up, others raked and plaza-like for the holding of concerts. The largest area is serialised into columns, in the manner of streetscapes, providing throughways for the crowds and vehicles of numerous exhibitions.

There are three municipalities: Congrès, Zenith and Expo.

Congrès – 18,000 square metres of multi storey framed building forms a block across the short dimension of the site. Elevated on columns, like a medieval bridge, it spans the distance with dwellings on top of it. One has to climb up into Congrès to arrive at its eating places, offices and lecture theatres. The entry ramp, rising and twisting against a wall overlaid with mirrors, provides a distorted and astonishing welcome to this part of the city. Here it feels rich and plush, carpeted in marbled resin, finished at one gable end in thick, faceted glass panelling – an area obviously for executives, bureaucrats and the well off.

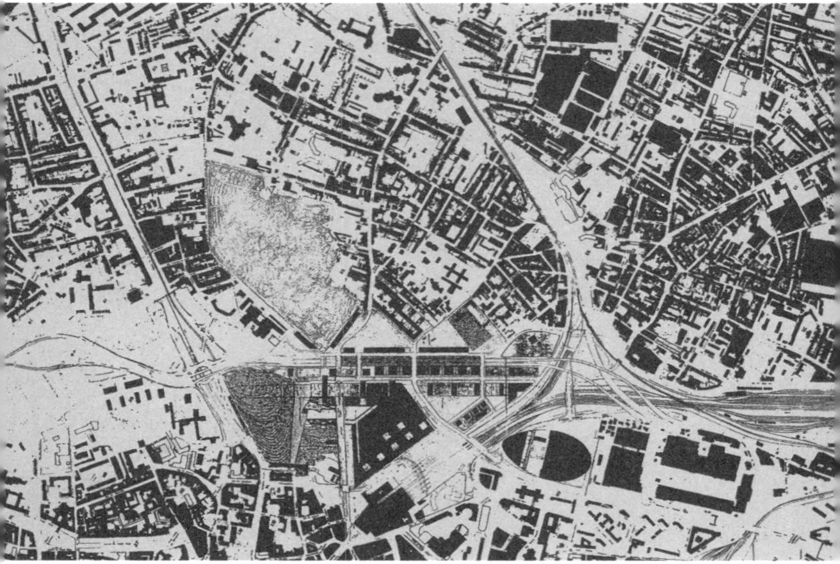

To the left of Congrès rises the more gaunt and denuded space of Zenith, a gathering place for mass spectacles and a site for rock concerts. Zenith is large and cavernous, housing a utilitarian network of steel roof sweeping over the concrete amphitheatre that offers a hardscape for today's rave music. Big metal stairs stick to the outside like New York fire escapes, zigzagging up the stone sides. Crowds spill out under the steep soffit of the main auditorium at ground level and exit or pass below the Congrès bridge towards Expo.

Expo is the largest area of this city. The 150 m x 150 m space is broken down into blocks of 24 m x 15 m. An area such as this could be featureless, with unlimited horizon and no definition of ground plan, but the columns here give scale. The close grid reduces the exhibition into smaller localities.

Removed from the immediacy of life down below, the roof above Expo becomes a grand abstraction. In wide-banded stripes, like the underside of a giant boat, it sails above the streets over the ground plan. Different to the brute metal textures that cover other such expositions, the timber of the roof-sky provides warmth and comfort; a feeling of permanence as a nice counter to the swarm of visitors below, looking for the latest product or style to come their way.

There are many commentaries, drawings and reports that complete a structural mapping of Congrexpo. But in these pages only the first log book is copied, highlighting the design of the Expo roof and noting the characteristics of Congrès and Zenith. Not included are the comprehensive tests carried out on the roof beams or a catalogue of the many early schemes, nor a full list of material specifications or construction sequences for the actual built project. Comprehensiveness is important, but in the spirit of this book, the exploration, the search and the enquiry, rather than the detailed end product, are stressed.

As with many journeys there are dead-ends and sudden turnings, from failed ambitions to particular insights that helped the design leap ahead. What sticks in the mind is the terrain of experiment borne out of forced expediency, matching low budgets and cheap materials to invention. Due to the fast schedule the pace was frantic and exhausting; and at times, Congrexpo seemed a dark and impossible journey into an unattainable interior.

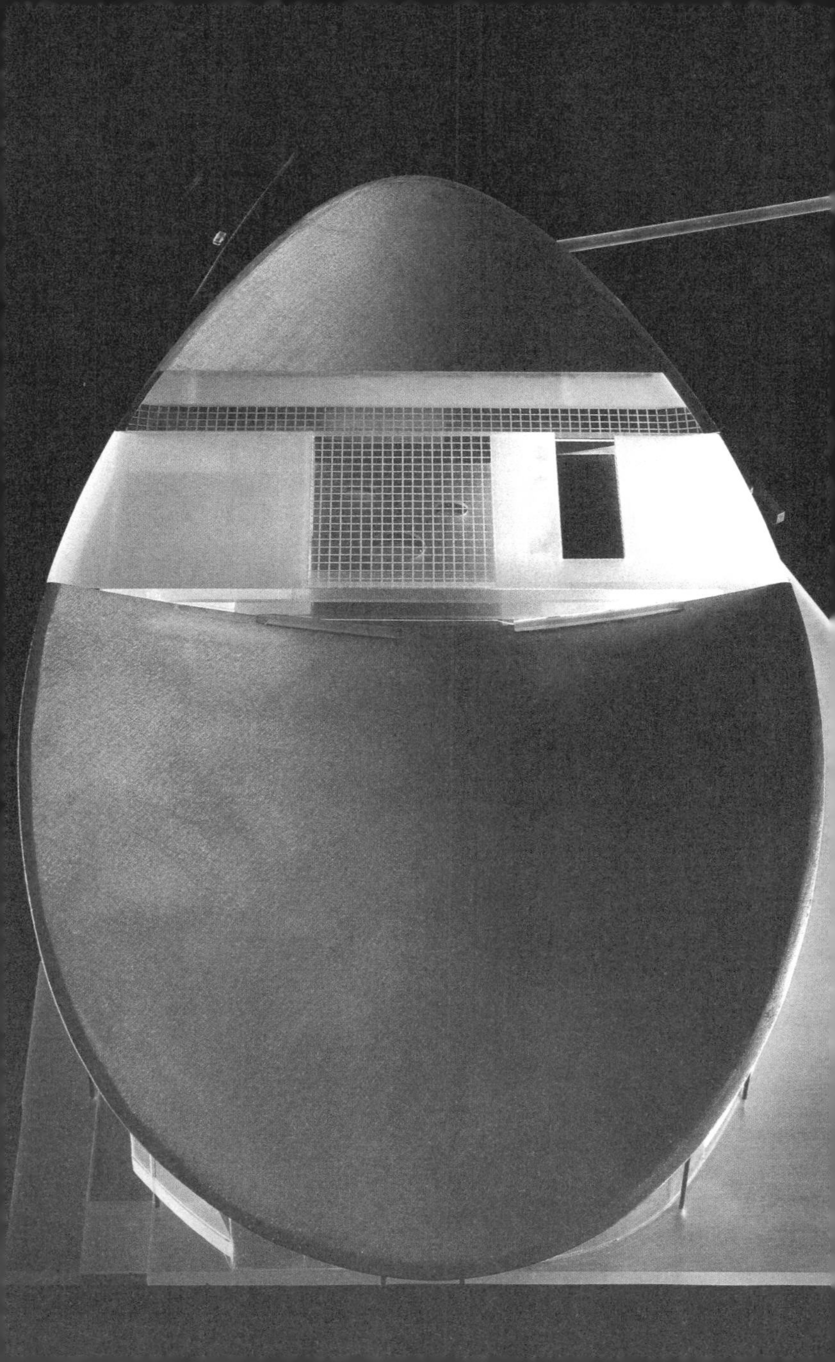

There are three program functions within; Music, Conference and Exhibition.

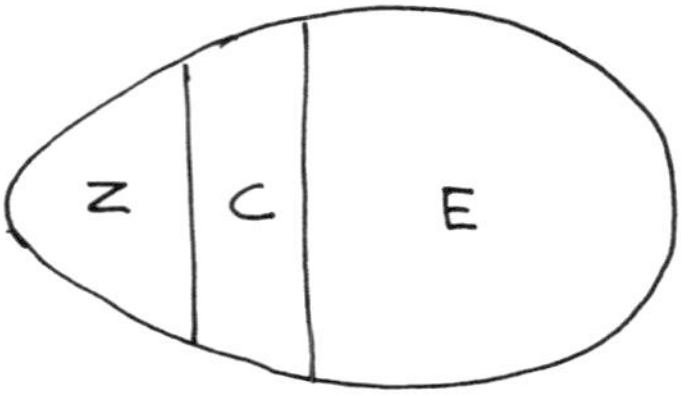

The parts call out separate identities, Zenith, Congrès and Expo but they come together in one adjacency and mix of culture and commerce.

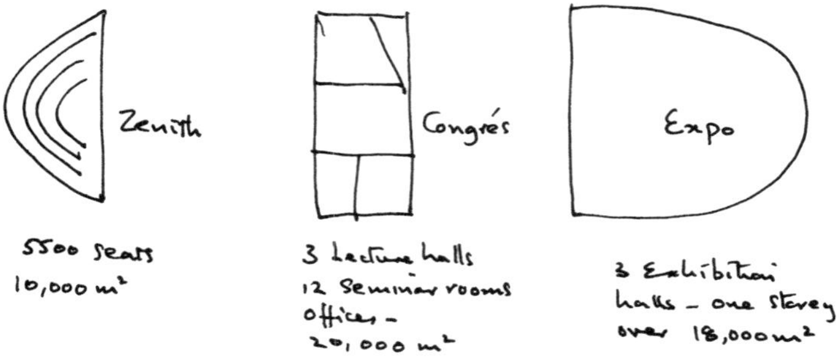

What binds the three programs is a unifying geometry, a dipping concave roof in plan that takes the shape of an ellipse. Early models show a flying saucer effect.

The question was what sort of roof to have, free span or something else?

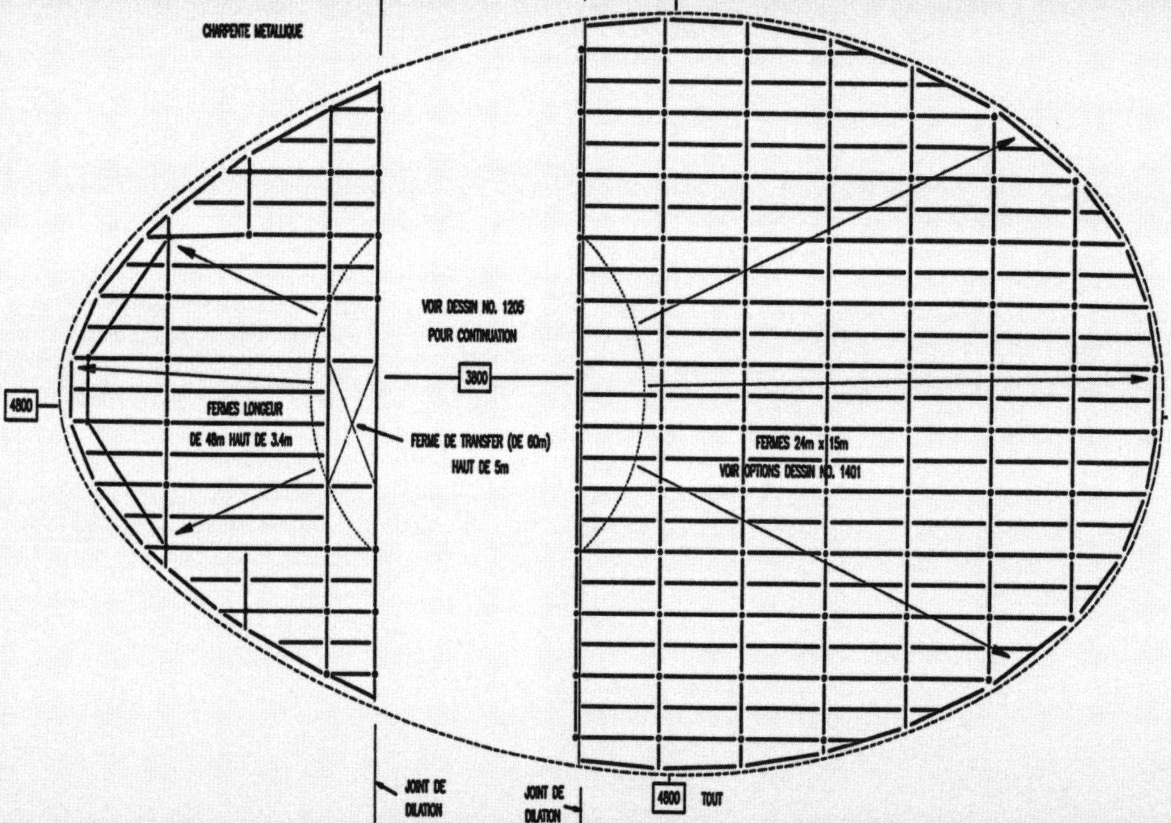

CHARPENTE METALLIQUE
VOIR DESSIN NO. 1205
POUR CONTINUATION
3800
4800
FERMES LONGEUR
DE 48m HAUT DE 3.4m
FERME DE TRANSFER (DE 60m)
HAUT DE 5m
FERMES 24m x 15m
VOIR OPTIONS DESSIN NO. 1401
JOINT DE
DILATION
JOINT DE
DILATION
4800
TOUT

The temptation was to go for the macro solution, to sweep across the space in one grand gesture, some sort of cable net draped over edge masts, tied down externally to the building line. But this meant anchors outside the site boundaries.

Another idea was a giant torsion ring with a roof diaphragm in between.

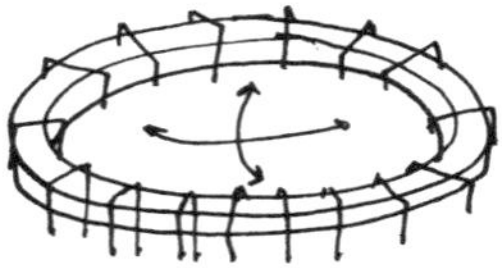

The ring could be developed into an edge zone, where all the plant could be located in a circumferential ring providing good service distribution possibilities.

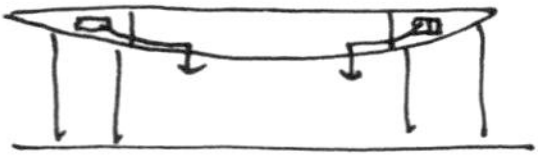

The roof membrane itself could be developed into a series of ducts, allowing air and light into the space below.

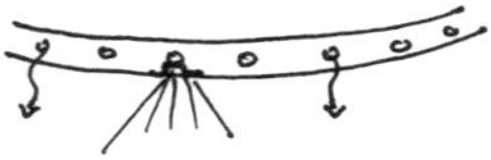

THE PARTS

Congrès, with its multi storey nature though, kept interrupting any grand idea for one roof solution. Architecturally, the roof could sweep through the Congrès area but structurally it seemed futile to look for one solution; single storey and multi storey did not mix.

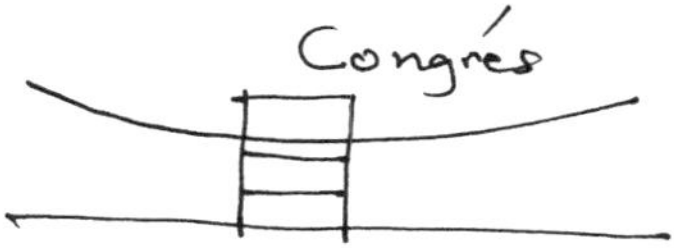

For the lecture theatres and seminar rooms of Congrès, a series of columns was introduced that went through to the ground. Since the mass of Congrès lifts off a vaulted soffit at first floor level, the columns acted like local piers under a bridge. For the Zenith Concert Hall, there was just clear span.

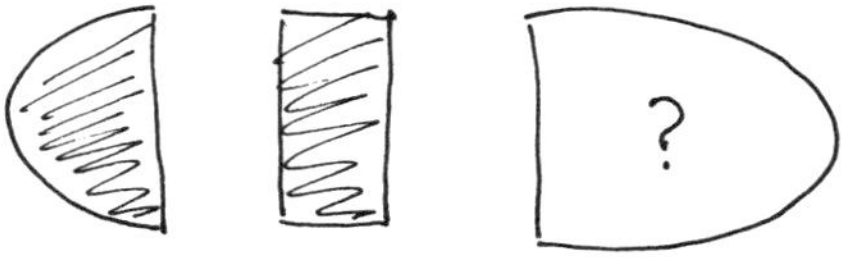

What about the Expo part?

We looked for a large span solution, but was such freedom really necessary? To achieve this great energies had to be expended on structure.

We decided instead to test a reverse concept – what was the maximum density of columns for such an exhibition space? After a series of studies the answer OMA / Arup came to was around 15 m x 24 m.

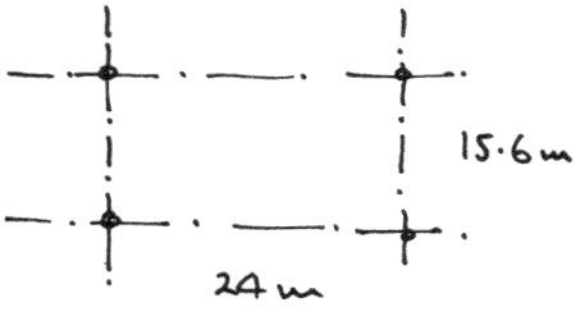

Questions were asked: could the lorries drive in and unload, would the exhibition consultants agree to the tight layout and lack of column free space? In the event, they did and the layout was accepted as feasible.

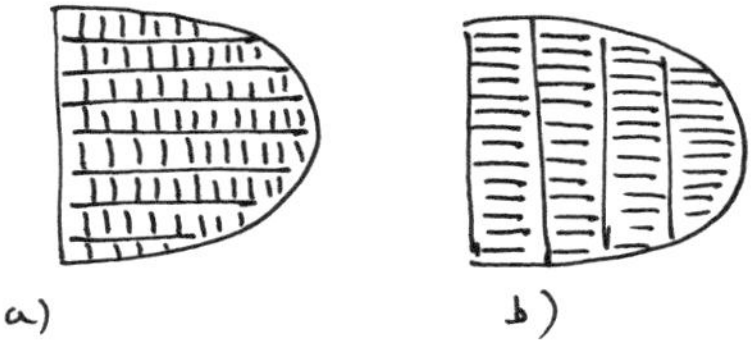

Models were built to investigate which direction the primary span should take. Framing plans with the main beam in the 24 m direction (figure a) proved to be more economical.

We had slipped here into the assumption that the roof was a metal deck on steel trusses – it meant a deep false ceiling to give the smooth underbelly Rem Koolhaas wanted.

But concrete, at a stroke, would realise the concave surface as ceiling and structure. Upstands could strengthen the slab as necessary to provide beam lines.

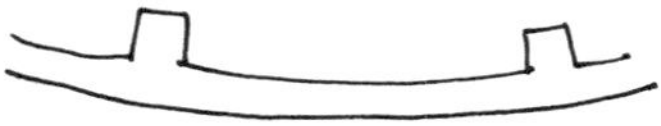

Air ducts could also be buried in the concrete to give good a/c distribution.

We thought we had the answer – that is until the Fire Officer insisted on barriers hanging down from the ceiling to contain smoke in reservoirs.

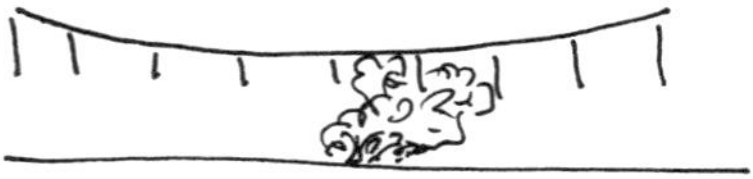

The unbroken sweep of any smooth surface would be destroyed by permanent fire curtains. Another approach was called for.

In negotiation with the Fire Officer the Arup team came up with the idea of breaking the ceiling zone into strips, allowing 50% free penetration for smoke.

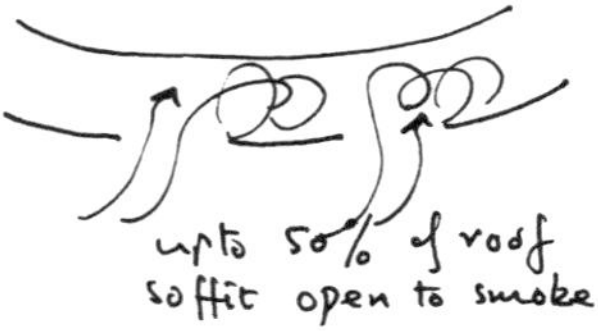

If the depth of the ceiling was 700 mm, sufficient smoke could be contained to remove the need for barriers.

This depth also made it possible to house a series of roof beams spanning the 15 m.

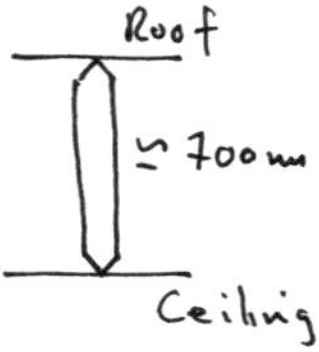

To break away from the typical response of steel and concrete I proposed that we use timber for the ceiling strips.

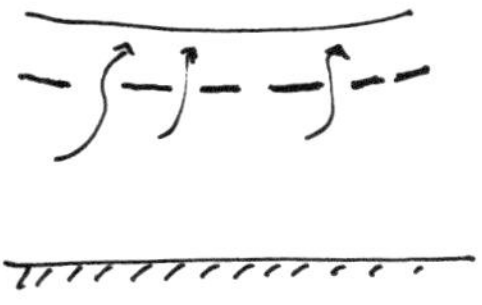

I saw the timber at first as cosmetic, as nice-to-have warm finish to a ceiling – the timber plank being attached to a steel truss.

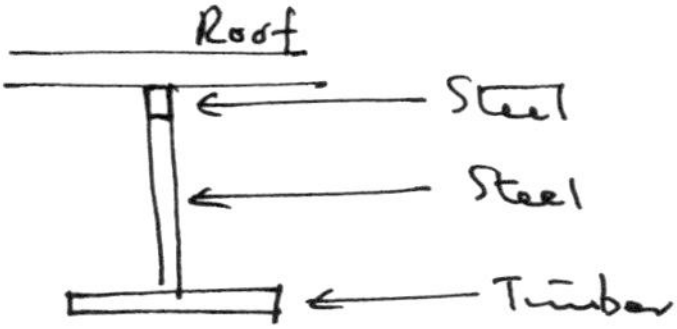

But this felt tame and wasteful. Why not use the timber itself as structure, as the tension boom of a truss? Suddenly the solution became more exciting – but the thought of a 'plank' being stretched out in tension worried us. It was so different to the normal idea of high strength steel acting in tension. But trees do it all the time, being subject to tension – we had to overcome our anxiety.

The idea persisted.

Gradually a very unusual hybrid truss was born where the compression chord became steel, the tension chord a timber plank and the diagonals in between a wave formed out of reinforcement bar.

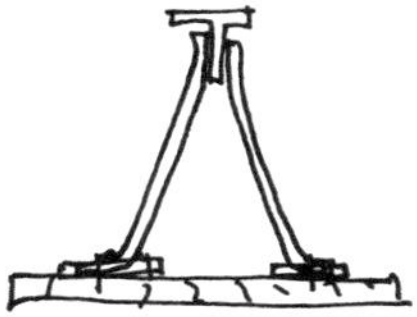

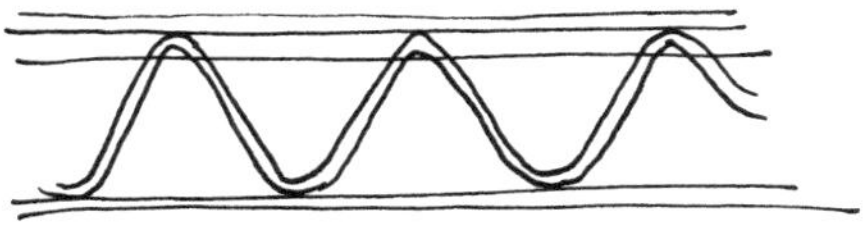

Koolhaas loved the idea, he called it the Arup roof. OMA built a model and the result was stunning, a striped effect giving the appearance of an unbroken surface.

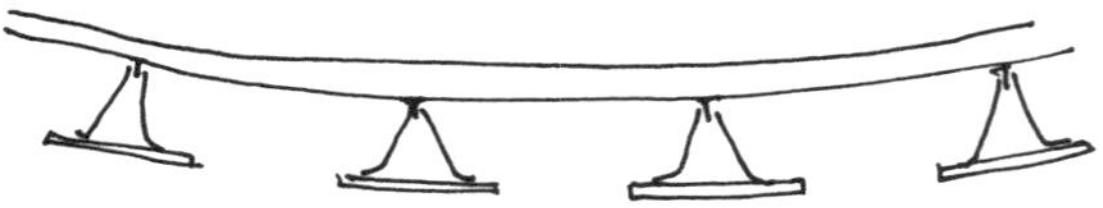

The roof looked like a giant boat hull. Connecting the timber planks to the shear webs gave a studded effect to the underside, as the silver bolt-heads were read against the warm grain.

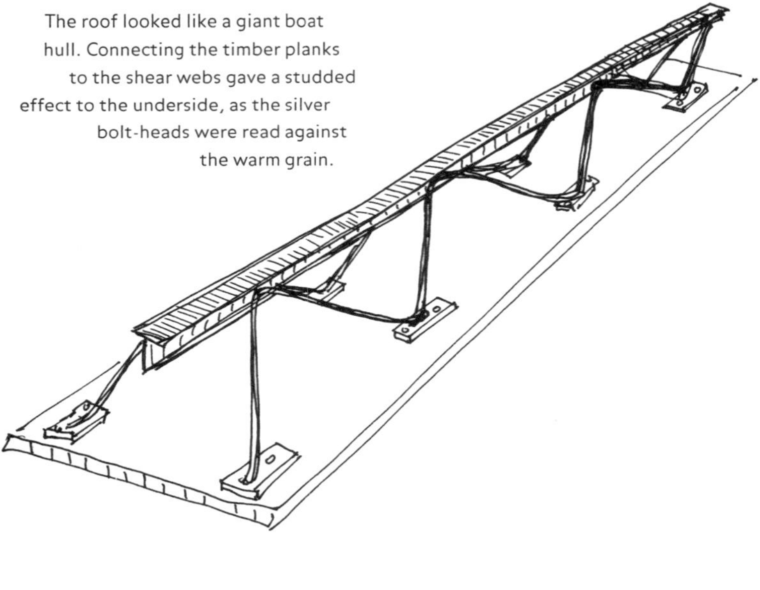

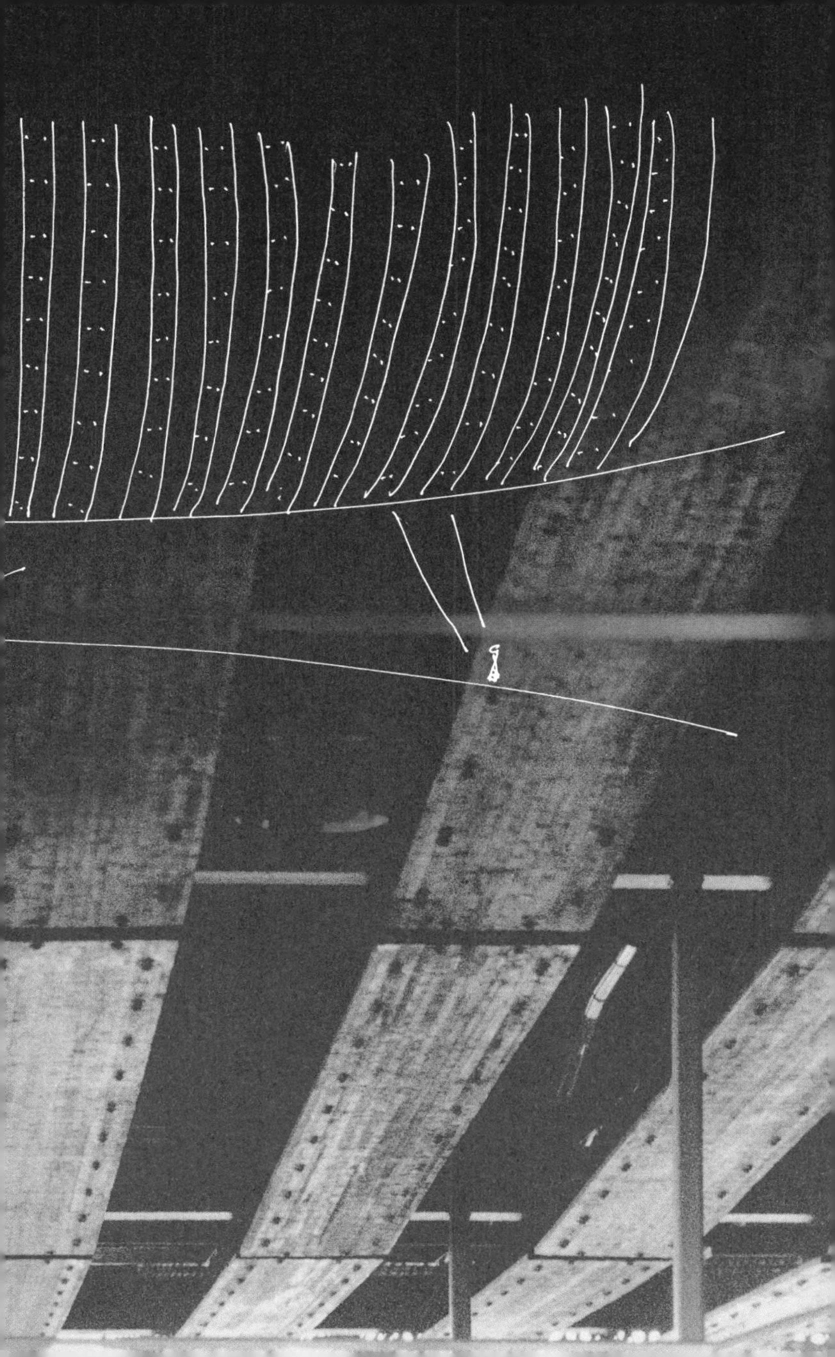

What was striking about the 'plank' was that it was put together by pressing several smaller pieces of timber in a special laminating machine. The strips went in one end, a finished timber plank came out the other.

The diagonals were welded onto the top steel tee section and arrived at site as an assembly ready for bolting to the timber strip. It was easy to build and put up. The whole enterprise was a 'do-it-yourself' kind of beam put together by a kit of parts; hybridisation ran free along the Expo roof. What was heartening was that the roof came within budget and what could so easily have been a deadening industrial type roof turned into the beauty of a laminated boat hull, bringing steel and timber together in very unusual circumstances.

Finding the hybrid 'do-it-yourself' beam was the highlight of the project for me.

Other aspects of Expo that are worth noting are the main beams, the columns with integral air conditioning systems, the bracing and roof geometry.

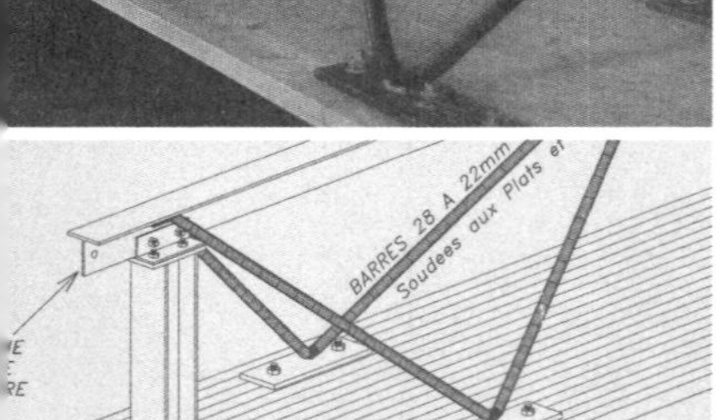

A tension tie drops down in a fine line below the soffit to be framed by two vertical struts along the 24 m span, to form a tie-beam for the principal line of support.

Disruption to the soffit is minimal.

The line of the tie helps break the space under the roof in a counterpoint to the sweep of the timber stripes. (At tender stage the tie was formed by rods, but changed later to the flat which was cheaper and better architecturally.)

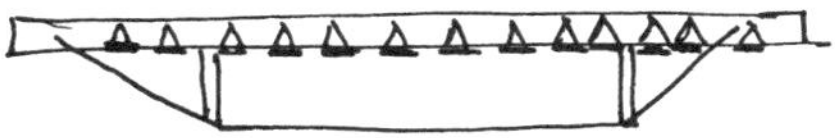

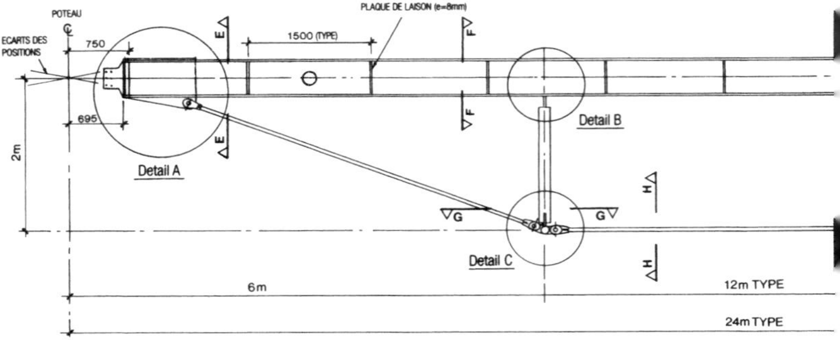

POUTRE TIRANTE TYPE DE PORTEE 24m TB1 (

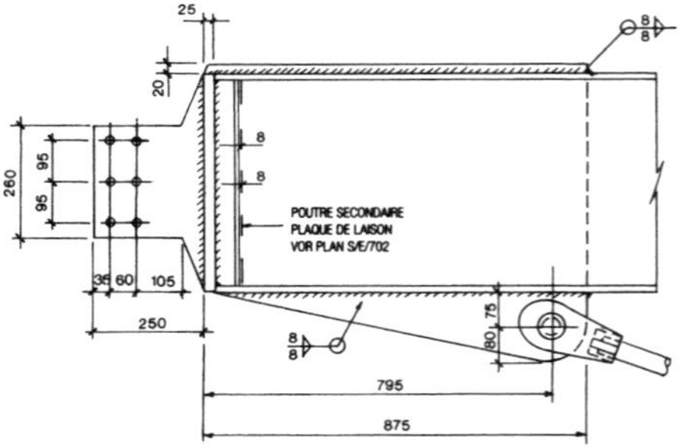

DETAIL A

(1:10)

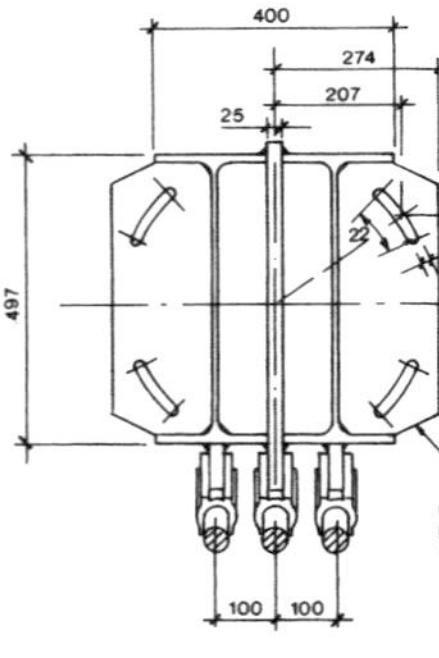

PLAQUE DE LAISON (e=8

POUR LES POUTRES SEC

1500mm D'ENTRE-AXES

COUPE E - E

(1:10)

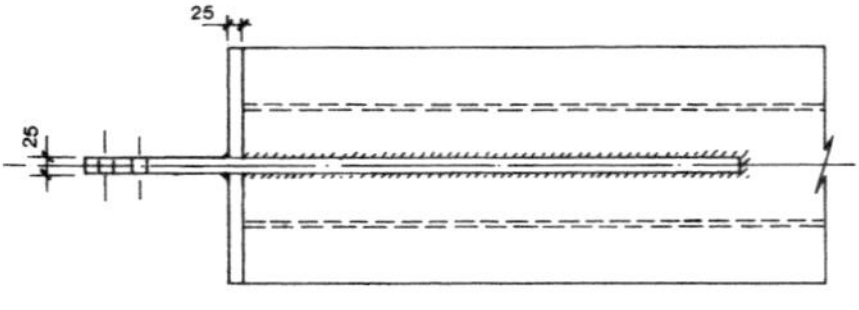

VUE EN PLAN - DETAIL A

(1:10)

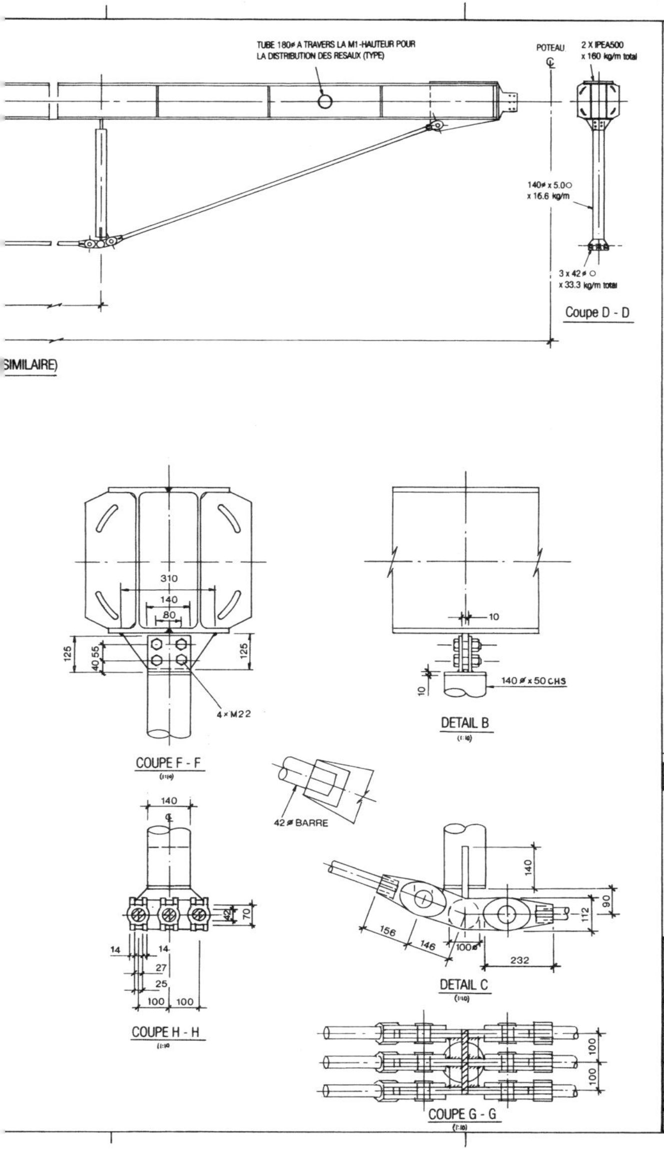

PLAN MARCHE
30.07.92

N

Z C E

EURALILLE
CONGREXPO
VILLE DE LILLE

EXPO
COUPES/DETAILS
METALLIQUES

Ove Arup and Partners International Ltd
ARUP

40103/03 | S/E/701

On a grid of 15 m x 24 m the distribution of air is very good if it mimics the column points.

The most compact solution is to place the air plant directly above the columns, and pass the air through the columns to discharge at the bottom.

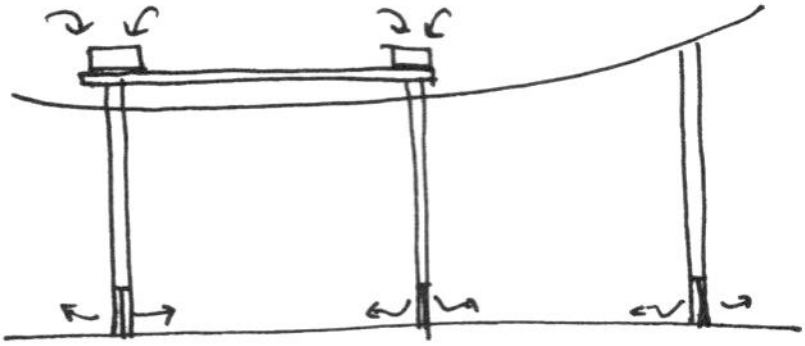

This concept of displacement ventilation is efficient for large spaces, discharging cool air where it is needed in the people zone. A top source would need much colder air to overcome the rising heat.

To allow the passage of air down the columns, a circular hollow section was taken and then joined to a cruciform which give four-way distribution at the bottom end, on plan.

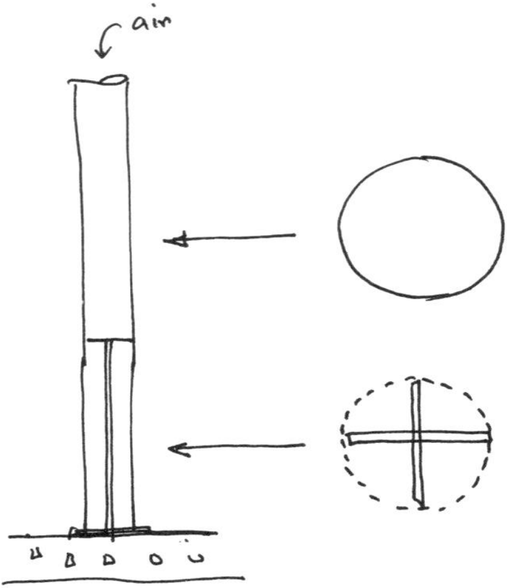

The transformation of circle into cruciform was done by welding the two sections within an overlap zone.

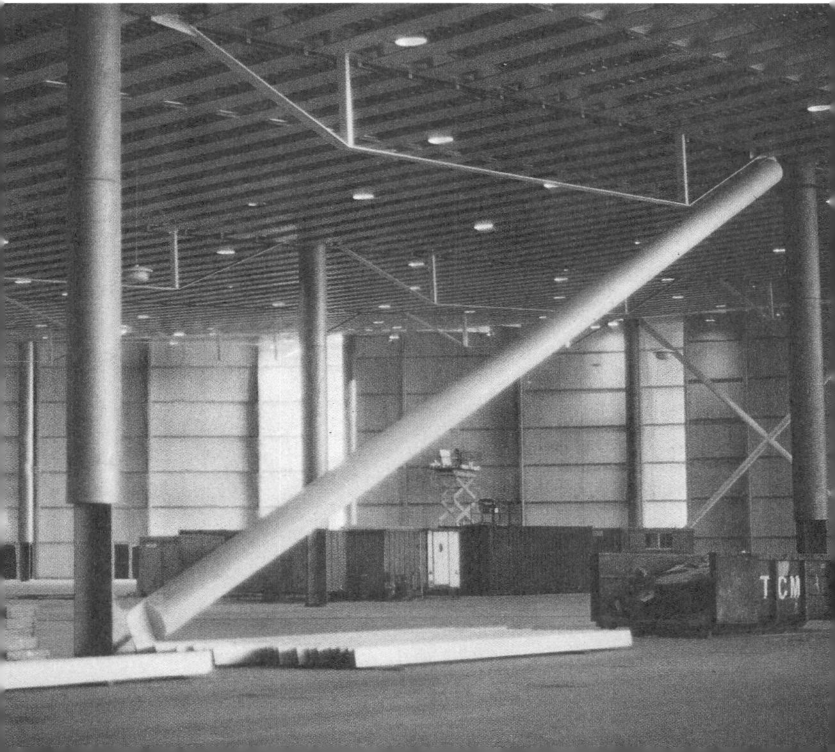
TCM

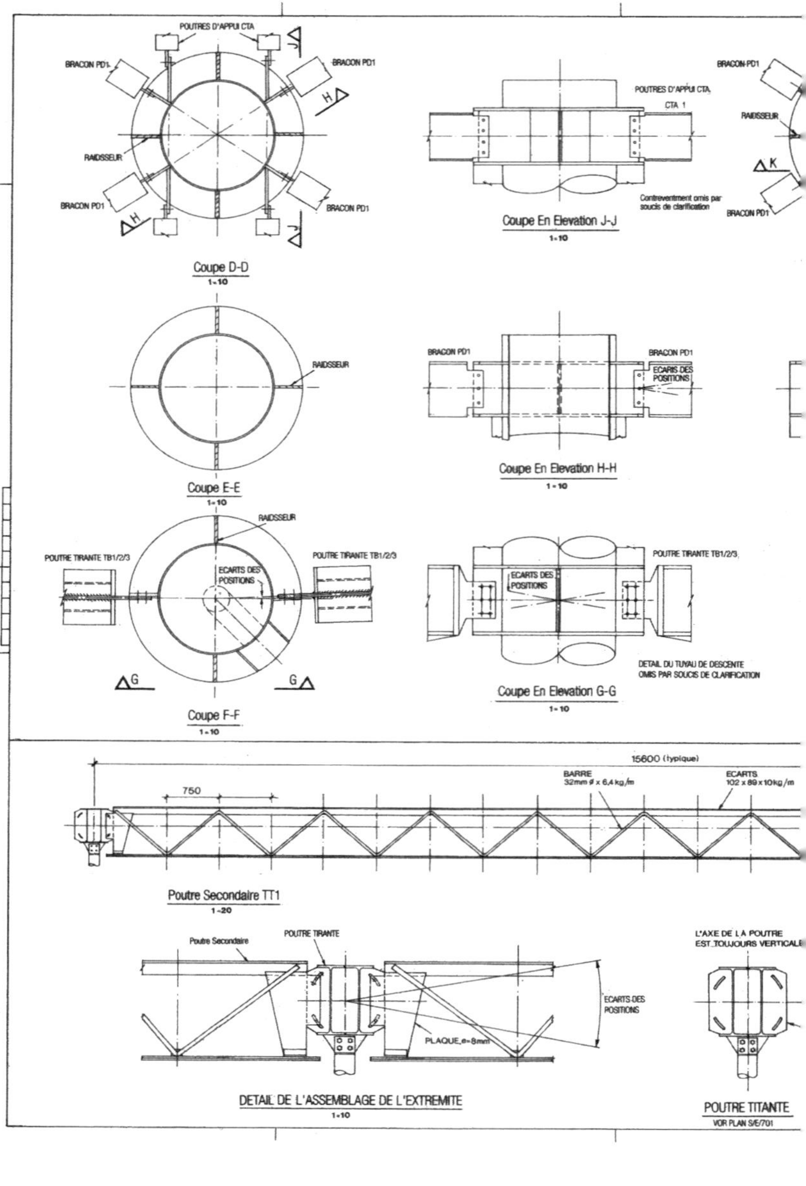
POUTRES D'APPUI CTA
BRACON PD1
BRACON PD1
RAIDSSEUR
BRACON PD1
BRACON PD1
Coupe D-D
1=10
POUTRES D'APPUI CTA
CTA 1
Contreventment omis par soucis de clarification
Coupe En Elevation J-J
1=10
BRACON PD1
RAIDSSEUR
BRACON PD1
RAIDSSEUR
Coupe E-E
1=10
BRACON PD1
BRACON PD1
ECARTS DES POSITIONS
Coupe En Elevation H-H
1=10
RAIDSSEUR
POUTRE TIRANTE TB1/2/3
POUTRE TIRANTE TB1/2/3
ECARTS DES POSITIONS
Coupe F-F
1=10
POUTRE TIRANTE TB1/2/3
ECARTS DES POSITIONS
DETAIL DU TUYAU DE DESCENTE OMIS PAR SOUCIS DE CLARIFICATION
Coupe En Elevation G-G
1=10
15600 (typique)
750
BARRE 32mm ø x 6,4 kg/m
ECARTS 102 x 89 x 10 kg/m
Poutre Secondaire TT1
1=20
Poutre Secondaire
POUTRE TIRANTE
ECARTS DES POSITIONS
PLAQUE e=8mm
DETAIL DE L'ASSEMBLAGE DE L'EXTREMITE
1=10
L'AXE DE LA POUTRE EST TOUJOURS VERTICALE
POUTRE TITANTE
VOIR PLAN S/E/701

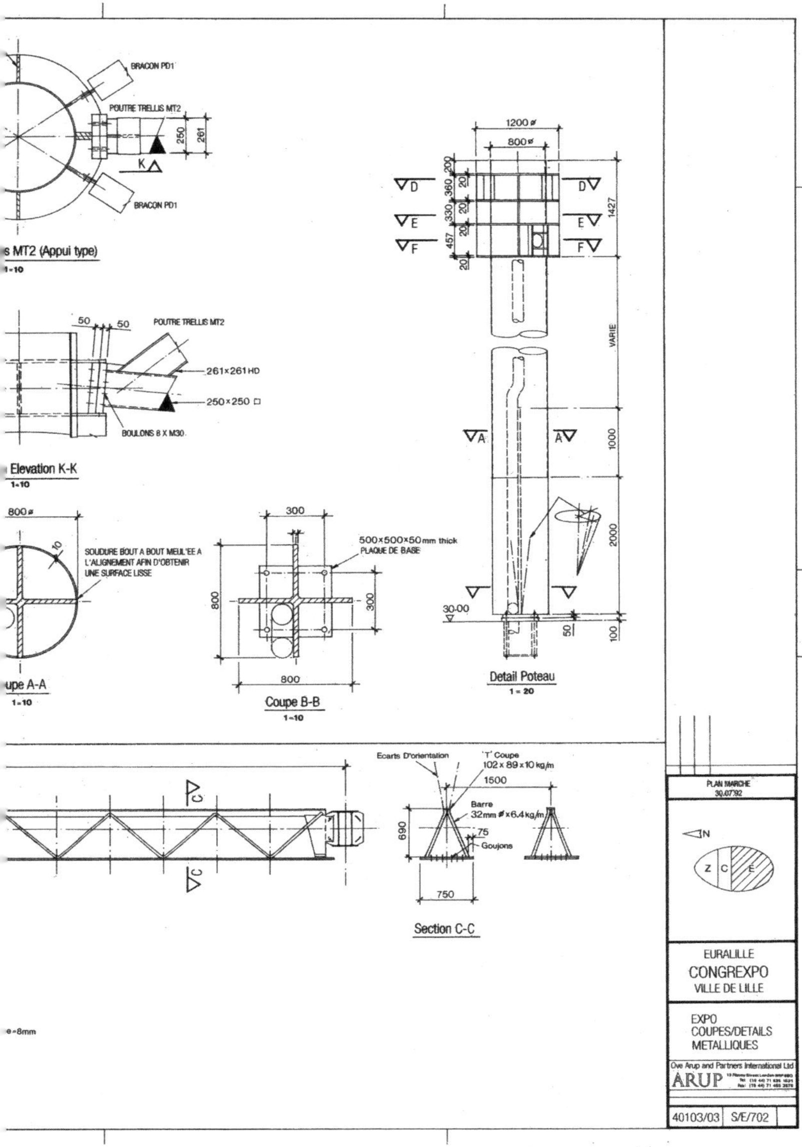
BRACON PD1
POUTRE TRELLIS MT2
250
261
K
BRACON PD1
s MT2 (Appui type)
1=10
50
50
POUTRE TRELLIS MT2
261×261 HD
250×250 □
BOULONS 8 X M30
Elevation K-K
1=10
800ø
10
SOUDURE BOUT A BOUT MEUL'EE A L'ALIGNEMENT AFIN D'OBTENIR UNE SURFACE LISSE
upe A-A
1=10
300
500×500×50 mm thick PLAQUE DE BASE
800
300
800
Coupe B-B
1=10
1200 ø
800 ø
200
20
360
20
330
20
457
20
1427
D
E
F
VARIE
A
1000
2000
30.00
50
100
Detail Poteau
1 = 20
C
C
Ecarts D'orientation
'T' Coupe 102 x 89 x 10 kg/m
1500
Barre 32mm ø x 6.4 kg/m
690
75
Goujons
750
Section C-C
e=8mm
PLAN MARCHE 30.07.92
N
Z
C
E
EURALILLE
CONGREXPO
VILLE DE LILLE
EXPO
COUPES/DETAILS
METALLIQUES
Ove Arup and Partners International Ltd
ARUP
40103/03
S/E/702

BRACING

To keep the hybrid timber beam concept 'pure' within the roof zone, the bracing was placed outside the roof.

A series of rings was formed on the columns to create two zones for connection, one for the roof, the other for the external bracing.

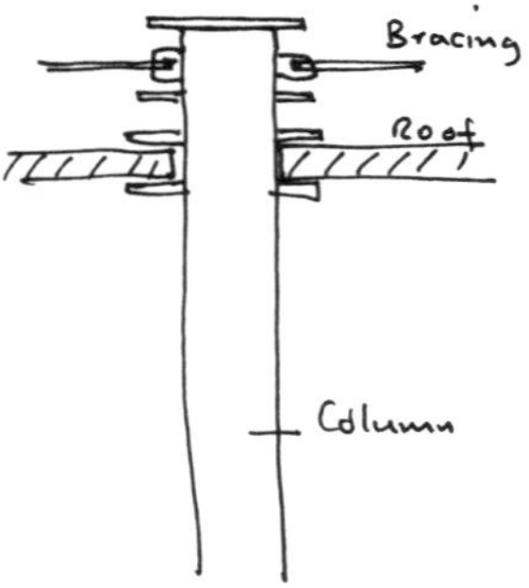

The bracing plan was straightforward, running in two orthogonal zones across the top of the roof, connecting into the top ring of the columns.

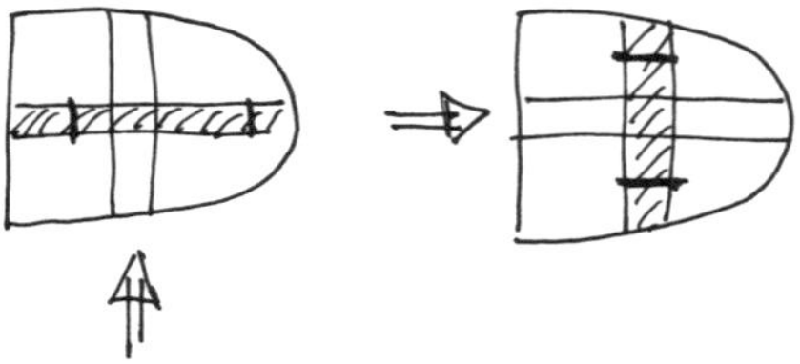

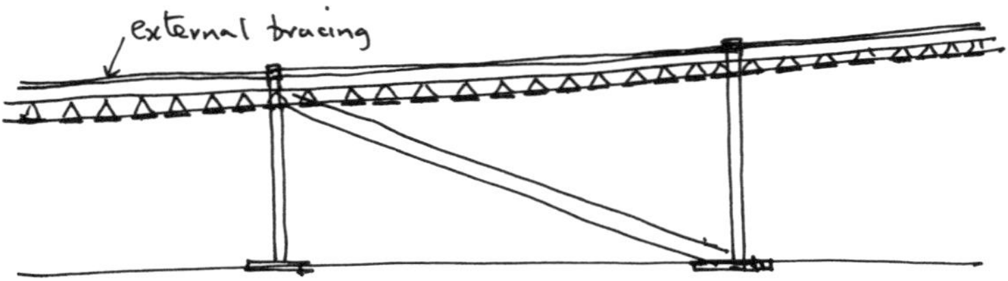

Some parts of the bracing were omitted for a more interesting pattern on the roof. Normally this break up of continuity would not be possible, advantage was taken here of the column being strong enough to allow the vertical displacement of axial force to take place.

Via local bending in the column section, the stability forces were taken down into the diagonal struts between ground level and roof. These braces were large diameter tubes, matching the size of the main columns.

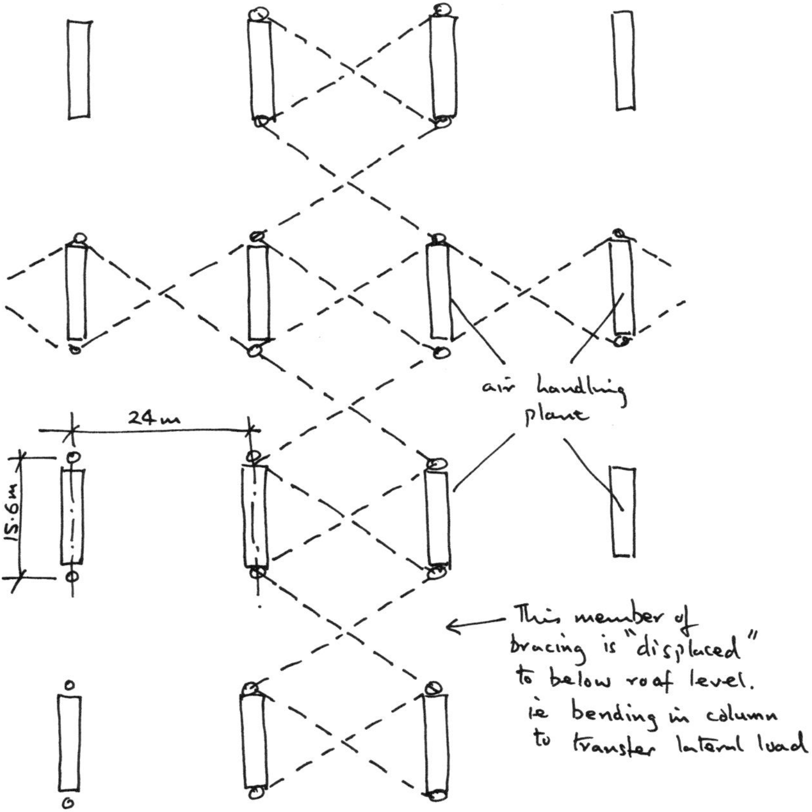

Roof top view of patterned bracing

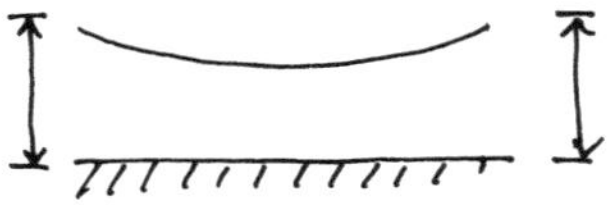

The outer edge of the oval shape was taken at a fixed altitude.

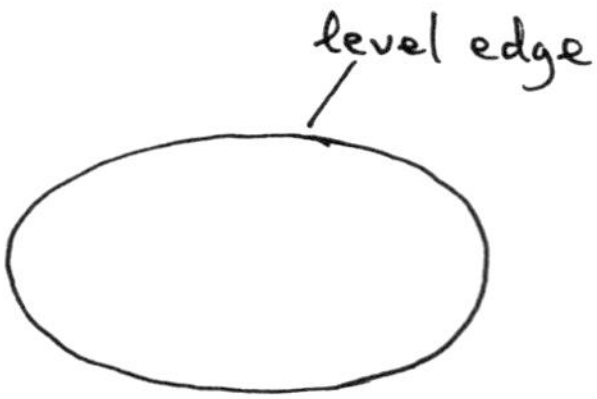

For the origin, a point off-centre was taken as the lowest point on the roof.

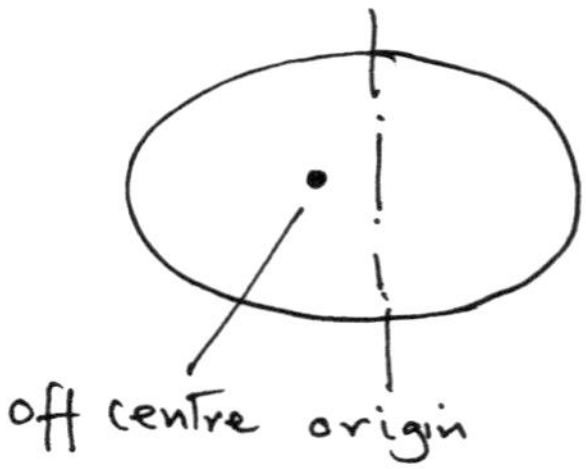

A series of contours were worked out, moving from the lowest point outwards to meet the level edge at the outermost rim.

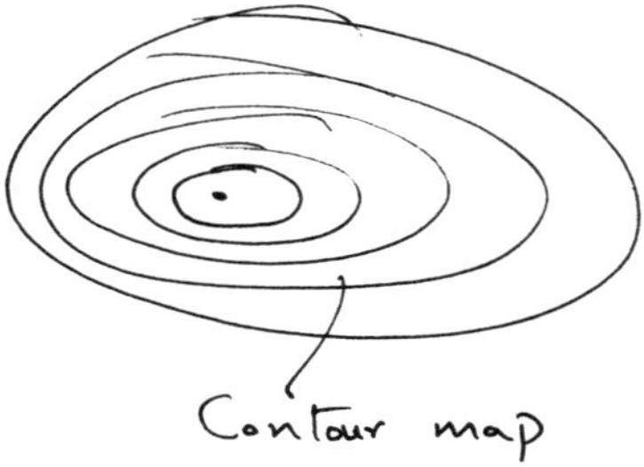

The resulting contour map looked something like part of a basic attractor out of chaos theory.

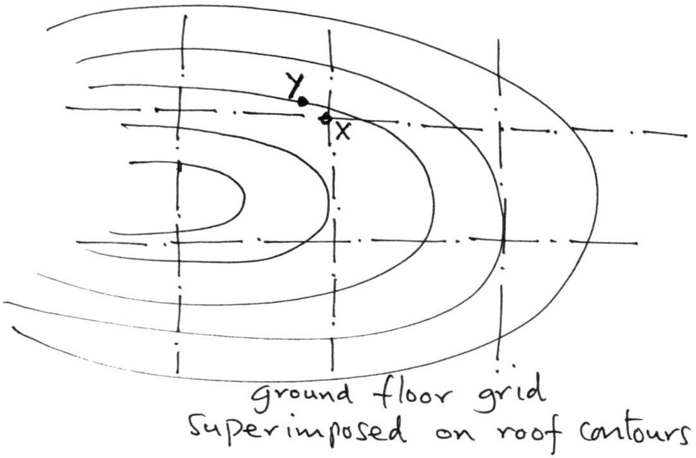

To keep the main roof members standard the columns raked in to take up the mismatch when the level ground floor grid was projected upwards onto the sloping roof. See points X, Y.

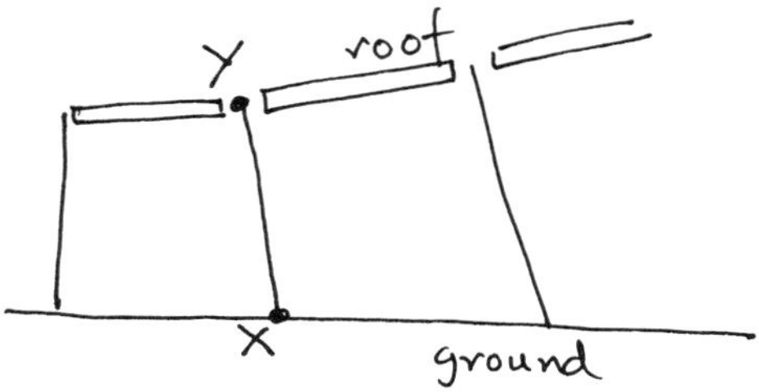

The building sits surrounded by velocity, its ground plan in the shape of an ellipse. It is huge; the Eiffel Tower being a measure of its length. The dimensions of the oval shape that one traverses are 245 m (length) and 150 m (breadth).

When the project was completed the city named it 'Lille Grand Palais'. The locals called it 'l'oeuf'.

And for the lowest of budgets, this low-orbiting egg provided a series of small miracles in its organisation, appearance and technicalities.

To those who observe the megapolis of Euralille, just up the road, as an alien landing, Congrexpo is its strange offspring. Its textures, shine and transparency are an obvious camouflage. Metallic/concrete/plastic, opaque/translucent – sometimes in grey light even foreboding – it keeps people guessing.

But, they argue, once inside it is bound to be something else.

309

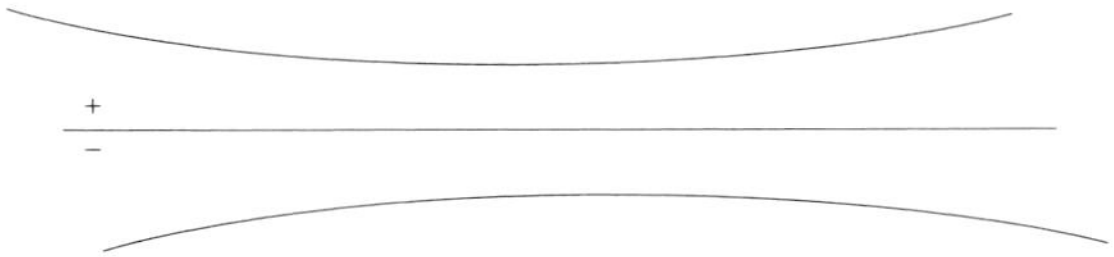

It is not just a bird that flies, the air allows an intersection.

We may know that an outspread wing on a thermal current supports the moment of falling to overcome the wrench of gravity, but such an effortless sweep creates a paradox. Where there was nothing the flight leaves a memory. Shape and volume come to the surrounding space, an action of the positive drawing out a hidden negative.

The mystery is in the unseen calculation of exact balance, of up versus down, of substance versus immateriality, of light against shadow.

In Lisbon, at the Expo '98 site, a similar event is taking place. Designed by Alvaro Siza, it is one of the purest statements in recent architecture. It is also a first entry into the act of structure.

The simplest representation of a structural element is the line.

That line turns into a drape for the canopy to the Portuguese National Pavilion. Like a necklace, the structure spans between abutments and defines entrance.

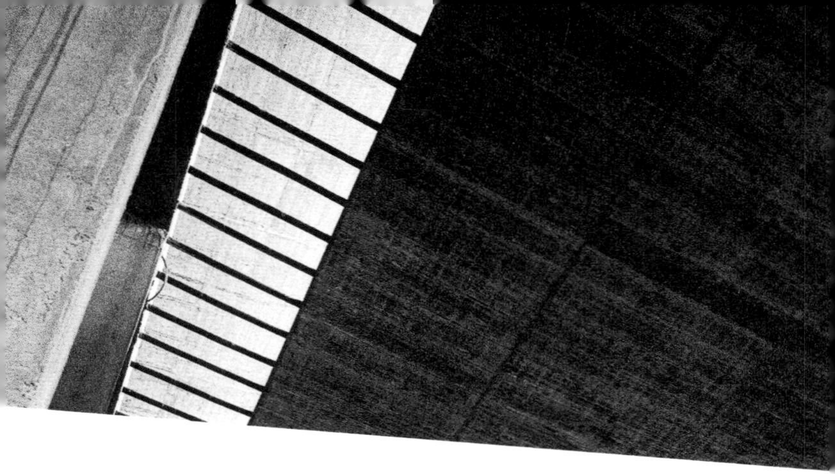

But the canopy is more than structure and shade. Its arc and flight give ceremony and celebration. Space itself is experienced as a vibration surrounding the trajectory. Made out of concrete, the curve flies seventy metres without apparent effort – from afar it looks as if it is made of paper.

And at the last moment of span, just before the safety of the vertical anchors, the form is cut. Lines of cables cross the void instead, pinning themselves to strong abutments. This de-materialisation is both a denial and a release. Weight vanishes and the mass hovers. Like the underbelly of some flying saucer the canopy floats. It is a trick of the light.

Where final closure and darkness should be there is only absence and innocent air. Across the gap, cables come into view as the end-threads of a story.

Structure is revealed as the true plot, the elemental line.

The juxtaposition of weight and solidity with that of vanishing causes disbelief, the shock of concrete flying the distance.

The assumption was to look for a high-tech answer, a net of wires tied to a lightweight skin-fabric or metal sheet. Wind reversals over such a span complicated the issue, needing more wires and struts externally to cope with uplift forces, spawning spider-like configurations. If a steel truss structure were to be hidden, buried within a top and bottom skin, then the thickness of the roof would have grown.

The alternative was to have hangers leaning out from the abutments, picking up the roof. Yet an axial configuration of hangers superimposed over the distributed and stretched out vocabulary of 'sheet' only seemed to confuse the eye. All attempts at light-weight answers compromised the elementary concept of drape.

The simplest idea then was to have the curve itself as structure but to choose a heavy material to give balance against wind uplift. The impossible thought of concrete entered at this point.

Having a thin concrete element span such a distance seemed outrageous, too heavy, and easily prone to cracking under high temperatures. There was danger as well from possible earthquake action, for Lisbon is in a seismic region, but the simple idea took hold – just one force line that does it all, material, form, structure, and finish.

ALCHEMY

Something had to be done to counter the extent of concrete heaviness. A lightness was needed. The answer in such situations is to invoke a contrary strategy – if there is weight to contend with, then bring in an opposite, non-weight; if substance is the concern, then splice that with non-substance, air.

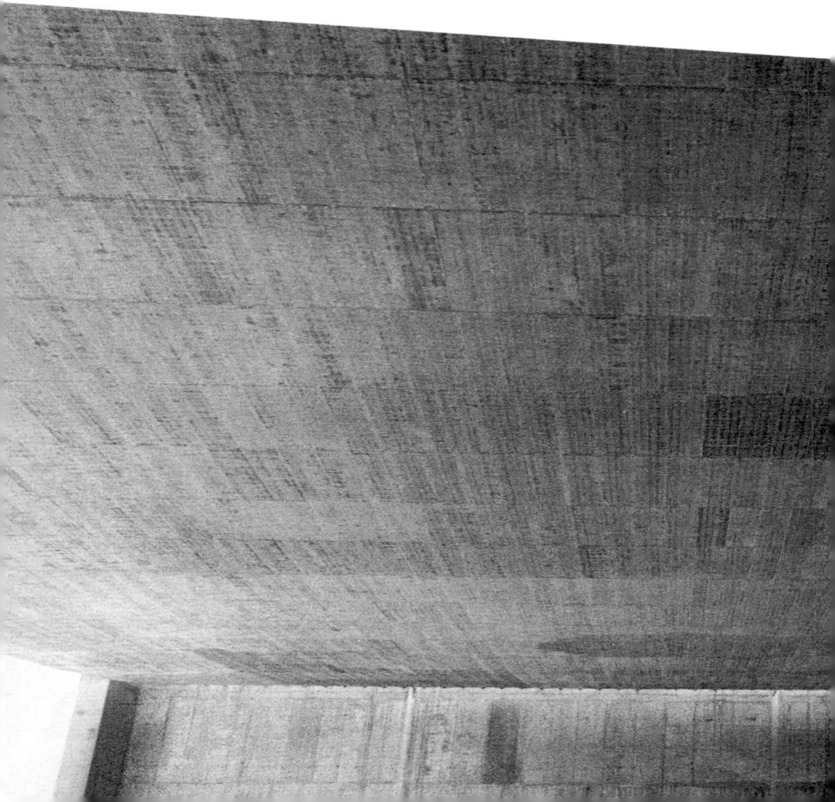

If one stands in the middle of
the plaza at the lowest point
of the catenary and looks upwards,
a thousand tons of crushing weight
is forgotten; the mass levitates.
The canopy disengages from
its end bearings.

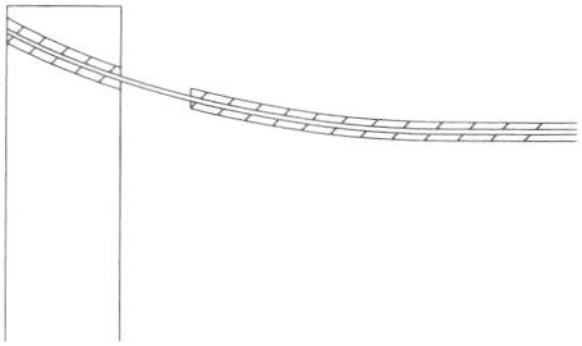

To add to the effect of lightness the material was made as thin as possible, only 20 cm of concrete over 70 m of span.

Calculations showed it could have been thinner but a certain point is reached when judgement and intuition start to give warnings.
In the belief that our estimate would better govern long-term performance we avoided the further enticement of shaving millimetres off the section.

IMPURITIES

Concrete cracks. Usually, it is micro cracking which in internal conditions is not damaging to the homogeneity of the material, but when concrete is exposed to the elements special care is needed. Cracks that propagate weaken the section, allowing moisture penetration and corrosion. The extent of cracking can be contained though by controlling tension stresses across the material section. For the canopy, we chose to limit crack widths to 0.15 mm, a fault line that could not be seen from the ground but one that would not impair long-term durability either.

A key decision in this respect was to de-bond the concrete; i.e. de-couple the mass from the load carrying system. Instead of concrete gripping the cable, an oiled sheath was provided for the cable to pass through, allowing the concrete to 'ride' the cable. As the cable 'slips' through the concrete, local effects of heat and cold and shrinkage over such a distance are easier to deal with. Concrete then becomes cladding and the structure is reduced to the cables themselves.

SECONDARY MATTERS

At first glance the drape looks simple to calculate and construct.

Surely the realisation is straightforward, a single curve in space – what could be easier?

The assumption may be true for the calculation of geometry and tension force in the cable, but simplicity vanishes when one considers the catalogue of disasters that could befall an exposed sheet of concrete over such a span. In aggressive environments of sun, wind and sea-air, intricate calculations need to be done to satisfy secondary concerns. Local vortex shedding, asymmetric patch loading, temperature differentials, spalling, and possible cable 'snap' from earthquake action, all complicate the plot. The justifications take time.

But the canopy has more to it than just technicalities buried in a concrete span.

In flying the distance, in dipping and intersecting an unseen matrix, space itself becomes tangible, growing into a hidden structure.

The canopy becomes a line in a bigger sculpture, part witnessed, part felt. The brute idea of concrete reverses into one of elegance and purity; the notion of mass turning into immateriality. The cut, playing on opposites, denies the continuum and serves up its own surprises.

ASPECTS OF THE SOLUTION

The curve is a minimum energy line, a natural fit to the suspension of weight distributed over a specific distance. Its shape is a mathematical function called a catenary, given by the equation:

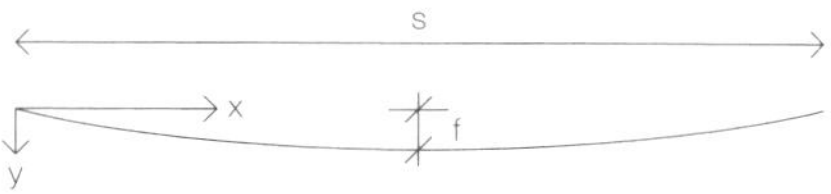

$$y = \frac{4f(sx - x^2)}{s^2}$$

In a catenary there is only axial force. The resultant horizontal tension at the abutments is obtained from the equation:

$$T = \frac{ws^2}{8f}$$

where w = unit weight. The smaller the sag f the greater the force. If the sag is zero and the impossible is asked of the structure, to hang something in a horizontal line, then T equals infinity. Conversely, if the sag is large, the tension is minimal.

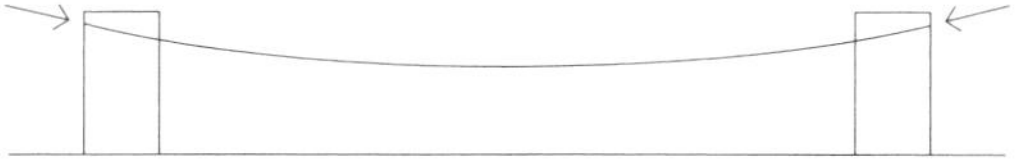

To keep the pure action of catenary at all stages the curve is projected right through to the abutments, which means the end anchors are lined up with the curvature.

Once the concrete is poured on the formwork and the cables fully stressed, the canopy lifts itself off the shuttering, as the structure is a self-balanced system.

The sequence of construction is:

Foundations:

Fins and anchor points:

Propping:

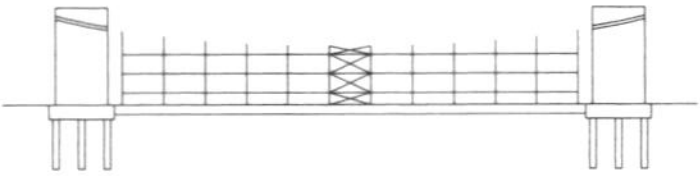

Formwork:

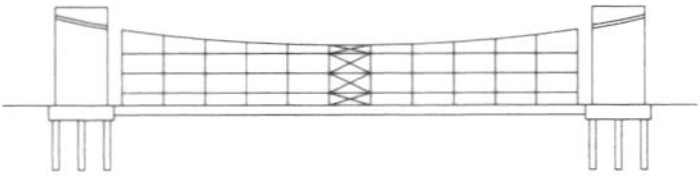

Cables and reinforcement:

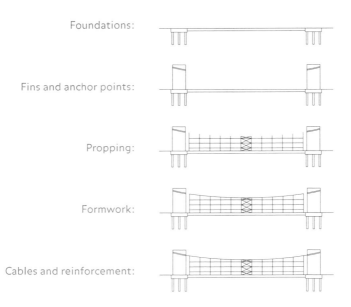

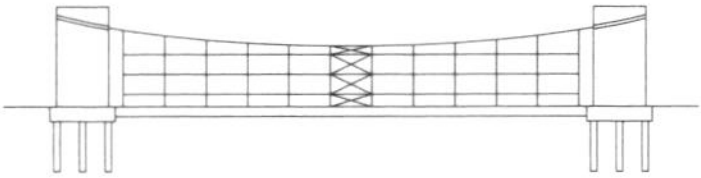

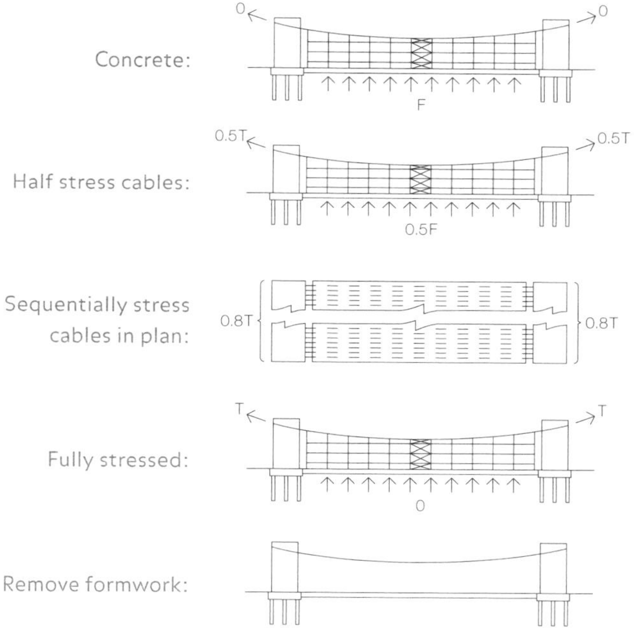
Concrete:
0
0
F
Half stress cables:
0.5T
0.5T
0.5F
Sequentially stress
cables in plan:
0.8T
0.8T
Fully stressed:
T
T
0
Remove formwork:

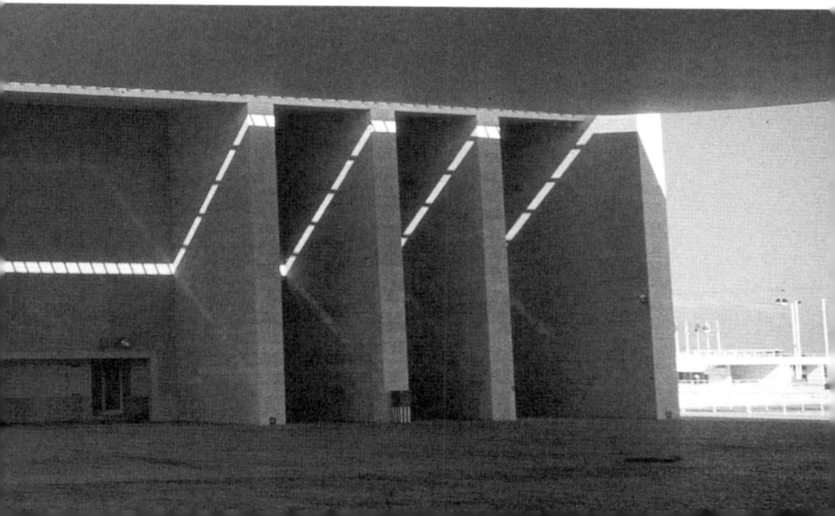

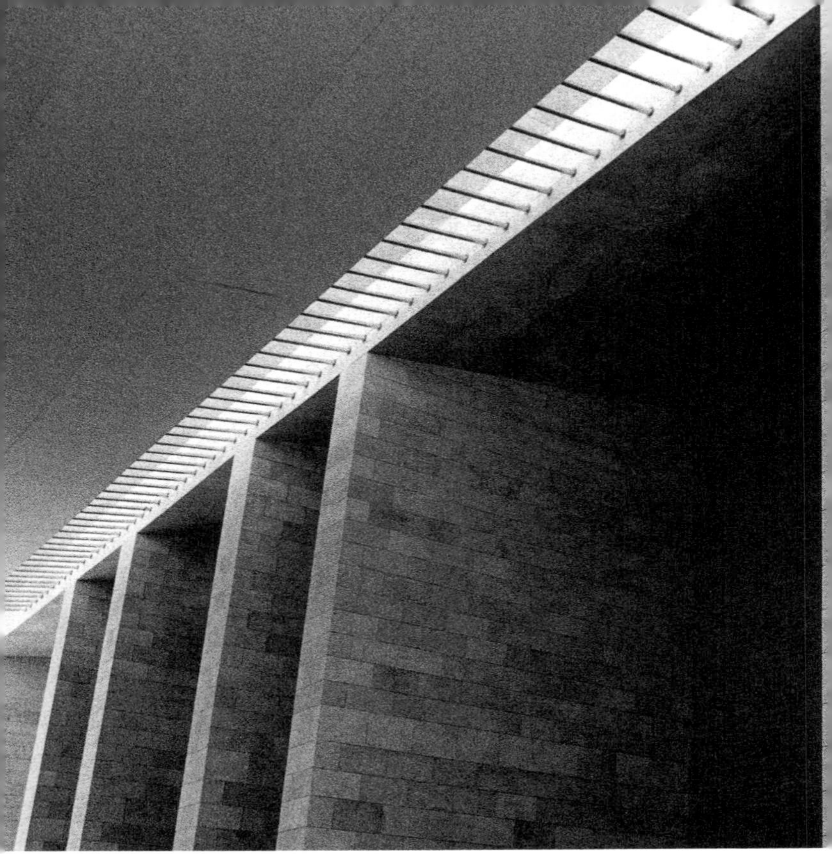

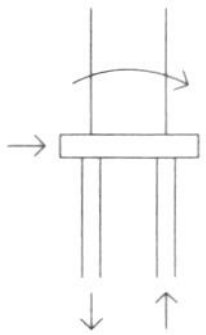

Cables pulling on the abutments give large overturning at the base. The bending moment is resisted by the push-pull action of the piles supporting the load. There remains a horizontal thrust to be carried to the foundations which needs attention.

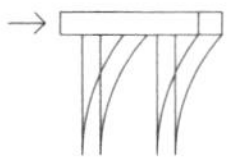

This force could be allowed to bend the piles over but the deflection and settlement is high – too much to accept.

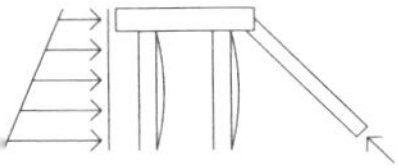

Alternatively, a raking pile could resist the thrust in a more direct manner. But considerable length of pile is needed for this solution which is costly. Additional horizontal load could be generated as well by seismic conditions which mobilise a wedge of soil impacting on the piles. This has to be resisted, giving further length and cost to the idea of raking pile.

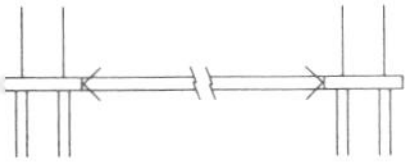

A proposal away from these complications is to put in place a series of ground beams across the length of span connecting one foundation with the other.

The ground beams act as struts. They hold everything together and complete a closed circuit for the load path. It is as neat as it is efficient. Everything ties together, balancing one against the other. A structural loop is created closing the tension force in the air to a reverse line of thrust mobilised below ground, connecting the abutments.

This play of opposites abounds in structural analysis, if there is an action here, then there is a counter-action over there – a finely honed system of checks and balances at all levels, from the macro to the micro, that takes care of equilibrium. For example, concrete in the abutments carries compression, and reinforcement buried in them transmit opposing tensions. Piles bear into the soil and the earth pushes back through an equal end bearing. And so on . . .

The canopy itself takes part in this game, with substance balanced by void, dark with light and mass set against weightlessness.

The Expo canopy is not just a first entry to structure but a metaphor for the very act of structure.

If a catenary is flipped over to serve as an arch, the compression in the arch is identical to the previous tension force of the catenary, provided the abutments are taken to be unmoving and stiff.

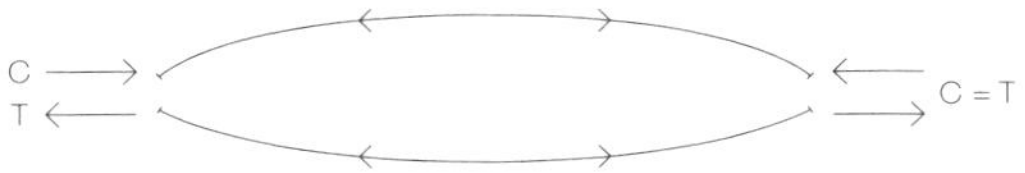

The horizontal becomes a mirror line.

If there is 'give' or yield in the foundation to an arch, then there is bending, and this becomes significant if the rise of the arch is low.

In tension, material is thinned out and stretched; in the reverse action of compression there is a 'squeezing' together. The same thickness of material in the catenary is not sufficient in the case of the arch. As the thrusts from the abutments climb up the trajectory there is the tendency for the material to fail by buckling, denying the force a continuous passage. As thin sections are weak in bending, the material fails.

The higher the rise of the arch the more the direct force and the lesser the bending. At full semi-circle height there is no bending at all. This is the inspiration for the hanging chain models that get flipped over to serve as vaulted ceilings and domes.

THE LINE OF FLIGHT

Is 'up' superior to 'down'?

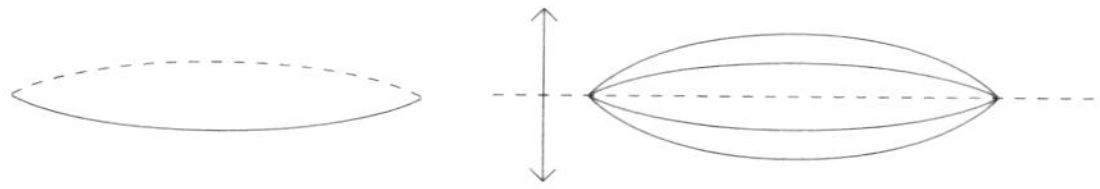

Should the Expo canopy have been a vault or a drape?

A deeper sag for the canopy could be described as 'unlovely'. Keeping the curve taut, as a line of low-flying tension, provides the dynamic, just as its exact reverse, the low thrusting arch, offers power to the eye.

Does the ratio of height at mid span to height of abutments govern the subjective view? Is h/H a key parameter for arch or catenary?

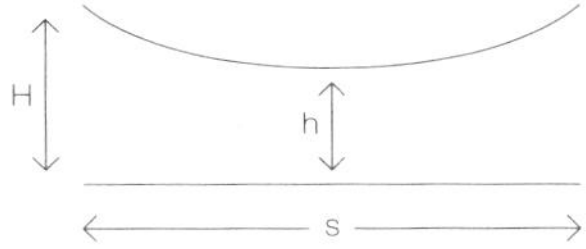

Is the ratio h/s more important?

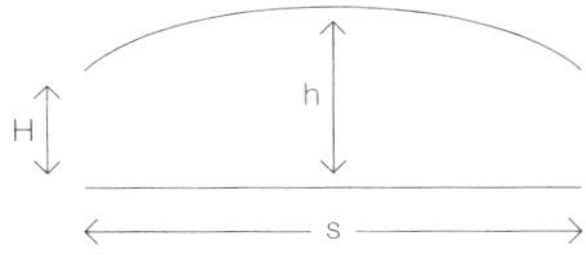

Is the dip or rise, f, the key factor?

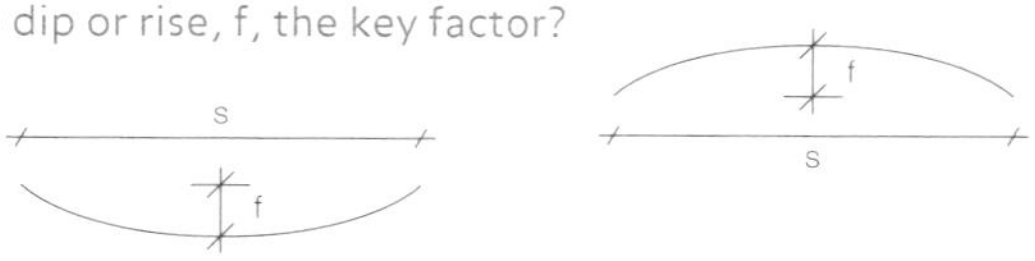

Ratios such as f/s or f/h must also be considered significant.

Do visitors to Siza's pavilion detect the line of the canopy as 'just right'? Is that estimation of 'correctness' in the flight given to the eye by only what they look at or is there a wider framing to the shape, an implied reflection or ghost image that adds value to the composition?

What if the ground has a counterpart to the design, a symmetry below, that completes the picture?

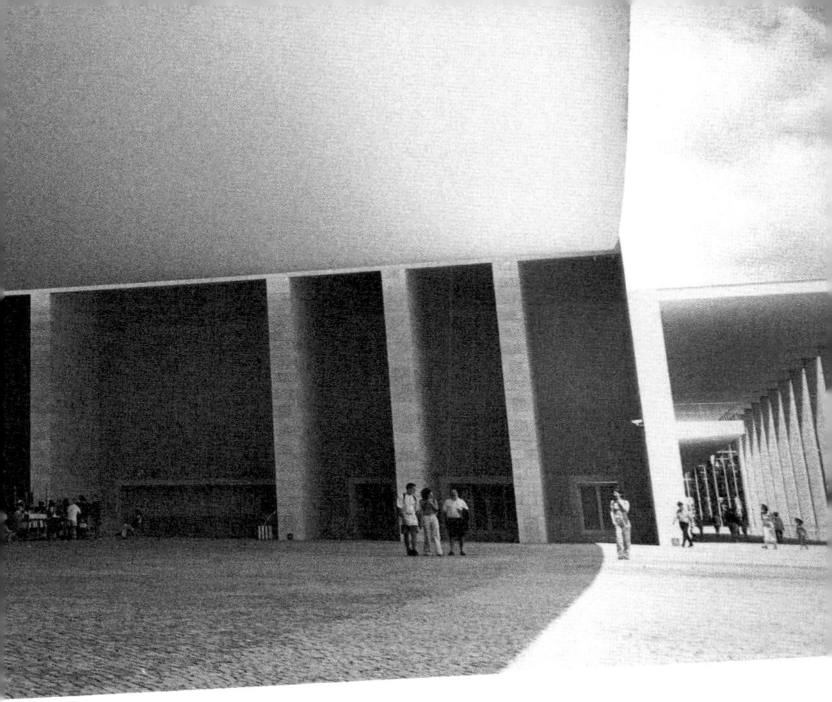

If the trace of the catenary and its reflection are joined, a rectangle can be drawn with vertices at the extremities of the curves.

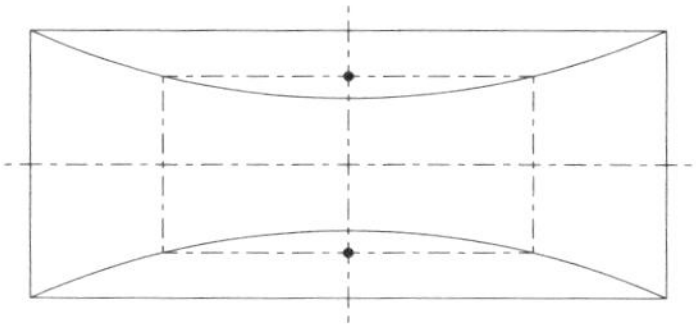

MOVING RECTANGLE

If a search pattern is set for a measure of proportion embedded in the geometry, the tracking of a rectangle that 'slips' and travels along the curves is worth following.

At the abutments the ratio of the sides of this rectangle is $^{S}/_{2H}$, (the overall span divided by the full height). And at the mid point the ratio vanishes, for there is no dimension of length to the rectangle at this location. What value does this ratio have when the horizontal of the rectangle passes through the curve's centre of gravity? For the Expo canopy this is 2.23.

The horizontal drawn through the centre of gravity of a catenary seems always to intersect the line of flight at a fixed location. No matter what the sag is, this distance in relation to span is the ratio 0.11 of span. Here is an invariant property, perhaps an essential clue.

But these concerns are to take the model at hand, a curve close to the ground. What about the rope bridge hanging high above the gorge, far removed from horizontal datum? If a hidden aesthetic is at work, may it not be in something to be found intrinsic to the properties and limits of the curve itself?

One idea is to link the sag of a catenary to a limiting condition with very little tension like a sag equal to half span. Flipping that curve over the horizontal gives an envelope of two curves. A rectangle joining up the centroids of this geometry has a ratio 1.7. Is the golden ratio somewhere behind this construction? Would a more squat interior rectangle produce an uglier line across space?

Another idea is to draw a series of catenaries of equal span about a common centroid – all trajectories pass through a point at 0.11 of span, though at different heights to the vertical. A limiting condition is then drawn, say, a sag equal to half span. If the Expo curve is then superimposed, its vertical offset at the extremity, from that of the limiting curve, is similar to the height of the canopy above ground at its launch point. Is it these parameters that give shape when drawing just by eye?

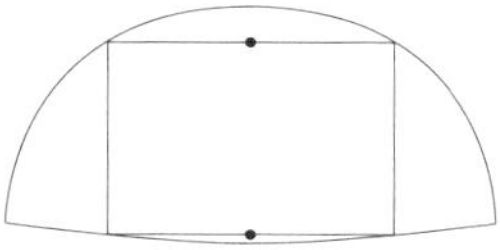

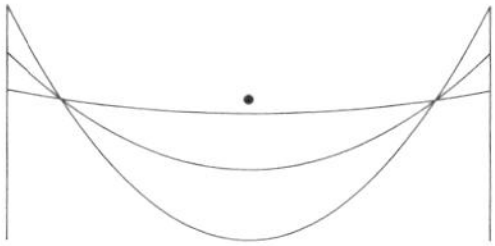

The structure becomes a template of parallel strokes; some deeper than others, some reflecting the converse action, of arch over the void. And the ground itself may attach buried shadow to substance.

Like a fantastic lens the curve focuses the abstract over the real and the speculative over the material.

Composition is an overlayering of the seen versus the unseen with potentiality set against the real. What is left in the mind is something different to the canopy, a sculpture of another sort, an unfolding series of *informal* cuts in an imagined space.

Like the bird in flight over the chasm, whatever we think, the idea is as much in the mind as in the curve in space.

Structure then becomes poetic licence – or a metaphysic in the science of architecture.

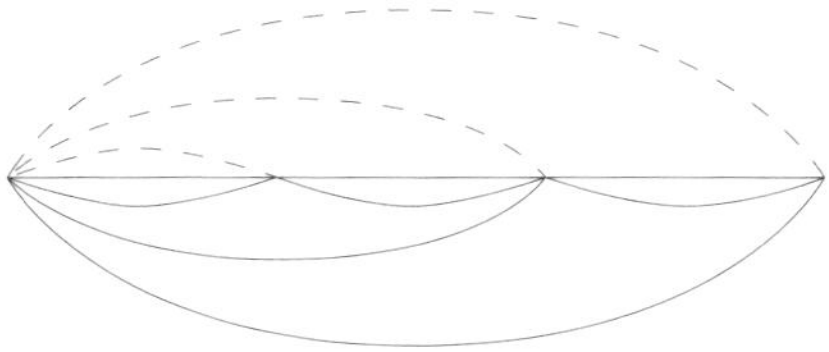

345

Structure is Flow in the Arnhem Interchange, not a framework as we know it but a generating diagram. Instead of joining points to lines a single thread loops and folds, stitching program demands to external configurations. Orthodoxy surrenders to improvisation.

In a free almost biological sense, far removed from the constraints of predictable structure, layering and folding take over and the concerns of a Newtonian mechanics fall away.

Like in a dream, structure traces an outline, opening and closing, crossing through space. The trajectory acts as catalyst and enzyme motivating flow and regulating realisable strategies. Offices, the free concourse area and a strict car park grid come together in one fluid concept, leading to both Cartesian and non-linear solutions.

The initial question between Ben van Berkel, the architect, and myself was how to integrate three separate layers of program?

Commercial offices

Concourse area

Basement car park

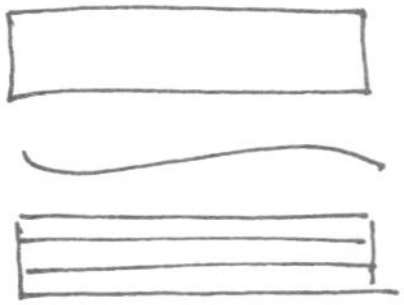

In each case the demand on grid was different – for the car park, a 15 m grid; for the offices a much smaller grid of 7–9 m; and in the concourse, a column free area.

How does one generate a compatibility?

A typical approach would assume space to be organised in vertical slices with the grids being taken as plumb lines. This means the lack of vertical continuity being taken out by transfer – the grids plunging down with load and the horizontal thickening up to bridge the mismatch.

Drive the predetermined car
park grid upwards through the
concourse level to meet the
office grid and have transfer
at office level.

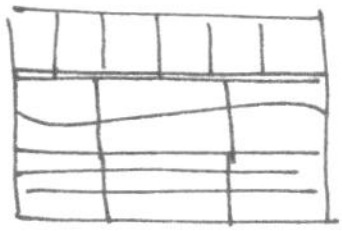

Let the concourse level take
out the clash of grids. This is
not a good strategy, as curvature
should not be adopted for
transferring point loads.

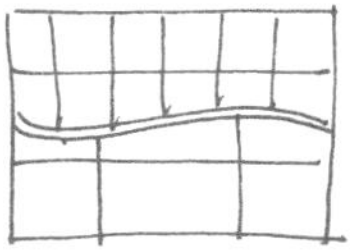

Allow the office grids to ride
through producing columns in
the concourse area, with major
transfer at the car park level.

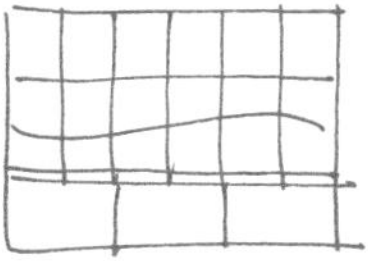

None of the proposals seemed right. Something more radical was needed, to progress the ambitions. We had the notion of seamlessness in our concept, was there a way out through Diagram?

We drew a line that moved up from the foundations to loop and coil over space.

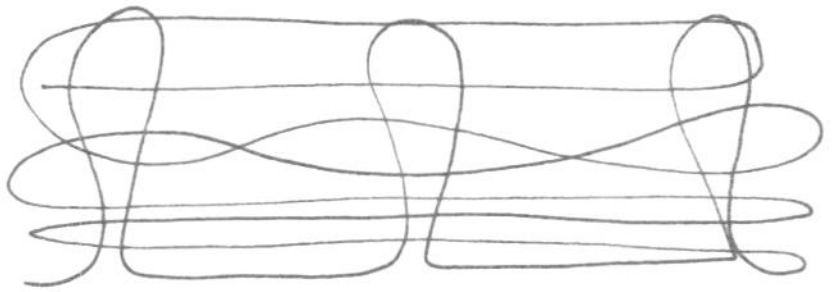

I felt that the single rows of column points at basement level should widen into zones, or regions, and initiate an upward movement. Rather than serve as limiting points the lowest contact surface should be the start-up, and not a dead-end. It seemed the natural thing to do. Instead of orthogonal framework, an improvising thread layered and crossed over itself to become the concept for structure, it was the strangest thing I had done yet to initiate a piece of construction.

MULTIPLE ORGANISER

And, with van Berkel, Diagram transformed readily into realisation.

Loops turned into inclined V-walls. In the car park, shelves or corbels off the walls supported floor decks; holes cut out of the Vs gave pedestrian access from one side to the other. Parts of the walls folded over and stretched or merged at concourse level. Higher up, the Vs reduced to columns offering spans of around 10 metres for the office levels. The need for transfer had disappeared.

The Vs offered architectural and servicing strategies as well: they act as 'People Collectors' – they conduct light down into the car park, offering vertical orientation for visitors. Air handling units located within the double-zone supply fresh air to the car park; and in the case of fire, smoke could be evacuated through these channels.

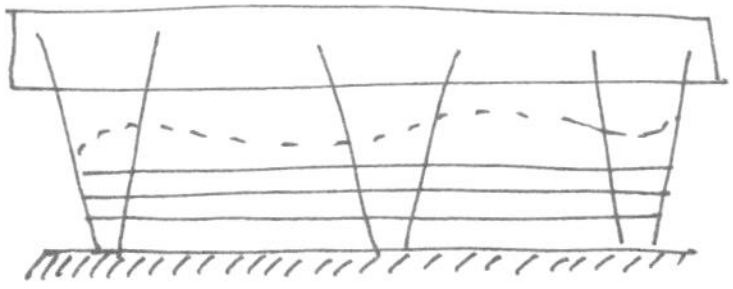

The Vs integrate structure, light, people and technical services.
They are 'Super Multiple-Organisers'.

CRASH ZONE

If the V-walls powered a vertical synthesis into the scheme then their horizontal path initiated a metaphor for the high energy curvature of the concourse level. The walls, on plan, were taken as moving lines – and allowed to crash into each other, initiating a 'crumple zone'.

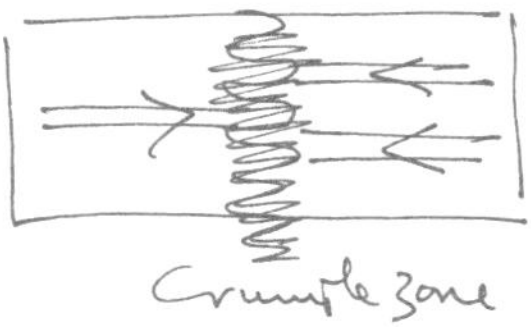

Imagine the concourse area and station roof being moulded and lifted from out of these melting energies. Walls begin to turn out of their plane, to fold and stretch, to vault and climb over the horizontal. The answers began to take shape from a mobility of plan as van Berkel wanted.

Computer videos ran . . .

How to keep the curvature as a natural consequence of the concept? For that, a merging was needed, connecting roof and floors into one network.

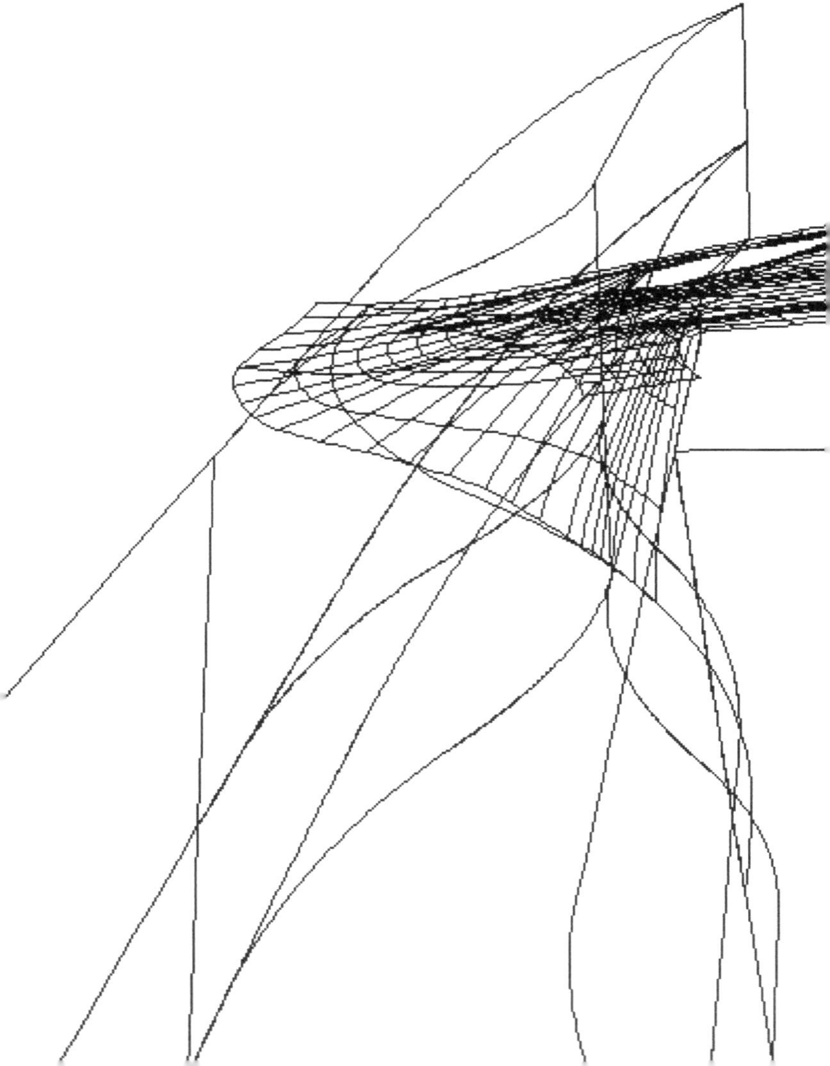

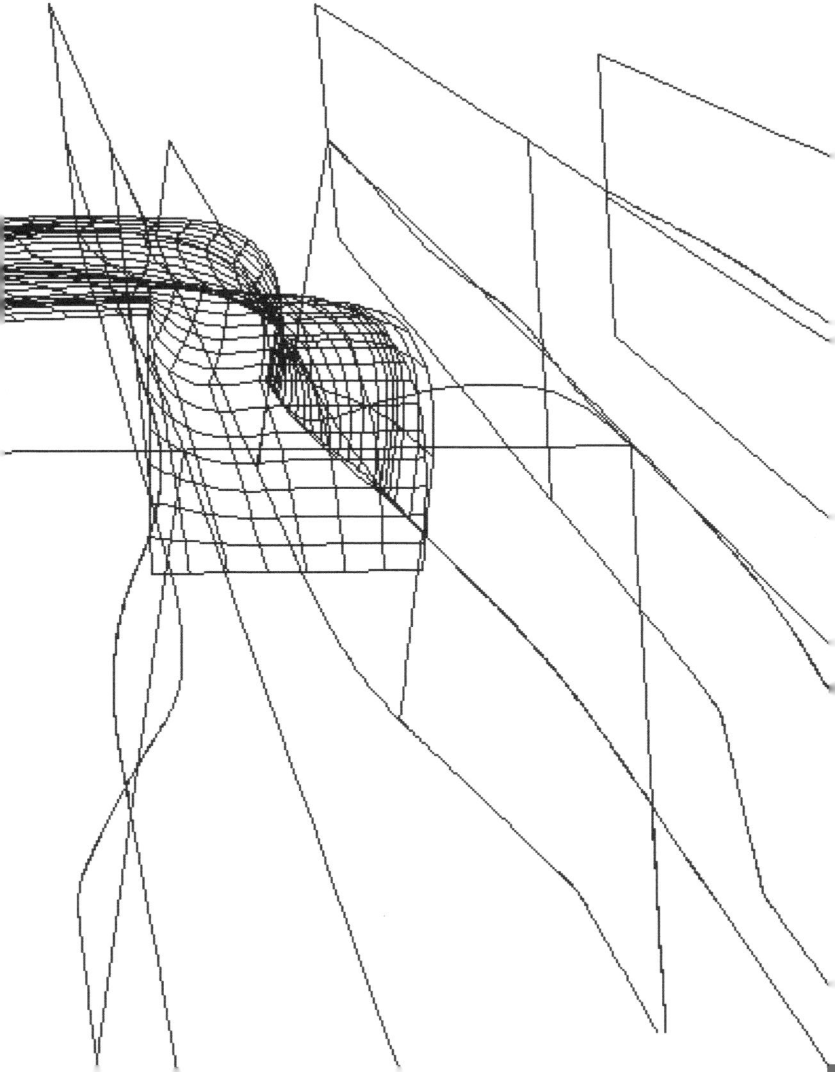

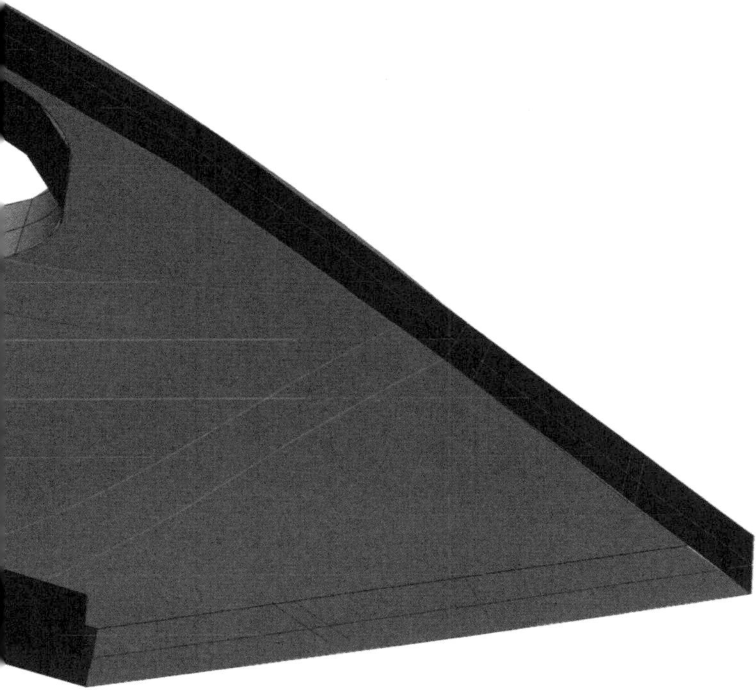

Drawing down the roof to the concourse area, in a twisting funnel, supercharged the tectonic.

Along the intertwined logic of a knot typology, a Seifert surface merged the horizontal with the vertical in one sinuous movement. The roof plunged through a vortex of column flowing out again as a diaphragm of the lower floor.

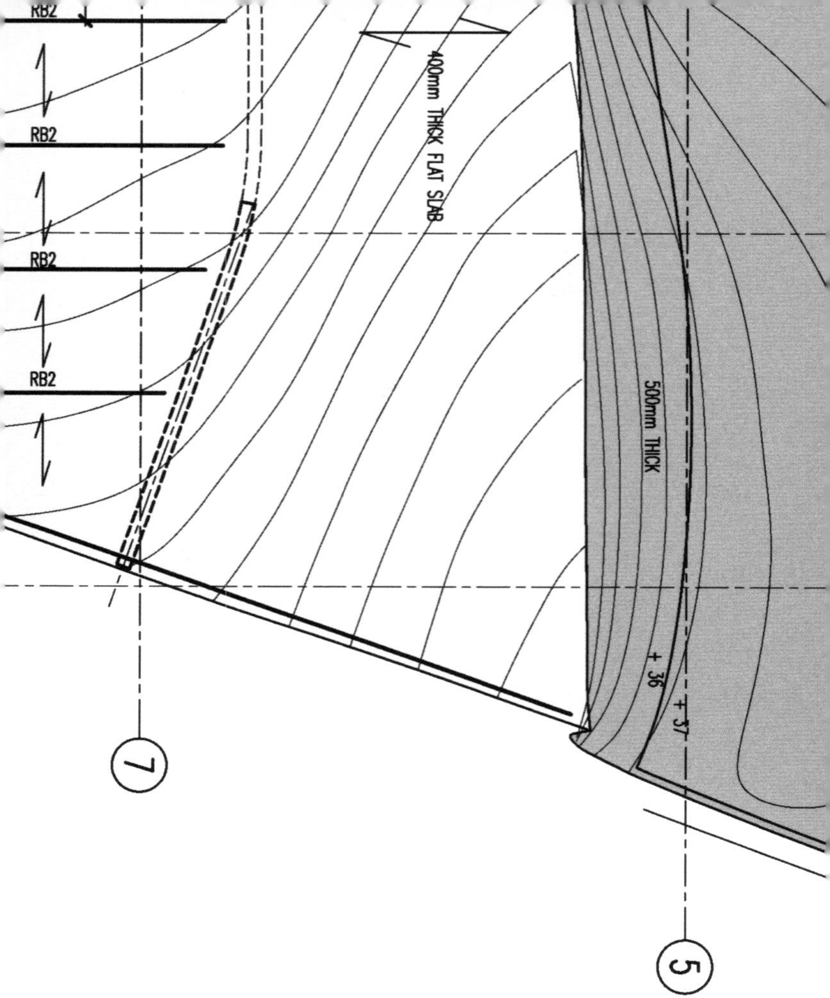

Structure travelled as border, defining the object territory as finite, but unbounded – a surprising butterfly pattern appeared on the roof.

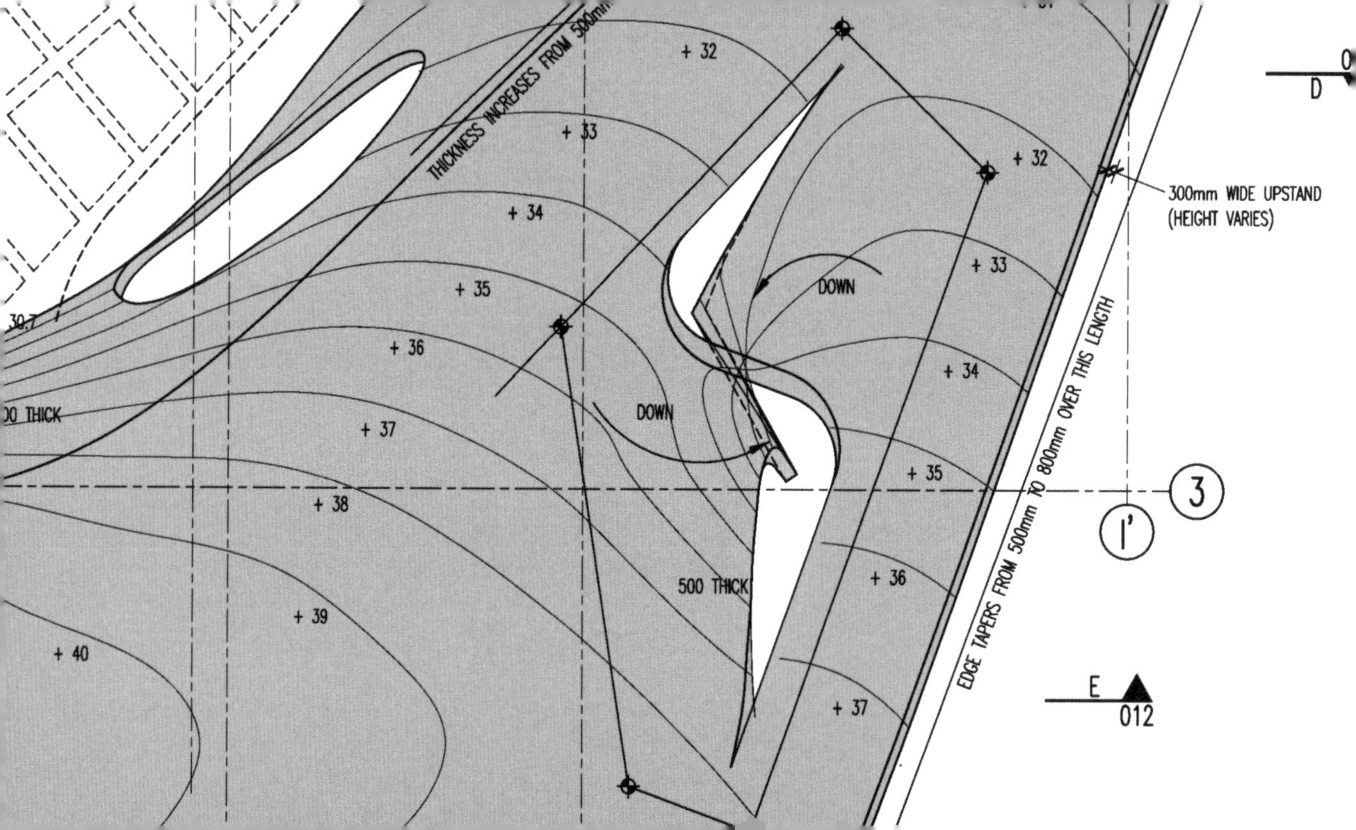
THICKNESS INCREASES FROM 500mm
+ 32
+ 33
+ 34
+ 35
+ 36
+ 37
+ 38
+ 39
+ 40
30.7
DOWN
DOWN
500 THICK
300mm WIDE UPSTAND
(HEIGHT VARIES)
EDGE TAPERS FROM 500mm TO 800mm OVER THIS LENGTH
3
1'
E
012
D

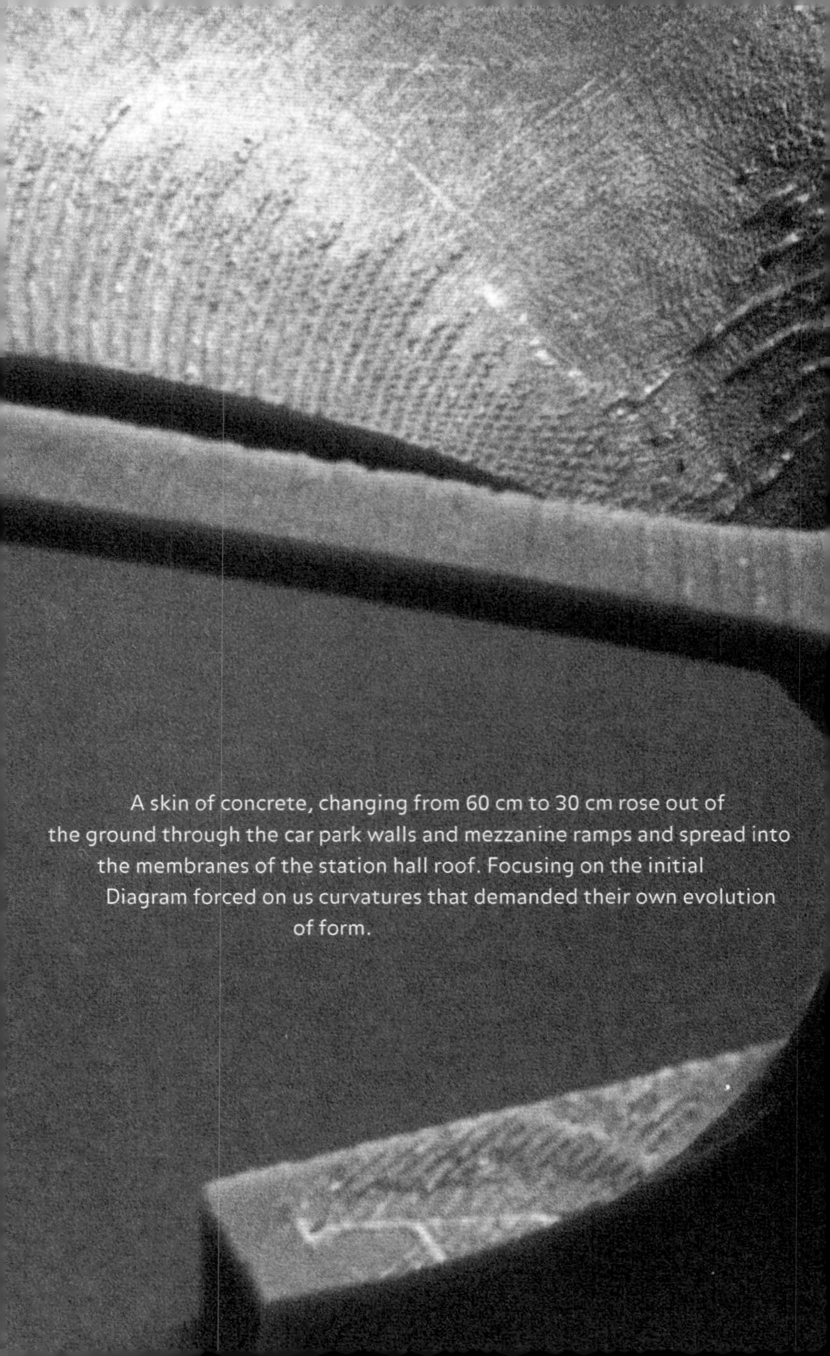

A skin of concrete, changing from 60 cm to 30 cm rose out of the ground through the car park walls and mezzanine ramps and spread into the membranes of the station hall roof. Focusing on the initial Diagram forced on us curvatures that demanded their own evolution of form.

Often free-form shapes are created with current software by pulling and shaping to please the eye. Then this superficial geometry is exported to rapid CAD / CAM realisations; but that does not necessarily develop an instinct for structure. To make meaningful structure out of folding typologies a different technique is needed, more of an interior concept based on generating line.

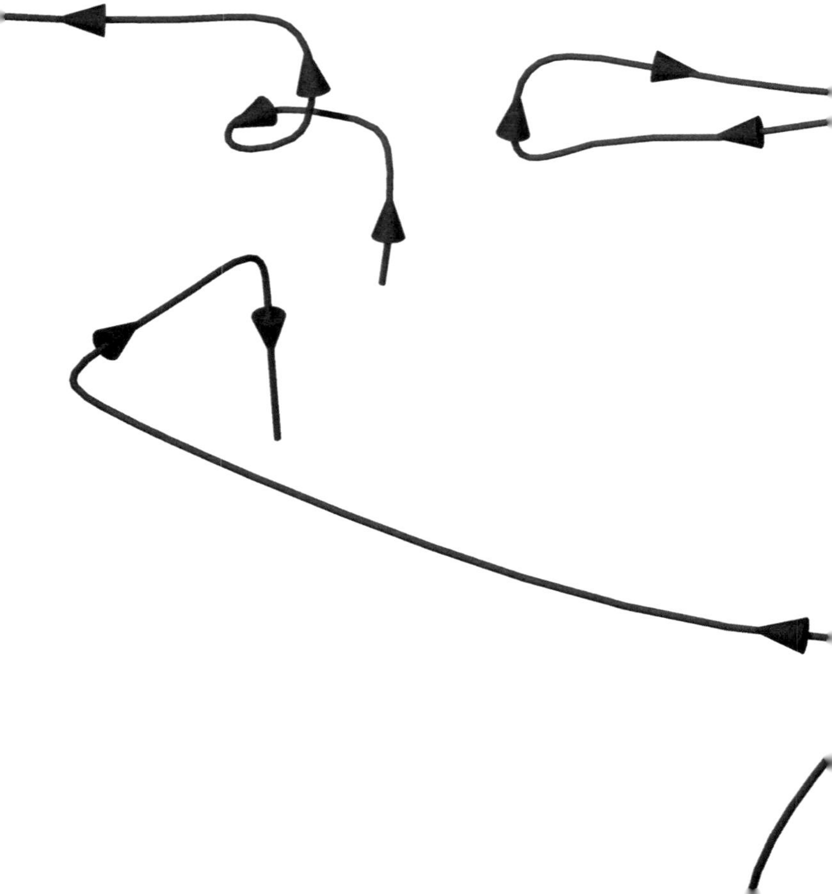

Consider a trial and error method that offers one such approach.

Draw by eye or algorithm free edges of the form – imagine them as supports. Trace their outline as if a piece of unfolding string.

Between these free lines, place an approximation of the surface desired, by crude patching.

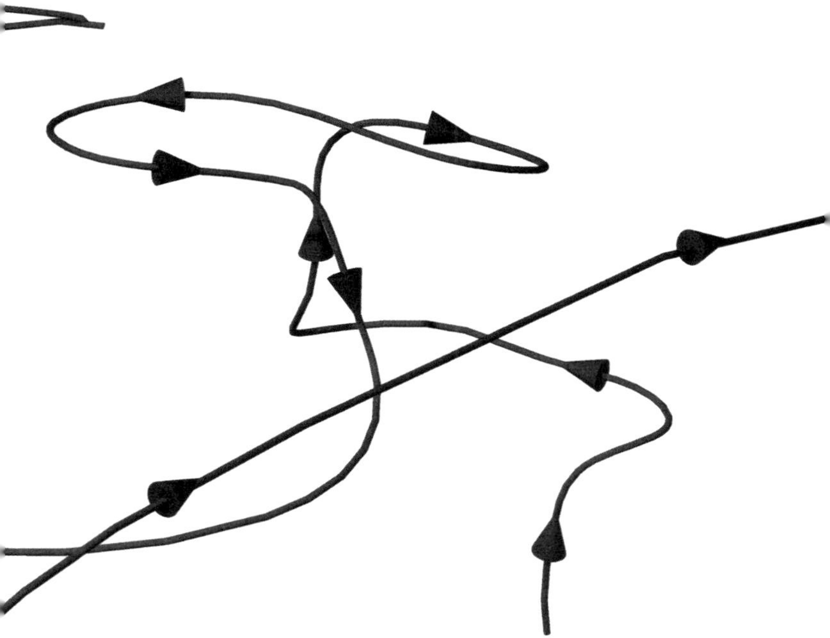

Facet the surface into sections, to fix planar elements to the preliminary curvature. 'Stretch' the facets into a minimum energy surface by pretensioning. If the spans are small, this tension is sufficient. If they are large, a tightening plus an upward pressure is necessary to smooth out 'wrinkles' in the surface.

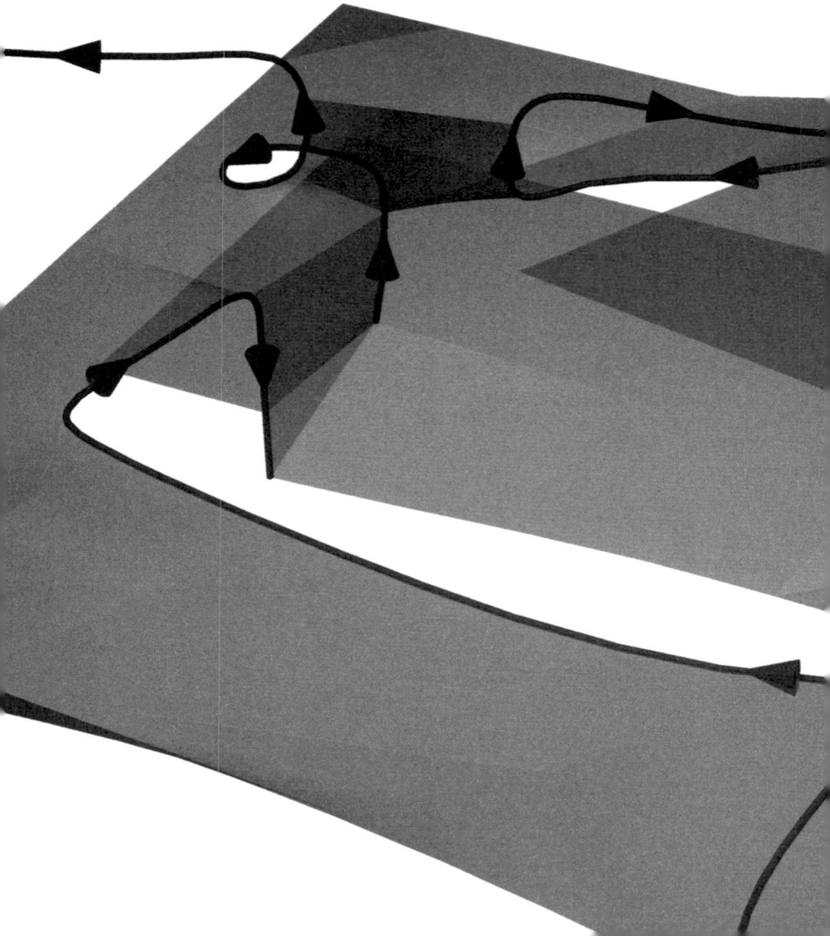

The sequence of solution is: form finding program followed by a non-linear curve fitting, then analysis, and back again to curve fitting, switching between the two until a satisfactory answer is found.

The surface produced is an optimum engineered surface, intact with the geometric definitions of its free edges. Now the 'strings' can vanish.

Note: 'free' edges could be artificially inserted over a sub-region of the form to work out areas of local geometry.

With this technique we look ahead.

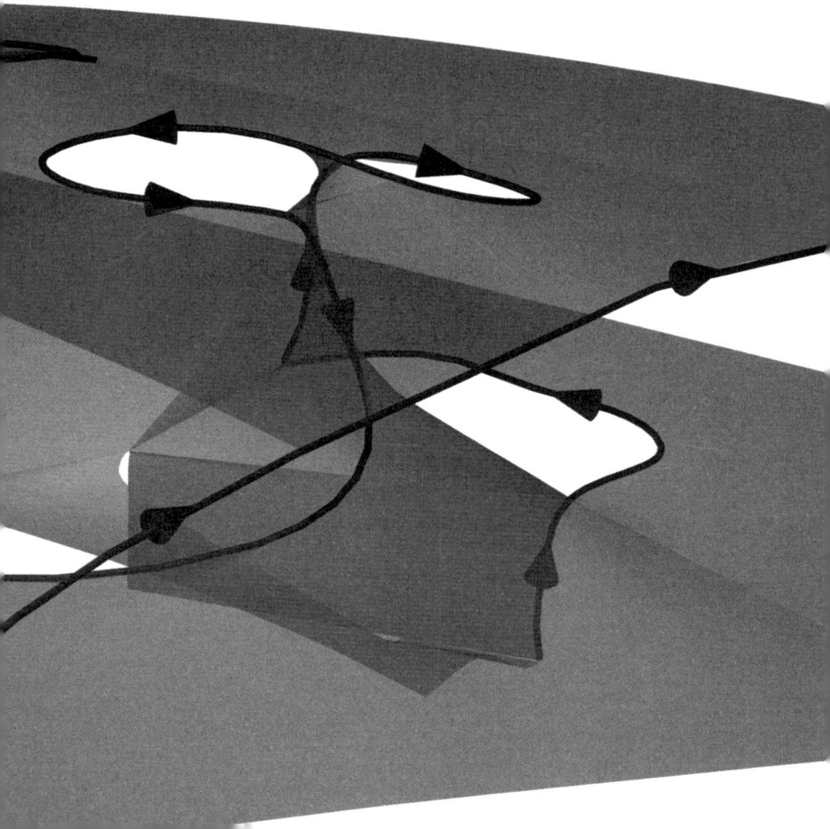

FREE-FORM DIVINING

Many a so called free-form solution is underpinned desperately by structure, the form is 'free' only to the extent of drawing the shape. No other meaning is attached to the outline; structure is put in hastily to stop collapse. The shapes may be wonderful but essentially they remain only 'cladding'.

To spend energy on promoting a free-shape only to forget its interior meanings and call on structure, late, to prop up the surface, seems a wasted opportunity. Every fold or contour is an opportunity for structure, finding the templates that promote complexity as an integral part of potential structure is difficult – but that too is the challenge.

NEW TERRITORIES

Form will come out of a concern with surface and travelling margin rather than a preoccupation with Plan, Line and Boundary.

What matters is pattern and its connectivity.

Clues to these solutions lie deep in nascent structure, in a shadow world of emergent patterns and geometric transients. In the very process of assembly a structural logic is seeded, if there is a connecting path there is a meaning.

When that connectivity is seamless, as in the Arnhem Interchange, zones of confluence, aggregations, overlaps and bandwidths, become a new language for structure. Architecture itself affects a transformation, and as Ben van Berkel says, becomes a new anatomy for engineering investigation

Sometimes, it is useful to look aside in a different direction. Investigating a strategy from another discipline helps – if nothing else, it's fun!

It struck me that making folds in space is like braiding, one layer over another.

If the Arnhem project is to do with mixing separate 'strands' of cars, trams, buses and people, a tectonic that intertwines these strands may be seen as an exercise in braiding.

A rule that links the number of braids (n) to the number of crossovers or folds, before the braids return to their original alignment, is given by:

Number of Folds = $n(n - 1)$

The rule links form and fold.

When the design is completed, we would have affected these strands of transport and people; according to the rule, there should be twelve folds to the form before the strands emerge again.

When this idea was introduced to the design team we were well into the scheme, there was no reason to embed a mathematical logic of braiding into the solution. We were busy chasing other metaphors – and it became a curious thought to leave to one side. Whilst we extrapolated and interpreted the flow diagram, no one checked to quantify the folds.

But I began counting . . .

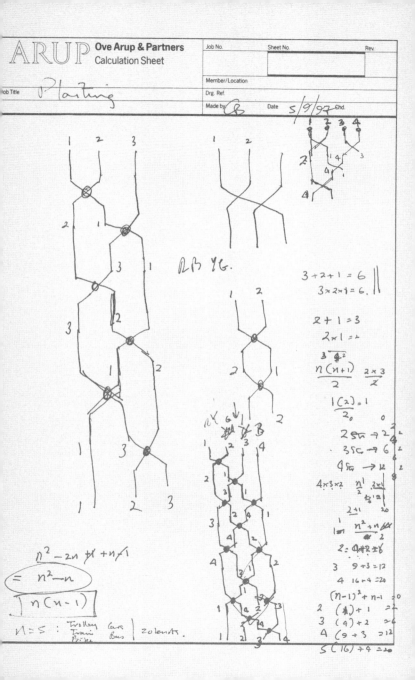

ARUP Ove Arup & Partners
Calculation Sheet

Job No.	Sheet No.	Rev.

Job Title: Plaiting

Member/Location:

Drg. Ref.:

Made by: CB — Date: 5/9/97 — Chd.

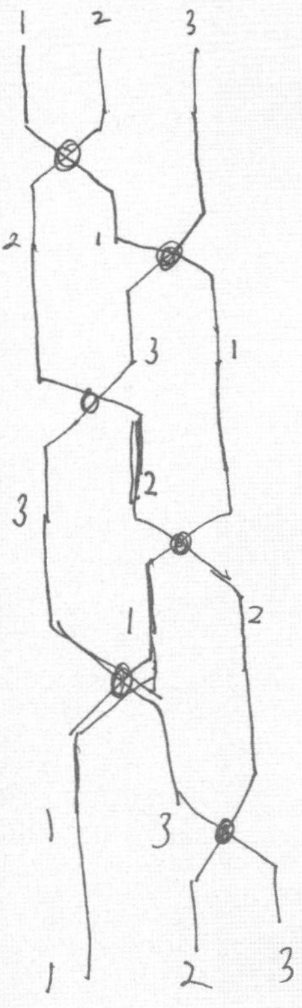

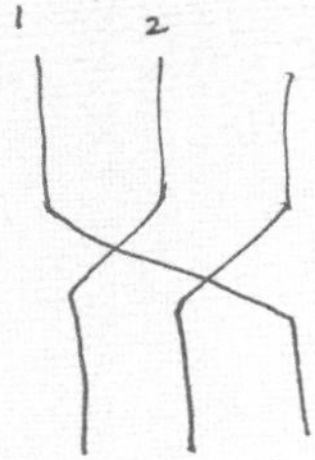

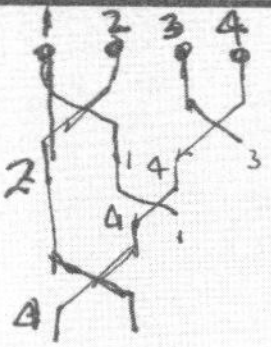

RB YG.

$3+2+1=6$

$3\times2\times1=6.$

$2+1=3$

$2\times1=2$

$\frac{n(n+1)}{2}$ $\quad \frac{2\times3}{2}$

$\frac{1(2)}{2} = 1$

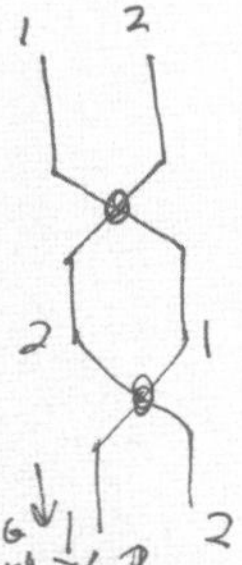

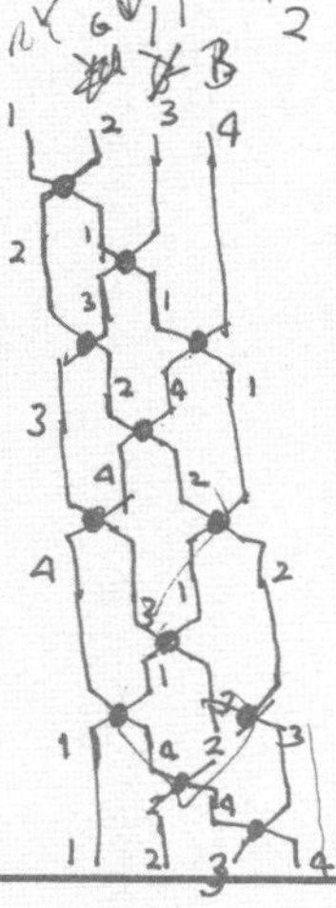

2 St → 2

3 St → 6

4 St → 12

$4\times3\times2$ $\quad \frac{n!}{2}$

$\frac{n^2+n}{2}$

2: 4+2 = 6

3: 9+3 = 12

4: 16+4 = 20

$(n-1)^2+n-1$ = 0

2: (1) + 1 = 2

3: (4) + 2 = 6

4: (9 + 3 = 12

5: (16) + 4 = 20

$n^2-2n+1+n-1$

$= n^2-n$

$n(n-1)$

n = 5 : Trolley, Train, Bike, Cars, Bus | 20 lends.

369

To awaken from a stasis of mind, I work the *templates* – a series of provocations that animate the idea of geometry as nascent, fluid, numbered and empowered with hidden strategies.

Investing the maximum potential into the minimum is the aim: if a grid is something ordered and fixed, it is also a map of the random – an ultimate scattering, without bias. In such start points, the metaphor overlaps with the concrete, the super-reality over the pragmatic.

Templates are like shadow plays, movements and projections of a dimension other than the one at hand. They are faint tracks leading towards an unknown region, the design space of one's imagination.

I

Laying down a grid should be a mapping of the possible, not a restraining order.

A grid is a necklace, folded in a certain way, which at any instant can be pulled apart and shifted dramatically – a moveable feast, not necessarily serious, fixed one moment, vanishing and refigured in the other. Each point on a grid is allowed a charmed life.

II

The point is source of local potential. It is an abstraction of higher energies compressed conveniently to nothing.

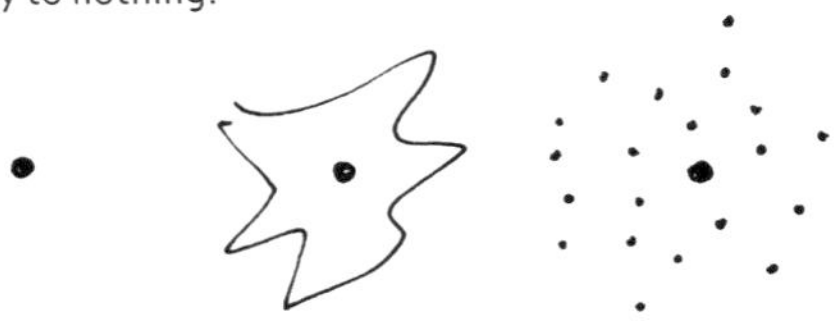

The point captures an average moment of scatter, like a star in the night sky is shorthand for a galaxy. The point is centre of action, also the virtual centre of local concentration where the entire weight of a body is said to act. Point is a drop of alchemy, the vanishing that is everything.

III

A line connects two points of potential. It is a current. It is also the meandering path of least resistance. It may be a direct connection, urgent and straight, or take a less obvious route, bifurcating, or folding over itself. The 'resistance' that configures the line is a function of the composition field generic to the solution. A reduced reality leads to the straight line, a compressed norm of hidden strategies.

A string or line is a travelling point.

IV

Connection becomes the meeting of several competing ideas, a moment of confluence.

The node is universal basin. The node is an infinite processor.

V

The point or line is a convenient map or projection of other domains. From a higher dimension to a lower dimension, points and lines carry code.

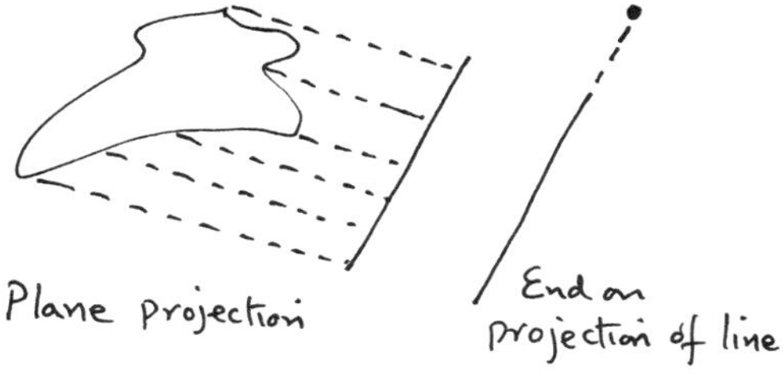

When a piece of 3D construction is rotated, at a certain moment a triangular grid is projected onto two dimensions. The shadow is a moment of rotation, a frozen instant of time.

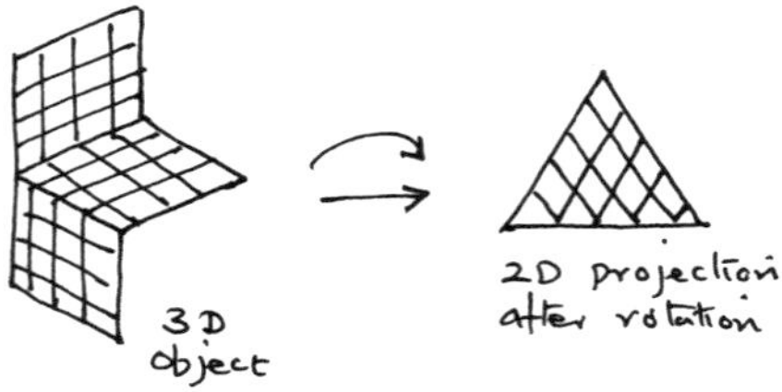

We cannot tell from the reduction what the whole is. We may only invest the maximum potential in the minimum movement.

Each projection is a loss of information. But what we see does not 'reduce' the object, its reality is all the more imagined.

VI

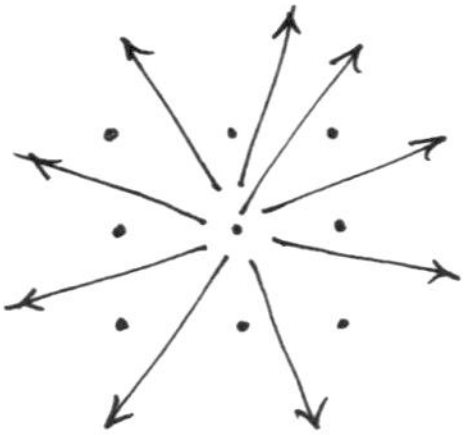

From one point in space, outwards, there are infinite pathways that never touch another.

Sight lines travel to unknown territories.

The grid is an infinite sieve.

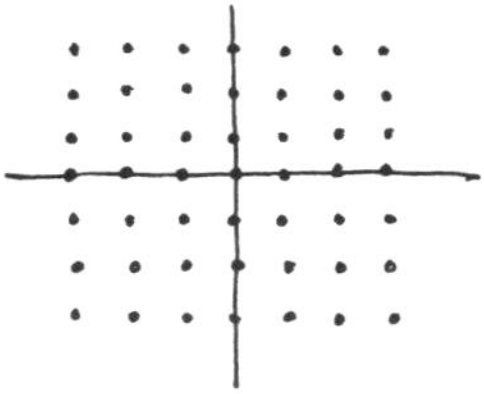

What if the grid is a template for numbers? Imagine every point on the x – y plane as a fraction, having coordinates like 3/4 or 271/272 i.e. x = 3, y = 4 or x = 271, y = 272 respectively. But however close the spacing between the fractions or points on the plane, another fraction can be found, which is even finer. These so called 'ratio-able' or rational numbers seem to fill up the plane. What can get through this tight packing?

Coordinates constituting irrational numbers do, (that is, numbers like $\sqrt{2}$ or $\sqrt{5}$ have decimal expansion that do not end – they are a finer subdivision of space). There are many more such points than the rationals. Irrational numbers constitute a higher order of infinity.

And there is yet another kind of number, the transcendentals, like π, that also run right through the tight packing of the rational numbers. If a circle is drawn of radius π centred at the origin of the axes, no point on its circumference would touch a rational number, however dense the field of points.

So the grid becomes an infinite sieve in the world of numbers, the simple integers surrounded by an indeterminate flow of unstoppable number strands.

VII

Prime numbers occupy a unique position in our number system. They are not compound and factorable like 6 or 133, (2 x 3 or 19 x 7 respectively) but are indivisible and non-composite like:

. . . 41 43 47 53 59 . . .

Primes are the fundamental building blocks of arithmetic. They have no hierarchy, no regular rule, and cannot be planned or predicted. They are the bar code of the abstract.

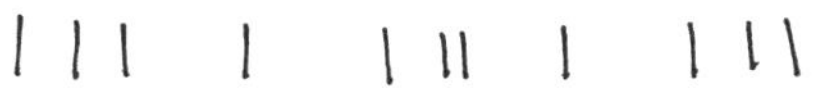

Primes shift and jump along the axis of integers at different speeds. The gaps are unpredictable, the pattern *informal*.

The world of mathematics may appear formal and rigorous to the outsider but at its numerate heart lies this primal river that remains essentially unknown. We can track its course but we do not know the motive power that gives it shape or flow.

What if there is a grid for primes – a projection from another more complex dimensional field we do not understand as yet?

VIII

We assume numbers like 1, 2, 3, etc... go on for infinity. If we place these numbers in a one-to-one correspondence with another set of numbers, say, like the even numbers, then these new numbers can be said to go on to infinity as well. This defies common sense for what we think of as 'fewer', the even numbers, are found to be as populous as the integers. Both sets of numbers are said to be enumerable to infinity.

1	2	3	4	5	6	·	·	·
2	4	6	8	10	12	·	·	·

Using such mappings, Georg Cantor (1845–1918), shocked the world with the idea of separate and overlapping infinities. His demonstrations gave to infinity a self-similar concept where a part has the character of the whole.

IX

Since a line has an infinite number of points, and a point radiates lines in an infinity of ways, a diagram can transform into a mathematical universe if each possible point is ascribed a number.

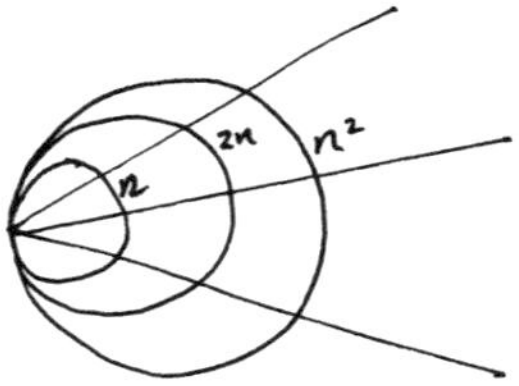

For example, a circle is a set of points which could be thought of as a set of numbers. In the diagram the inner circle is the set of integers 1, 2, 3; the second circle, the set of even numbers for example, the third circle a set of square numbers, ...and so on.

1	2	3	4	5	6	·	·	n
2	4	6	8	10	12	·	·	2n
1	4	9	16	25	36	·	·	n^2

The numbers of each series may get larger but the count of the events on each circle is the same; the radiating lines running through the circles govern this, yielding an equal infinite number of intersections through each circle.

To capture the full range of numbers, negative numbers should be allowed into the picture. The circles need reflections.

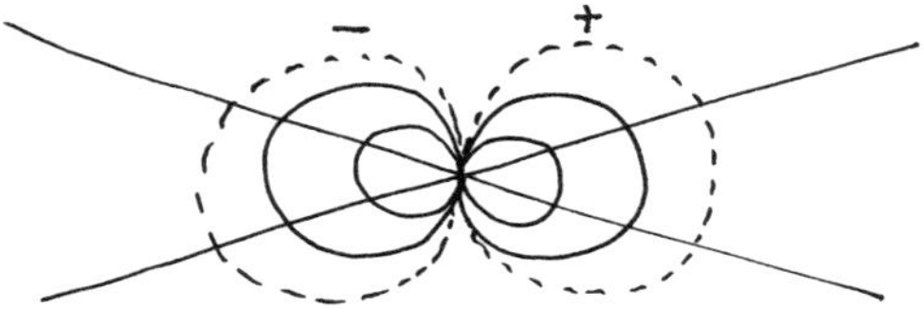

Since there is no difference between plus or minus infinity in terms of quantum, the circles do not touch or cross but *flow* one into the other.

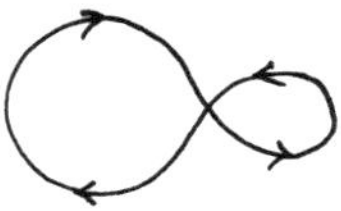

Number fields are not static. Our multiplication tables for example are algorithms that radiate to infinity and their structure may be represented in similar overlapping circles (see Bibliography – 'Number 9: The Search for the Sigma Code').

x

From a topological point of view a straight line is a circle. They are both continuously connected and one is the inversion of the other.

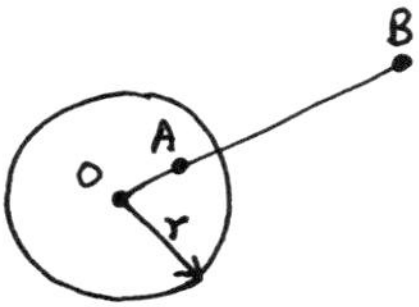

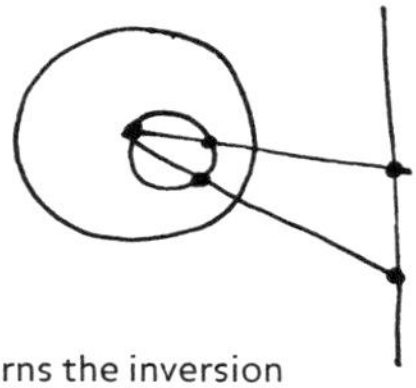

The expression that governs the inversion is given by OA x OB = r^2. When OA is small, OB grows large. Contiguous circles passing through point O invert to parallel lines spaced apart.

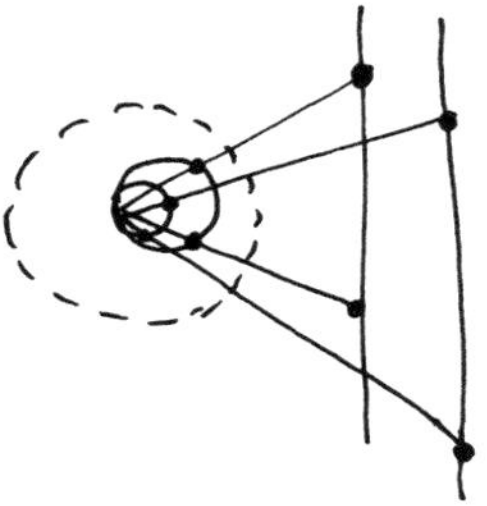

Circles through O at right angles to each other produce orthogonal grids. Note that the algorithm $OA \times OB = r^2$ 'empties' all the space out of the bound circle into the plane outside.

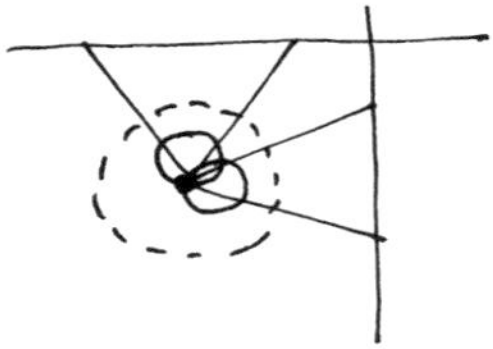

There is infinite space outside the circle but paradoxically so is there within the circle. Like a fractal concept, of similar embedments at different scales, infinity provides regions of boundlessness in local concentrations of the finite.

SHIFTING BOUNDARIES

XI

Imagine a magic string that may fold into a square or rectangle or twist over into a loop.

The fold-over gives rise to ambiguities. Is the diagram one idea or two separate regions? We know it is one idea because the piece of string was folded over itself but to an outsider this is not obvious. The diagram could be two separate loops joined at the centre.

If the cross-over point is not fused or merged, which way does the piece of string go at the crossing, under or over? One is in 'front', the other is 'behind'. In a multi-sequence of folds and overlaps, in the making of a knot, important topological information is contained in what is front or back. The direction of twist to a surface is governed by which crossing is over or under. (See ARNHEM pp. 354 ff. for a simple knot becoming structural column, wall and slab.)

XII

A transformation of this idea can be developed by a generative line, folding in its trajectory but never crossing itself. The 'cells' of the ensuing diagrams give rise to interpretations of 'IN' and 'OUT', as alternate chequerboard sequences.

'IN' and 'OUT' become qualities of certainty within a specific frame of assumption and their connectivity is an incident of fold – they don't stand alone as concepts but are wound together in a thread of guesswork. The many become one.

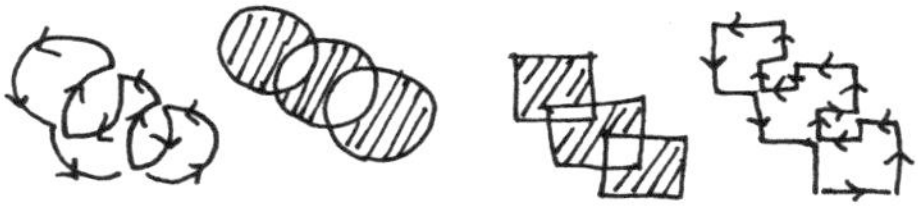

XIII

A string loops and folds and is compressed so that one loop touches another. The contact points merge or fuse – the curving lines 'straighten' out to produce the familiar configuration of truss.

If the loops compress further and the contacts harden, other configurations arise.

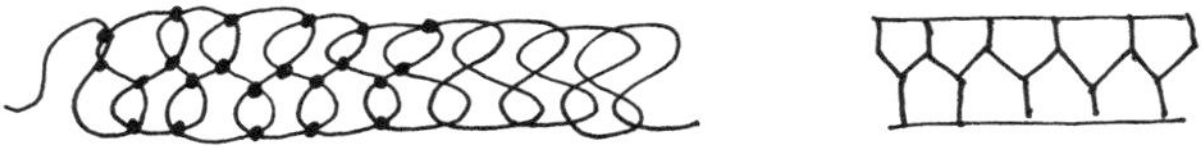

The different rates of compaction of a travelling wave produce a variety of networks.

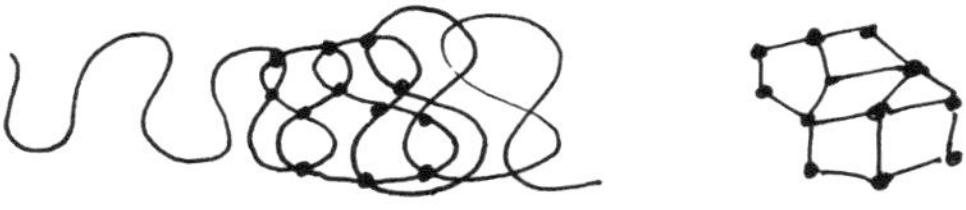

The arrested movements at any moment are structures, ordered by chance and carrying a memory of the shaping, but hidden, force field.

A travelling line may hit a force field of orthogonal properties, which in plan would force a circuit at right angles around corners, never leaving the horizontal plane.

The trace could branch and draw other circuits, or be ordered to jump the vertical to elaborate further circuits at each new level. The linking vertical lines from one plan to another will be a climbing set of diagonals. A traditional building frame could grow in this manner.

XIV

A 2D framework may be viewed as a projection of a more complex 3D network.

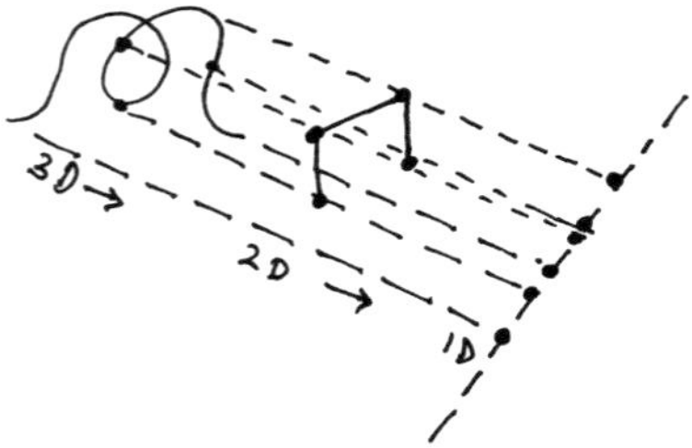

(If we see prime numbers as nodes along a line, we cannot understand them fully, for we do not see into the more intricate network that may hold them. See template VII.)

SYSTEMS AND ANALYSIS

XV

René Descartes wed arithmetic to geometry. He proposed two lines, at right angles to each other (the X and Y axes), with a point on the plane being described by two, coordinate, number values. 'Cartesian' meant a precise, numerate, picture.

The coordinates of a point P are (x, y) – the values of x and y being mutually exclusive. That is X and Y natures do not mix but cohabit. As one entity, P is hybrid.

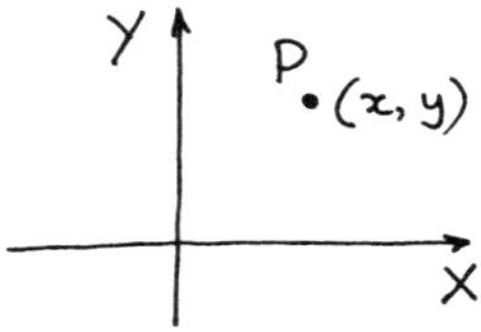

The generator of Cartesian space, a straight line, can only be defined in relation to the juxtaposition of two points P_1, P_2. If their coordinate values are $P_1 = (x_1, y_1)$ and $P_2 = (x_2, y_2)$ then the straight line between P_1 and P_2 is said to have the gradient or slope $(y_2 - y_1) / (x_2 - x_1)$.

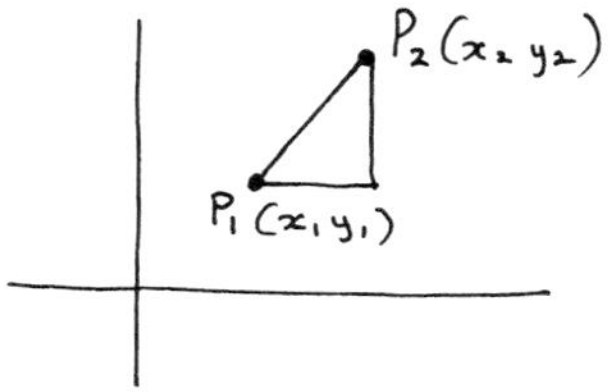

As the value of a slope is a constant along the line it need only be sampled locally, anywhere, to produce the value.

In the basic premises of Cartesian geometry there are the characteristics of local, hybrid and juxtaposition, innate to the concept of the *informal*. This is a surprise and a sign that Order, as we define it, is only a subset of a wider domain.

The slope of a line on the Cartesian plane may be viewed as a compound construct, as a combination of the simultaneous movement of two points, one on each axis at constant speeds though the speed may be different on each axis. If the point on the x axis moves faster, the line will 'lower' itself and flatten. If the dot on the y axis moves faster on the other hand, then the slope will increase and the line would rise and be steeper.

But if the imaginary dots should accelerate or decelerate, in relation to each other, then a curve results on the x – y axis.

Nothing is static, even in Cartesian space.

XVI

A moving point C, between A and B, at different moments, produces various proportions.

In general AC/BC has different values producing arithmetic means, geometric or harmonic means or the golden section dependant on where C is taken. When AC = BC, the point C represents the arithmetic mean between A and B. If AC x AB = BC^2, the geometric mean is obtained. If B is rotated 90° to AC and the rectangle completed, its proportion is equal to that of the golden ratio when AC = 1.618 BC.

Proportions may be interpreted as frozen instants of time.

XVII

Why would we assume that a phenomenon close to us should project unaltered to the infinite? But the cornerstone of Euclidean geometry does just that, the mighty intellectual framework of Euclid's theorems are built on ten 'self-evident' truths or axioms. The second axiom states that a line may extend, unstopped, to infinity. The fifth axiom states that through a point juxtaposed to a given line, there is only one line that can be drawn parallel to it and that these parallel lines never meet until infinity.

If a line is defined as the shortest distance between two points, on the surface of the globe there are no parallel lines, for on our globe the shortest distance between two points is on a great circle. These circles all meet at two points, the poles.

On the face of the globe, a triangle has more than 180° to the sum of its internal angles, on such a curving surface the greater the size of the triangle drawn the greater the sum of angles. If we could imagine a contrary surface, or a concave curvature, then a triangle drawn on it would have less than 180° to the sum of its angles – Bolyai (1775–1856) and Lobachevsky (1792–1856) independently proposed a geometry which they called hyperbolic, that had such properties and a surface which gave through a point on it many parallel lines in relation to a given line. Bernard Reimann (1826–1866) proposed a different elliptical geometry, more akin to the properties of our globe's surface, where there are no parallel lines through a point. Einstein's space-time geometry, which is finite but unbounded, was built on Reimann's ideas.

The entire debate over the last two thousand years on the nature of geometry is a question of locality and juxtaposition, relating to the definition of a parallel to a given line.

XVIII

We assume three orthogonal directions to describe space. Computation is easy this way, for a line at right angles to a plane has no shadow or projection. Each dimension is independent of the other. Classical physics and Newtonian science built on such flat and linear models. Time was conveniently added as another, fourth, independent axis in the popular imagination, so that space-time was visualised as the sum of four 'orthogonal' parts. But space-time is one thing, inextricably wrapped with energy densities and related curvatures.

Reimannian space that describes this phenomenon, is a function of the topology of an object (its connectivity) and the distances between its points. This combination of distance with the invariant quality of the object under deformation classifies the object in multi-dimensional space.

Space-time is a hybridisation arising from the juxtapositions of such local energy densities (or masses) populating the universe. The projections of this complex world may be seen by us like shadows on a wall. In our 3D world some of the information is lost but we can imagine its intricacy.

Space that is finite and unbounded is an astonishing interweave producing strange 'ins' and 'outs', dense knots and black holes. In turn this maybe a projection down of a more complex space, the mathematical imagination that occupies our mind.

XIX

When entering a design there are several stages to unravel; a composition field, pattern, the choice of connectivity, geometry and, finally, material.

The overlaps to structure are:

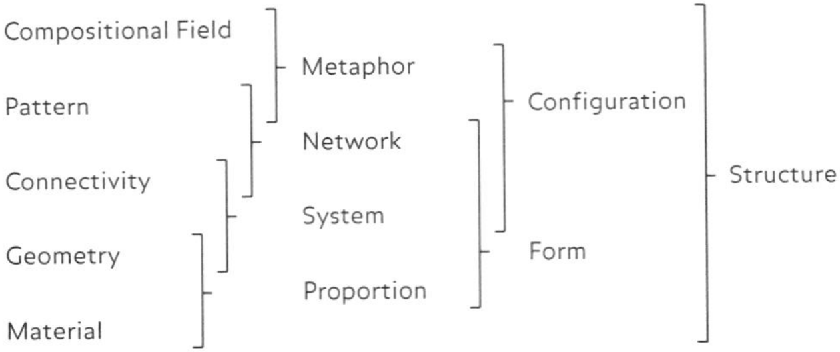

XX

Something dramatic happens when we contemplate the analysis of 'structure'. The world loses its substance: walls, columns, floors and beams shrink and dematerialise to leave an imprint on a small skeletal drawing. The structure becomes just lines connecting nodes – a virtual diagram. The line has no real thickness and the node no size, they are mathematically dimensionless entities of point and line. Precisely because a framework has no substance we can give it any properties we like: weight, area, stiffness etc. Armed with such properties the structural diagram becomes a potent machine, waiting for a set of actions.

To energise the diagram there has to be another dematerialisation, this time of people and furniture and the gusting wind to obtain a set of loadings, as shown by arrows.

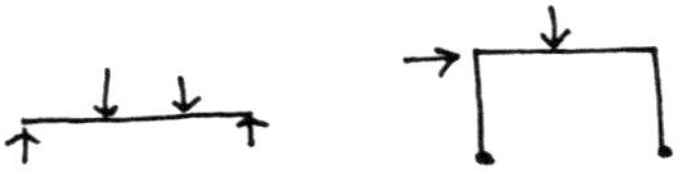

The arrows are forces. No one really knows what a force is but conveniently force is deemed to act at a point, in a certain direction, its efforts transferred through a dimensionless point of contact. Because the force is a virtual carrier, it can carry any loading. Its only descriptor is number.

The diagram becomes *limit,* and then *threshold* as calculations run through. In a zone of purest abstraction analysis begins. In this world no clock keeps time – the forcing actions are instantaneous and the response of the structural network, immediate.

But there is a further layer of abstraction to consider, the formulae. At this ultimate end of affairs there are no diagrams, only symbols. We are at the cross-over points where the discrete turns into an algebraic continuum, where equations define channels of information. The formulae are only 'seen' by the numbers.

Then we exit, back to the discrete, via resultants, which through interpretation yield size and proportion, and then connection, framework and system. Finally we get back a building on a drawing board or computer screen.

If one studies the standard equations of structural mechanics, it is no surprise that their character of hybrid entities, local variable powers and juxtaposition of terms is *informal*.

XXI

The equilibrium of forces is fundamental to all aspects of structure. Without it there would be no coherence. Joints would spin and elements not stick together, 'things' would fly apart.

Two forces F_1, F_2 acting in a plane may be balanced by a third force F_3 in opposition. The diagram that pictures this equilibrium is a triangle of forces.

The concept of equilibrium is hybrid.

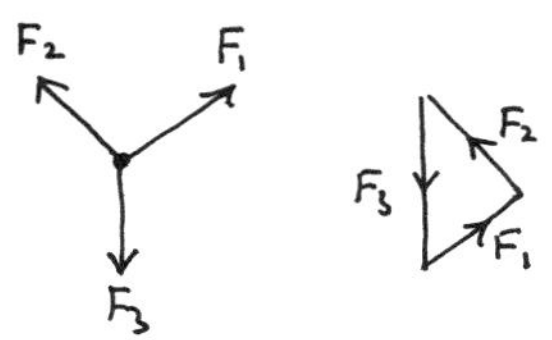

One of the great secrets of the universe is how it achieves balance, interior adjustments that provide symmetries, not of the static bilateral kind but dynamic weaves that stitch and match cross-currents or oppositions. A fundamental law is the Conservation of Energy, which in turn gives rise to conservation of momentum; from that, projected down further, we get equilibrium.

Force is a vector that can be projected onto component axes in three mutually perpendicular directions.

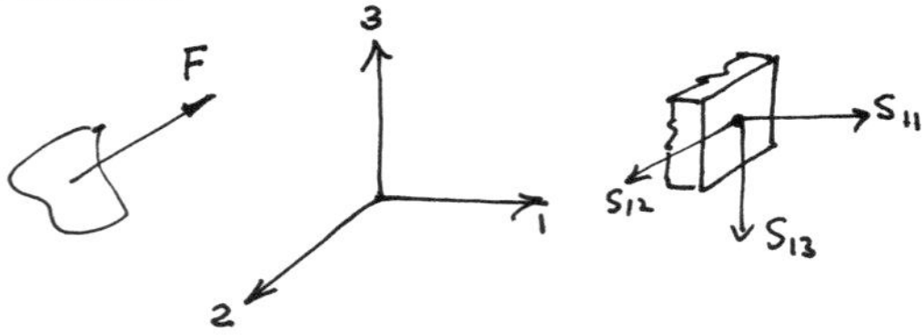

If a body is subject to stress, a unit cube is sampled within it to define the general state of stress. On each face of the cube there is an axial stress normal to that face and two shear stresses acting along the face, at right angles to one another. The coordinate axes are given numbers 1, 2, 3.

The axial stress is labelled S_{11}, S_{22}, S_{33} the subscripts denoting face 1, direction 1, etc. and the shear forces are labelled S_{12}, S_{23}, etc. with S_{12} meaning face 1, direction 2.

The mathematical picture of the simultaneous set of actions is:

The array is that of a matrix.

$$\begin{bmatrix} S_{11} & S_{12} & S_{13} \\ S_{21} & S_{22} & S_{23} \\ S_{31} & S_{32} & S_{33} \end{bmatrix}$$

There is no hierarchy since the set of stresses are projections of the one, general, vector in space. The matrix represents a complex set of 'shadows'.

Along the diagonal of the matrix from top left to bottom right are the direct or 'pure' normal stresses to the face of the cube. This leading diagonal, as it is called, has an important role in the subsequent resolution of the matrices, it acts as a kind of conduit for the channelling and optimising of calculations.

XXIII

A structure is a network of adjacencies.

Each element or adjacency has a stiffness K, dependant on its immediate connections. Each 'cell' of structure has a series of such local stiffnesses to be considered. When the 'cells' are put together, the array of stiffnesses may be assembled into one large matrix within which the smaller matrices of each cell nest.

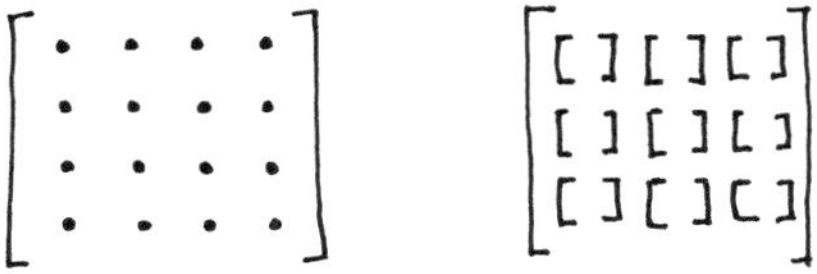

The matrix becomes a series of overlaps.

The collation can be given a generic symbol [K] for stiffness and operated on as if the matrix is a mathematical entity. Similarly the external forces could be written as another matrix [P] and the resulting deformations produced by the forces as [D].

Then the equation [P] = [K] x [D] describes the action of structure.

The matrix [K] is a function of the network or connected geometry of the particular structure. Since the mathematics is based on idealisations, [K] *is quality of pattern.*

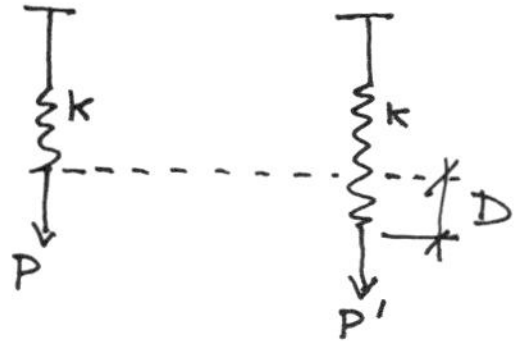

In a spring, where there is only one degree of freedom, there is no adjacency in the configuration and the bracket sign of the matrix, denoting simultaneity, disappears.

$$P = KD$$

The equation is linear. For a given stiffness of spring, if the pull of force doubles, the extension doubles.

XXIV

A generating line of structure, may crank, flex or branch.

This can happen in plan or elevation
or both at the same time.

The motif may repeat in a regular
rhythm or overlap.

Structural lines may bifurcate and
come together again.

The zone created gives extra stiffness. If the diagram is an elevation, the structural cell may transmit load in a direction out of the plane of the paper. This direction may crank or flex or branch as required.

Moments of reverse curvature in
elevation produce structure.

Peaks and troughs couple to produce 'beam' action out of the plane of the paper.

As the ideas overlap and the possibilities increase, the idea of 'line' disappears. Zones and surfaces take over. Column, beam and slab and wall become interpretations of a continuity. Ultimately plan and section lose their traditions.

XXV

If *local*, *hybrid* and *juxtaposition* are the interior characteristics of a design, the notation of their interdependencies may be assembled by a 3 x 3 matrix.

L_L	L_H	L_J
H_L	H_H	H_J
J_L	J_H	J_J

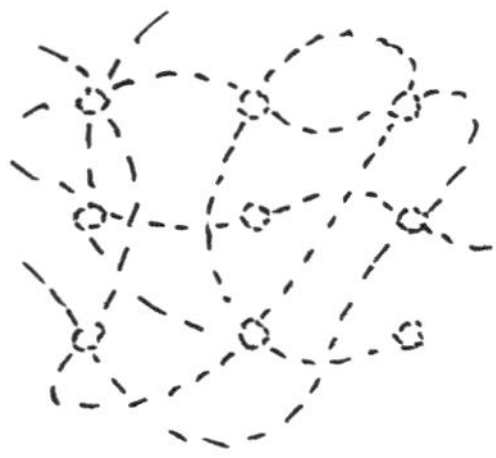

The leading diagonal $L_L - H_H - J_J$ denotes the pure nature of each characteristic. Entries off the diagonal describe mixed qualities, where H_L is primarily hybridisation but having a local effect; whereas L_J is a local action spreading the nature of a juxtaposition.

This informal matrix is equivalent to the 'stiffness' of a structure. It can lead to loose and flexible or narrow and rigid answers. External constraints may be viewed as forcing actions [P] and form as 'deflections' [D] arising from these actions. They are both collations of simultaneous activities and can be ascribed matrix notation. What negotiates between the two is I, the *informal*.

The equation is [P] = [I] [D]

To design, we engage the *informal* in a series of complex cross-multiplications. Like with structure, design is a series of adjacencies, of buried codes and local starts and aggregate resolutions; locked into it, at every level, are the characteristics $L_L - H_H - J_J$

XXVI

The ultimate matrix of simultaneous information is the DNA spiral. On its twisting threads lie the genetic codes that produce life.

Recent research shows that DNA winds around lumps called histones to make structure like a bead necklace, achieving a high density of compaction. The molecule itself is a twin thread of intertwining helices. Each thread is a backbone of phosphates and deoxyribose to which four bases, Thymine, Adenine, Cytosine and Guanine are attached in random arrays. The bases link up in pairs. Their specialised couplings bring a dynamic symmetry to the configuration.

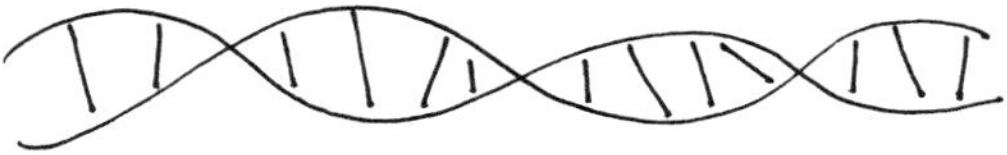

Cytosine with Guanine, and Thymine with Adenine.

The 'messages' from the base chain is read in adjacencies of three. Millions of such messages run to instruct the genes.

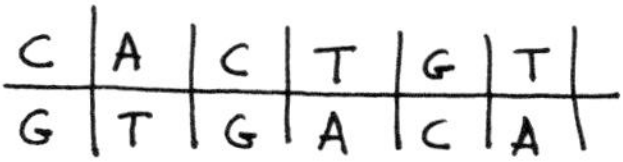

The bases themselves are complex structures of protein molecules which offer a 'loose' hydrogen bond to link across space, attaching one base to the other, forming the 'ladders' of the helix. The local condition of this free hydrogen atom is crucial in clipping together the helices.

From local bases to arhythmic serialisation, from juxtaposition to strands of hybridisation, the molecule appears *informal* in assembly. DNA is a magic configuration.

XXVII

Patterns are magical marks, open pictures for the mind to travel through.

Akin to the visible spectrum in electromagnetism that colours our imagination, pattern offers structure, to the realm of ideas. In this region metaphor is at one end, concrete realisation at the other. A contemplation of one leads to the other.

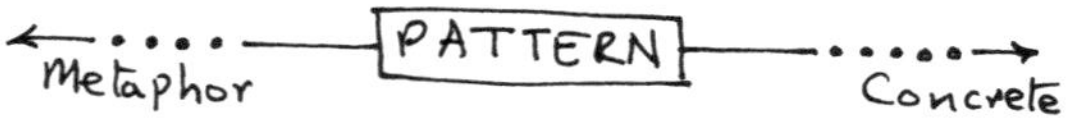

To give meaning to pattern we impose scale – a molecule map or a road map – but pattern is invariant; a fix at one level raising a speculation at another. A meditation on pattern suggests connectivity – and in here are the archetypes of structure, the networks of configuration.

The diagram acts as catalyst, and continues its private haunting, attacking certainties. Whatever is seen in a reduced reality seems to have a ghost in another dimension – the mystery denies dogma as a natural state. Mind seems to have its own subversive structure: to find out, I run the templates.

Note: In starting a design there are static certainties and dynamic improbabilities. Because a building is a structure there has to be a static certainty; because a building is a piece of architecture there is an unpredictability.

In mathematics, differential equations which describe the world have two parts, a particular solution alongside a more generalised expression – a cohabitation of the specific with the generic. The generic informs the class of solution and lends character, but the exact answer is shaped by the particular solution which just fits the boundary conditions of the problem area. What we begin to see as reason, or order, is a particular area of logic mixed in with a more general region of instinct and intuition. Our mind engages that multiplicity and learns and grows.

393

THE AUTHOR

Cecil Balmond has been working with the international firm of consulting engineers Ove Arup and Partners for the past thirty years, on a variety of prestigious and award-winning architectural projects. He was born in Sri Lanka, where he studied at university, before leaving for further education in England. His interest lies in the genesis of form and the overlap of science with art, using music, numbers and mathematics as vital sources. He was Saarinen Professor at Yale, and Kenzo Tange Visiting Critic at Harvard. He is a member of the Arup Main Board, and lives in London.

KEY TECHNICAL CONTRIBUTIONS

Maison a Floriac: Robert Pugh (Project Engineer), Ted Weicker, Heracles Passades (Special Analysis)

Kunsthal: Clinton Tang (Project Engineer), Mirvat Bulbul; Geementewerke – Rotterdam (Construction Documents), Peter Schilperoot (Project Engineer)

Sports Stadium, Chemnitz 2002: Bob Lang (Competition), Toby McLean (Roof algorithm)

'Spiral', V&A Museum: David Lewis (Competition), Bob Lang (Scheme Design), Francis Archer (Algorithm, Scheme Design)

'Fractile', V&A Museum: Francis Archer (Fractal Design and Development)

Congrexpo: Robert Pugh (Project Engineer), Rory McGowan

Portuguese Pavilion, Expo 1998: Fred Ilidio (Project Manager), Andrew Minson (Project Engineer); STA Lisbon (Construction Documents)

Station Arnhem Centraal: Charles Walker (Project Engineer), Francis Archer (Seifert surface), Gwenola Kergal (Computer Graphics)

SELECTED PROJECTS

Carlsberg Brewery: Phase 1, Northampton, 1974, Knud Munk (ex Utzon). Conceived, designed and completed in 107 weeks. A tour de force in big structures at speed.

University of Qatar: Qatar, 1980, Dr Kamel El Kafrawi. Assembly of octagons and infill squares over huge plan area using minimum number of precast concrete panels.

Stuttgart Staatsgalerie: Stuttgart, 1984, James Stirling & Michael Wilford. Complex collage of column/wall interactions in postmodern icon. Curved glass wall. No expansion joints in 110 m square plan.

Dutch PTT Pavilion: Holland, 1987, Frank and Paul Wintermans. Demountable visitor stand. Won the Dutch award for steel. A first adventure into high tech.

Latina Library: Italy, 1987, James Stirling & Michael Wilford. A study in composition of circle and rectangle in plan against pitched roof elevation, with interior ziggurat spirals for book search.

Hague City Hall: The Hague, 1988, Rem Koolhaas. First competition win with Koolhaas. All steel building – project given ultimately by city to Richard Meier.

Palazzo Citterio: Brera Museum, Milan, 1988, James Stirling & Michael Wilford. Complex refurbishment including new build library plus courtyard covered by light weight skin. Still awaiting planning approval.

Bibliothèque de France: Paris, 1989, Rem Koolhaas. Competition. Giant series of deep beams allowing freedom in vertical plane for cut outs to allow invasions from public program.

Congress Centre: Agadir, 1989, Rem Koolhaas. Far out compelling fantasy of cellularisation superimposed over free form arch structures.

Zeebrugge Ferry Terminal: Zeebrugge, 1989, Rem Koolhaas. Competition. Capsule out at sea – ambitious, mix of concrete, steel and light-weight fabric.

Kunsthal: Rotterdam, 1992, Rem Koolhaas. Art gallery with structure as episodes. A catalogue of juxtapositions.

Abando Transport Interchange: Bilbao, 1994, James Stirling & Michael Wilford. Large 160 m roof over heavy civil engineering type construction (scheme design).

Congrexpo: Lille, 1994, Rem Koolhaas. Three in one building with hybrid roof of timber and steel in unusual configuration.

Musikhochschule Stuttgart: Stuttgart, 1995, James Stirling & Michael Wilford. Follow on adjacent building to art gallery, completes an unique composition with central tower being positive counter to hollow drum of former.

Sport Stadium Chemnitz 2002: Chemnitz, 1995, Peter Kulka with Ulrich Königs. Competition win for the athletic games 2002. A break from the traditional stadium design. Job stopped, lack of funding.

Thyssen-Bornemisza Museum: Madrid, 1995, Rafael Moneo. Refurbishment of old palace into art gallery for Baron Thyssen's private art collection.

Jussieu Library: Paris, 1996, Rem Koolhaas. Spiralling floor ramps – with permeable façade. Competition win.

ZKM: Zentrum für Kunst und Medien, Karlsruhe, 1996, Rem Koolhaas. Release of the cross-section due to stacking alternate floors with storey height Vierendeels. Halfway through detail design job cancelled.

Ferry Terminal: Yokohama, 1997, Foreign Office Architects. Competition win. Doubly curved, metal structure, stiffened through bifurcations.

Universal HQ: Los Angeles, scheme design 1997, Rem Koolhaas. Large office project for media giant, with inventive seismic resistant configurations.

Maison de Floriac: Bordeaux, 1998, Rem Koolhaas. Floating box in a new typology. A transcendence over Villa Savoye.

Portuguese Pavilion: Expo 1998, Lisbon, Alvaro Siza. Concrete canopy that flies like a bird.

Theme Park: Yverdon, 1999, Ben van Berkel. Ectoplasm of structural nodes anchoring free-flowing warps in between. Competition entry

Portuguese Pavilion: Expo 2000, Hannover, Alvaro Siza. Free-form fabric roof inspired by shifting grid of numbers.

Chicago IIT Campus: Chicago, 2001, Rem Koolhaas. New student centre against backdrop of Mies with elevated elliptical tube carrying the metro across the roofscape.

Imperial War Museum: Manchester, 2001, Daniel Libeskind. Structured steel shells clad in concrete, supporting each other in interconnecting shards.

Summer Pavilion: Serpentine Gallery London, 2001, Daniel Libeskind. Eighteen turns of structural planes in echoes of the V&A Spiral form.

Dutch Embassy: Berlin, 2002, Rem Koolhaas. Labyrinth of shear walls, tunnelled out for spiral of circulation.

Prada Store: San Francisco, 2002, Rem Koolhaas. Multi-perforated exterior skin which offers structure and seismic resistance in strong earthquake zone.

Graz Music School: Graz, 2003, Ben van Berkel. A spiral winding longitudinally that overlaps itself, providing unusual spatial template for an improvisation on materials and form.

Jewish Museum: San Francisco, 2003, Daniel Libeskind. Twisting rectangles intersect with each other and masonry fabric of old power house. Intersection leaves complex void to overcome in the transmission of seismic loads.

Arnhem Interchange: Arnhem, 2003, Ben van Berkel. Seamless structure. One skin of concrete provides inclined walls, ramps and vaulting roof.

Casa de Musica: Oporto, 2003, Rem Koolhaas. Prismatic concrete box with intervention of skewed single props to stabilise steeply inclined walls.

Seattle Library: Seattle, 2003, Rem Koolhaas. Floating slabs of program held together by diagonal meshed seismic system.

Uffizi Canopy: Florence, 2003, Arata Isozaki. Slender steel and stone canopy to Alberti's building.

Guadalajara Student Centre: Mexico, 2004, Daniel Libeskind. Intersecting rectangular volumes – this time the void at the cross-over is made into a positive solid to resist seismic forces.

Chavasse Park: Liverpool, 2005, Philip Johnson and Studio Baad. Structural arch strands with pure tension surfaces in between in large free form steel mesh over shopping mall.

Denver Art Museum: Denver, 2005, Daniel Libeskind. Interdependent forms with large cantilever that vanishes, from solid to glass.

Victoria & Albert Museum: London, 2005, Daniel Libeskind. A three-dimensional wrap in space with self-stabilising walls. Another kind of movement takes place on the walls, the tiling pattern of a fractal.

BIBLIOGRAPHY

Gaston Bachelard: *The poetics of space,* Beacon Press (Boston), 1969

Cecil Balmond: *Number 9,* Prestel, 1998

Stephen Barr: *Experiments in topology,* Dover Publications, Inc, 1985

Jacob Bronowski: *The origins of knowledge & imagination,* Yale University Press, 1918

J W Dunne: *An experiment with time,* Faber, 1958

E H Gombrich: *Norm and form,* Phaidon, 1966

John Gribbin: *In search of the double helix,* Black Swan, 1993

Rom Harrè: *The philosophies of science,* Oxford University Press, 1965

Stephen R Holtzman: *Digital mantras,* MIT Press, 1995

Carl Jung: *Man and his symbols,* Picador, 1978

Wassily Kandinsky: *Point and line to plane,* Dover Publications, Inc, 1979

David Kuelle: *Chance and chaos,* Penguin, 1993

Hans Lauwerier: *Fractals,* Penguin Books, 1991
Lucretius: *On the nature of the universe,* Penguin Classic, 1951
Eli Maor: *To infinity and beyond,* Birkhäuser Boston, Inc, 1986
Jacques Manod: *Chance and necessity,* Fontana Books, 1974
Marvin Minsky: *The society of mind,* William Heinemann Ltd, 1987
M Mitchell Waldrop: *Complexity,* Penguin, 1994
P Morrison & P Morrison: *Powers of ten,* Scientific American Library, 1982
Lorraine Mottershead: *Sources of mathematical discovery,* Oxford, Basil Blackwell, 1978
Clifford A Pickover: *Keys to infinity,* John Wiley & Sons, Inc, 1995
Ilya Prigogine & I Stengers: *Order out of chaos,* Flamingo, 1985
F L Schauermann: *Theory and analysis of ornament,* Sampson Low, Marston & Co, 1892
C Stanley Ogilvy: *Excursions in geometry,* Dover Publications, Inc, 1990
J W N Sullivan: *The limitations of science,* Mentor, 1963
Tjukurrpa: *Dreamings,* Prestel, 1994

ILLUSTRATION CREDITS

ACKNOWLEDGEMENTS

A team of four people have made this book possible – it began with Christian Brensing and a discussion many years ago in Berlin about a book on my ideas and project work. I invited Christian to act as Editor and to give the book a sharp focus. He introduced me to the designers Michele Jannuzzi and Richard Smith who translated the stories on the projects into a seamless innovation of text and image, adding 'structure' of another kind to the content. Margaret Cashin completed the team in producing the manuscript and acting as the most perceptive of sub-editors, providing guidance through all the ups and downs and U-turns. These four pulled, shaped, and gave imagination to a book well beyond the limitations of my first draft. Sebastian Campos, Edoardo Cecchin, Robbie Mahoney, Helen Rattigan and the rest of the team at Jannuzzi Smith helped realise the design of the book, and the expertise of Martin Lee ensured that our production ideas became reality. Thanks also to the Prestel Team: Urban Meister who championed the book and gave it initial definition; Christopher Wynne for his pivotal role in moving the book forward and acting as final arbiter on the text; and Meike Weber who worked with great diligence and commitment on the production helping to turn our editorial and design ideas into excellent results.

A special thank you to David Turnbull and Jane Harrison of Atopos for valuable criticism on the theoretical chapters of *informal*. But none of the work in these projects could have been done without the talented project teams I worked with at Arup. I am indebted to the leaders of these teams: Francis Archer, Fred Ilidio, Bob Lang, Rory McGowan, Andrew Minson, Robert Pugh, and Charles Walker, for their creative contributions. To Francis and Charles a special thank you for helping me reach further into the complexities of 3D form generation and surface modelling than I could have on my own.

My appreciation to my wife Shirley and children John, Sarah and James for allowing such an imposition as a book to enter their lives again, and for allowing me to chase my private demons in the completion of this work.

Prestel Munich: Königinstrasse 9, 80539 Munich
telephone +49 (0)89 3817 090
fax +49 (0)89 3817 0935
www.prestel.de

Prestel London: 4 Bloomsbury Place, London WC1A 2QA
telephone +44 (0)20 7323 5004
fax +44 (0)20 7636 8004

Prestel New York: 175 Fifth Avenue, Suite 402, New York, NY 10010
telephone +1 (212) 995 2720
fax +1 (212) 995 2733
www.prestel.com

Design: Jannuzzi Smith
Editor: Christian Brensing
Copy editors: Margaret Cashin; Christopher Wynne
Production coordinators: Martin Lee for Jannuzzi Smith; Meike Weber, Prestel
Origination: ReproLine, Munich
Printing and binding: fgb · freiburger graphische betriebe
Typefaces: Balance; Neue Helvetica
Paper: Munken Lynx 130 gsm

Library of Congress Control Number: 00-104160
Deutsche Bibliotek CIP-Einheitsaufnahme data
is available

Printed in Germany on acid-free paper
ISBN 3-7913-2400-4